CLOSE CONTROL

Managing a Maximum Security Prison — The Story of Ragen's Stateville Penitentiary

Cover print: Stateville photograph compliments of the Illinois Department of Corrections.

CLOSE CONTROL

Managing a Maximum Security Prison —
The Story of Ragen's Stateville Penitentiary

Nathan Kantrowitz

Harrow and Heston
PUBLISHERS
Guilderland, New York

Harrow and Heston, Publishers
1830 Western Avenue
Albany, N.Y. 12203

Library of Congress CIP:

Kantrowitz, Nathan.
Close control: managing a maximum security prison :
the story of Ragen's Stateville Penitentiary / Nathan Kantrowitz
        p. cm.
      Includes bibliographical references and index.
      ISBN 0-911577-31-9 (hard : alk. paper) -- ISBN 0-911577-35-1
(paper : alk. paper)
          1. Ragen, Joseph E. 2. Illinois State Penitentiary (Joliet, Ill.)
3. Prisons--Illinois--Personnel management. 4.Prisons--Illinois--
Officials and employees. I. Title.
HV8332.K36   1996
365' .977325--dc20   96-32680
                                           CIP

Contents

In memory

Lucy Floren Sassaman
1904-1964

THE TIP OF THE ICEBERG

A national survey of 31 state and federal correctional agencies, conducted for this study, found that prisoners killed 8 staff and 69 inmates in 1984. Agencies also reported 5,350 inmate assaults on staff during that year. Statistics show the number of violent incidents has remained relatively constant. Nationwide, during 1986, 39 state and federal correctional agencies reported 6,194 non-fatal assaults on staff occurred; 102 prisoners and 2 staff were killed by inmates.

> R.A. Buchanan, C.A. Unger, and K.L. Whitlow (1988)

Officials say that assaults on inmates and guards at high-security Federal prisons rose nearly 20 percent last year...

> *New York Times*, January 24, 1995

One inmate was stabbed to death Thursday night at Auburn Correctional Facility and another died on Friday in a fight at Attica Correctional Facility that injured a third prisoner.

> *New York Times*, August 20, 1995

List of Figures

List of Tables

Biography of a Book, with Acknowledgements

This book began in 1957, nearly 40 years ago. I was a graduate student who took an interim job, not knowing that it would provide me with an education in prisons, politics, and ideology. Don Pappenfort, my fellow graduate student at the University of Chicago, introduced me to Hans Mattick, then Assistant Warden of the Cook County (Chicago) Jail. Hans told me there was a vacancy in his old position as Sociologist-Actuary to the Illinois Parole Board at the Stateville-Joliet Penitentiary which was a good job for a graduate student and I might find it interesting. He suggested I apply, but not to use his name. I later learned that he and his mentor, Joe Lohman, then Sheriff of Cook County, were at opposite political poles from the Republican Governor and his Parole Board; they were also at odds with the conservative Democrat who was Warden of the prison, Joseph Ragen. Mentioning their names would have been the end of my application. Thus it was I began. A sociology student majoring in population studies, with no interest in prisons, no courses in criminology, and intending to keep the job for a year or two.

My first and perpetual debt of gratitude goes to Don Pappenfort, who started me on this journey and who for 40 years, until his death in 1995, was my closest friend, my guide, and my critic.

During my six years employment at the prison, the people who made this book possible were the convicts, especially my clerks. Over the years, 19 prisoners, (two to four at a time), were assigned by the custodial staff to work in the office for me and another sociologist. It was these men, their friends, and friends of these friends who became my basic sources for documents, (some "borrowed" from the Warden without his knowledge), interpretation of these documents, events in the prison, and much information. I had little say in who my clerks would be, for they were assigned by a captain. Sometimes he assigned friends of my clerks, sometimes not, and this unpredictability helped keep me from becoming insulated within a clique of friends. Many other inmates were my guides, especially those who helped me with research projects. Some were those assigned to Stateville's Television College who volunteered to work on my research projects during the summers of 1960, 1961, and 1962; some worked in nearby assignments; a few who spoke frankly were among the approximately 4,000 inmates I interviewed for parole or who applied for Executive Clemency. Ultimately, this study describes the Stateville Penitentiary of 1957-1963 as experienced and understood in bits and pieces by numerous convicts and me, and then shaped by my imagination. My analysis did not exist in the minds of any of the inmates, or indeed of the custodial staff, including Warden Ragen, that prison's creator. This account of Stateville did not exist in my own mind during my employment there, but was shaped upon reflection—six years later—when I wrote the first draft of this book.

During those years, David Maurer, late Professor of Linguistics at the University of Louisville, Kentucky, cajoled my wife Joanne and me into an interest in criminal linguistics. His influence led to our survey of prison language in *Stateville Names: A Prison Vocabulary* (see Kantrowitz, 1969, 1973). Perhaps to make up for leading us astray, Dave wrote the letter of support responsible for the only financial assistance this research has had, a one year fellowship during the 1969-70 academic year from the Ford Foundation to analyze our linguistic survey. That assistance was crucial in giving me an uninterrupted block of time to concentrate at the right moment: those few years removed from Stateville had rendered me de-institutionalized and allowed some perspective on the experience, which was still recent enough that my memories were vivid. With that grant, I spent a year at Oxford, writing the first draft of this book.

At that time, Nigel Walker, then Reader in Criminology and Director of the Penal Research Unit at Oxford University, very kindly extended his support and hospitality, even to personally finding housing for my family. I wish to thank the Fellows of Nuffield College who extended to me their privileges as a Member of the Senior Common Room, and Gillian Frisby, who typed the original 1969-70 manuscript in those pre-computer days.

The 1969-1970 manuscript was an extensive work. In order to achieve my goal of making the inmate world and its language understandable, I had to provide the context, which was Warden Ragen's regime. But I had not studied Warden Ragen's regime of control as much as I swam in it, immersed in endless revulsion and fascination. It was rather like living just inside the edge of one of Dostoyevsky's novels. My notes were not those of an academic observer from afar, but of a busy bureaucrat who sometimes felt unhinged by it all. Thus, when I came to sort out my thoughts as I sat looking out at the English countryside, I did indeed construct Warden Ragen's regime from my imagination. But in essence, no analysis of a prison regime is generically different, whether academic or journalistic. As I hope to make clear, the organization of a maximum security prison does not exist in the same social time and space as, say, a factory or a school. It is a secretive, conspiratorial, and violent world in which recalcitrant inmates are not expelled. In many prisons, a mistake or a betrayed confidence can inflict a terrible ostracism or violent death on an inmate. And because it is so cramped a world with no privacy, mistakes and betrayals rarely remain secret.

When I came to revise the 1969 draft into something short enough to be published, I recreated Warden Ragen's regime as a book in its own right, a draft I completed around 1976. I would like to thank Darlene Mack and other secretaries who typed pieces of that manuscript at Kent State University, Ohio.

At that time I was a Professor of Sociology at Kent State University in Ohio. Although I had blundered into that intellectual backwater, I was fortunate to teach with Professor George Pownall in his Corrections M.A. Program, an island of excellence in a sea of dross. For those years I had George as a guide to academic criminology, a critic in revising the original manuscript, and a colleague in teaching. I am grateful for George's help over these past 25 years and his sometimes scathing criticism in re-thinking this final revision, as well as a critical reading of the manuscript by Kady Pownall.

I sent prospecti of the 1976 manuscript to all U.S. academic presses, and I appreciate that the editors of the presses of the Universities of Pennsylvania, Florida, and Penn State were kind enough to consider the manuscript. I cannot say the same for the academics whom they called on for guidance, except for the only one who recommended the manuscript, Professor Daniel Glaser, of the University of Southern California.

Dan, who had been one of my predecessors at Stateville, urged the University of Pennsylvania to publish what he said was an important book, and added six white-hot single spaced pages of helpful criticism. From then on, it was all downhill. A second, anonymous review, which was characterized as "garbage" by Robert Irwin, the press' director, spent 500 words calling the manuscript unsophisticated, limited, unsupported, and emotional. (These were the reviewer's kinder encomiums.) Still battling to get his editorial committee to approve, Robert Irwin sent it to a third reader. He then had to give up, for he reported, "The third reader was more hostile than the second, and, as a condition for delivering his report, the vicious son-of-a-bitch prohibited us from showing it to you."

The editors of the Penn State press gave up after an academic, in 200 words, called my manuscript "boring" and reported, "I have never known anything but one-man prison control so this supposedly 'unique' approach to control does not impress me as being any radical change from the status quo." Similarly, the University of Florida press editors sent it to an academic who in 2,000 words, mainly attesting to his own importance, dispatched it to manuscript purgatory.

So ended my quest for the academic grail. In 1978, when Robert Irwin reluctantly signed off, he prophesied, "Somewhere there's got to be a publisher to bring out the book." I would like to thank Graeme Newman who, in 1994, decided to do so.

Other thanks for help over the years go to so many I can only apologize to any whose names I omit. Special thanks go to Mara Dodge, Tom Spitznas, and Betsy Sterling of Prisoners Legal Services of N.Y. for material and criticism. Also, Richard Allison, Phil Burno, Bill Drennan, Lucia Capodilupo, Jess Maghan,

Lola Odubekun, Mike Reynolds, Terry Rosenberg, and Tony Scocco. I gratefully remember the presence of the late Herb Scott, my colleague as sociologist at Stateville during 1962-63. Officials of the Illinois Department of Correction include Wardens Thomas Roth and Salvador Godinez and their staffs, who permitted me to visit the Stateville Penitentiary in 1991 and 1994, and Nic Howell of Public Information in Springfield who searched the files for possible photographs of Warden Ragen's period.

I would like to thank the staffs of the various libraries who were helpful: among public libraries, The Harold Washington (Chicago) and the New York Public Library, and the Warner in Tarrytown, N.Y.; among Universities, Columbia, Illinois at Chicago, Phyllis Schultz of the Criminal Justice Library of Rutgers University, and Tony Simpson of the Lloyd Sealy Library of John Jay College, CUNY. Also, Scott Forsyth and the staff of the U.S. National Archives in Chicago. Bernice Maluke did much of the typing from typescript to disk.

This book is dedicated to the memory of Lucy Floren Sassaman, who was surrogate mother and mentor to my wife and me for nearly ten years before her death in 1964. That warm and loving, hard-headed Minnesota Norwegian, schooled in the Farmer-Labor Party and tempered by the Depression of the 1930's, guided two young and naive people in the ways of the world. We depended on Lucy for support and guidance all through the turmoil of those Stateville years.

Finally, I would like to acknowledge the help and virtual co-authorship of my wife, Joanne. She lived through the years at Stateville, and since then tolerated files cluttering the house and obsession cluttering my mind. Moreover, it was her own linguistic research to which I contributed the fieldwork that formed the basis of the book I intended to write in 1969 on the inmate social world.

And our sons, Alex and Ted, who grew up with this work in all its manifestations, and never ceased to be fascinated with Dave Maurer, Uncle Don, George Pownall, and the arcane world their parents had once inhabited.

My gratitude extends through the years to all these people. Only I can be responsible for any unintentional errors.

Nathan Kantrowitz
Tarrytown, New York
1996

Preface

Introduction

The killings which plague American prisons underline in blood our concern with controlling those men whom we have sentenced to iron cages. The lack of control also encompasses stabbings and beatings, rape and sexual abuse, extortion, malicious degradation of their fellow convicts, and such constant inequalities as the need to be strong or well connected to obtain decent food or clothing, when available. All these may be the lot of the average convict. This is the reality of a world in which the convicts pay for the warden's lack of ability to control the institution.

How are we to control these places? In theory it is simple, for the warden controls the guards so the guards control the inmates. The inability to do this has been a sorry failure of many wardens. Many believe it is impossible, especially in the large maximum security state prisons which are the cesspools of our great cities. Nor are academics of help, for they miss the point that prison control must be an interconnected system of control in which the web of restraint must be based on the everyday trivia of serving food, washing sheets, mopping floors, and buying candy, in order to suppress the horrors of rape or murder. Academics describe maximum security prisons as institutions governed by a warden who adjusts to fiefdoms run either by his staff or by inmate leaders and gangs. In reality, prison control is an interlocking interdependence controlling the minutiae of every day life. Only this control immobilizes the potential convict power to control other inmates.

This study describes what is necessary for any large prison to be rigidly controlled. Such control aims to eliminate violence, sexual abuse, extortion, the demeaning of inmates by guards or other inmates, and the gratuitous inequality of the strong over the weak among inmates themselves. But it must begin somewhere in reality, for we must demonstrate what some have indicated is not possible without brutality: that such control is more than hypothetical. The reality we shall describe was very real in the Joliet-Stateville prison of Warden Joseph E. Ragen during the time of my employment there during 1957-1963. We shall describe and document this system of close control based on punishment of guards and inmates alike, and on a monopoly of physical violence, which is not the same as brutality. Stateville had little of that.

In addition to describing his system, we will derive some ways in which that system could serve as a basis for control in today's maximum security prisons. Briefly, the general system of control that we derive from Warden Ragen's

Stateville consists of nothing very exciting, for it is essentially a spartan leisure society for the convicts, obtained by paring down and simplifying the operations within the prison so power can be centralized within the capability of the average warden. Today's taxpayers have poured so much money into prisons that the illusions of an earlier generation about "upgrading" the quality of maximum security prisons are now over. Today's taxpayers are in the process of rethinking their largesse. Maximum security prisons henceforth are likely to be massive warehouses. Custodial staff jobs will be good jobs for working class men, while convicts hopefully will be able to exercise what is their central right—to be kept physically in good health, but otherwise left alone. We should emphasize that the control we envision diminishes power all around—to inmates, to guards, to professional staff. To be effective, power must be centralized in the warden.

We have to face a major social issue: that maximum security prisons will be those few institutions of a state's prisons which will be so rigidly controlled. This will lessen the need for the exceedingly expensive "super max" prisons holding small numbers of inmates under permanent lockup, where prisoners are confined to their cells as many as 23 hours a day for years on end. Such places are a modern adaptation of the earliest prisons of the 18th century "Pennsylvania" system which kept men in permanent isolation.

The maximum security prison allows other prisons in a state to remain more flexible and humane, which is what we mean when we speak of "medium" and "minimum" security prisons. If we do wish to control maximum security prisons, then we face a practical issue: how do we gain the acquiescence of the guards to bend under such a yoke, and how do we simplify their organization so control is within the ability of the average warden? As we point out in the Conclusion, the social issue requires a political will from the citizenry to move the politicians of a state. The solution to the practical problem has its own price.

Consequently, although this study is pointed toward students of corrections, I hope that a wider audience of concerned citizens, journalists, and administrators find it useful. Our prison, the Stateville prison, was the largest institution (nearly 3,500 convicts) in the Joliet-Stateville Penitentiary complex which also included the smaller and older Joliet prison, a reception center, and a 2,000 acre farm. This complex housed almost 5,000 inmates.

The time was 1957-1963. This was at the height of its close control under Warden Joseph E. Ragen and his successor and protegé Frank Pate, who took over in 1961 after Ragen was named Director of Public Safety for the State of Illinois. Warden Ragen at this time maintained a rigid and effective control over his guard force and the inmates, a feat accomplished almost exclusively by punishment. At bedrock, his base was a monopoly on face-to-face physical violence, something which is the basis of all control in maximum security prisons. Usually violence is within the power of many guards and inmate gangs in prisons which degenerate to a Hobbesian world of brutality and nastiness. This was not the case in Warden Ragen's Stateville. His monopoly of violence and centralized control over the guards led to the paradox that he created a moral society. Both inmates and guards hated it and chafed under his yoke, but they accepted it as "fair."

In effect the very rigidity of control made for real justice, for the weaker among the inmates were protected from the strong. During the Ragen era, Stateville inmates had to be careful that they might lose their afternoon's recreation if they talked in line at the wrong moment, but they had little fear of stabbings or rape by other inmates. Before and since the Ragen era, they might talk all they wish and ignore line-ups, but they might also fear for their lives, and they might fear violence from guards and guards from them. Prior to Ragen's control, Stateville was virtually run by the inmates and plagued with violence. As his regime developed over the years, he dominated the institution. By the 1970's, only a few years after he and his protegé Warden Pate departed the scene, Stateville returned to its old fearful self. The Ragen era had passsed.

Outline

The intellectual structure of this study is simple, for we must document that the warden controlled the guards and they in turn controlled the convicts. The difficulty comes in documenting this, for the evidence is limited and flawed. Inevitably, ours becomes something of an exercise in higher journalism in which the interpretive and subjective becomes a major part of the presentation. You should not expect to accept an author's conclusions without some feeling for his integrity, intellect, and experience. The touchstone is evidence defined in such a way that the reader accepts it as realistic or fair; I hope you will accept my own.

With these problems in mind, I have organized this study to begin autobiographically with the history of this book and that of my descent into the world of the Stateville Penitentiary during 1957 to 1963. After that I describe the basic task of the warden: to synchronize men and their behavior in time and space, so the prison runs day-by-day. Control is won or lost on this microscopic and perhaps mundane level, which is covered in Chapters 3 and 4. After this discussion of the ecology of the prison, six chapters provide objective evidence: Chapters 5, 6, and 7 discuss Warden Joseph Ragen's control of his guards, based upon all punishments meted out to them during a five month period in 1958; Chapters 8, 9, and 10 discuss the subsequent control of the inmates based upon all major punishments ("Merit Staff" reports) meted out to inmates during 12 months in 1959 and 1960. Following this section, we return to a more interpretive synthesis. Chapter 11 explains the inmate economy, how Warden Ragen controlled it, and how Warden Pate finally bankrupted it to gain greater power over the inmates. Pate did this by manipulating the central bank of the inmate economy, the inmate commissary. Finally, in the last chapter I try to answer the question, "Where Do We Go From Here?" by discussing what lessons we may learn from Warden Ragen's system, the relevant issues of public policy, and how it might be possible to apply some methods from Warden Ragen's regime to prison control in general.

Inevitably, this is not an objective study in the same sense as say, medieval history, where all evidence is available to all. But within my limits of perspective and evidence, I have tried to explain and document a unique system of control in a way that allows us to outline the general requirements to duplicate it. Obviously, creating such a closely controlled prison does not preclude other kinds of prisons, which may range to totally treatment-oriented institutions or more humanitarian alternatives to incarceration such as probation or community-based corrections. Consequently, this report is not a blueprint for a state's corrections system. While the closely controlled prison I describe is necessary, it should be but one part of a penal system.

A Note to the General Reader and Teachers

This book was written for the general reader (with whom I include introductory undergraduates). So that detail does not overwhelm, I suggest you begin with the "Biography Of A Book" and Chapter 1, "The Accidental Observer," so you can understand how this book emerged. Next, Chapter 2, "Chicago's Criminals, Politicians, and Joseph Ragen's Career," will enable you to understand Warden Ragen and his world.

Chapter 3 is the first of two on "The Round Of Life: Controlling Time and Space." Chapter 3, "An Overview," might be read by the general reader by turning to "Warden Ragen's Stateville" for an understanding of how a prison operates. For undergraduates, the entire chapter discusses how ideology influences academic research, and how it has created a body of misinformation about Warden Ragen's regime.

Chapter 4, "Stateville's Schedule In Detail," the second chapter of "The Round Of Life: Controlling Time and Space" can be left to advanced students (with whom I include those employed in corrections).

Chapters 5, 6, and 7 explain how Warden Ragen controlled the guards. Chapter 5, "An Overview," serves to explain the basics to the general reader; the details of Chapters 6 and 7 will be more useful to advanced students.

Chapters 8, 9, and 10 explain how Warden Ragen deployed his staff to control the inmates. The general reader will be interested in Chapter 8, "An Overview," which outlines how control was organized, and Chapter 9, "Violence," which gets to the bedrock of control in a maximum security prison. Chapter 10 will be of interest to advanced students.

The text of Chapter 11, "The Inmate Economy," should be read by all, while the two appendixes will be of interest to advanced students.

Finally, Chapter 12, the "Conclusion," poses the question—and my answers—to the general reader: "Where Do We Go From Here?"

In brief, an undergraduate course might include the text (and exclude the appendixes) of chapters 1,2,3,5,8,9,11,12.

1

The Accidental Observer

M Y DESCENT into the prison world of 1957 was shaped by my job as Sociologist-Actuary for the Illinois Parole and Pardon Board at the Joliet-Stateville prison, located 35 miles southeast of Chicago. I interviewed prisoners who were about to see the Parole Board. As I have recounted in the Acknowledgements, I had no background or interest in criminology, but with some curiosity I took the job. I intended to stay one year, but I stayed for six.

I and another sociologist interviewed 125 to 150 men per month and dictated reports for the Parole Board which provided a brief social background, a summary of prison adjustment, an actuarial score stating the chance of parole violation, and a personal evaluation of whether the inmate was a good risk to complete parole successfully. To carry this out, we had a suite of 3 small rooms inside the maximum security area of the prison, and 2 to 4 inmate clerks who transcribed the reports.

Finding and keeping these clerks satisfied was a crucial part of our duties, for convicts who could read and write at a high school level were scarce, and even scarcer were those who could touch-type and spell correctly from a dictation tape. This was the pre-computer and pre-xerox era, so all typing and clerical jobs in the prison were done on manual typewriters with carbon copies (*flimsies*). Our office had a lot of competition from custodial offices and factories where the Warden could pay them wages (*pay jobs*), while we could not.

During my six years, most of the 19 inmate clerks who passed through my office could have had their pick of prison clerical jobs. Often, we could not trust one of the clerks: he could be dangerous because he was naive, or because he was a *pipeline* to a Lieutenant or one particular chaplain close to Warden Ragen. With the others, we tended to form a secretive society. (I have omitted or disguised the names of everyone in this book with the exception of Joseph Ragen and his successor as warden, Frank Pate.) We guarded ourselves with a bland exterior

1

from prying by other inmates, guards, and the problematic chaplain. I use the term "guard" and sometimes its less common synonym "officer" in this book because those were the terms used during my employment in Stateville. These names did not have the pejorative connotations at that time that some corrections officers feel they have today.

There were official and unofficial perks to the job. The office was equipped with an air conditioner and a television set (not at all common appliances in 1957). We smuggled cigarettes and food in regularly and letters out occasionally; our clerks could *score* for food from the Officer's Kitchen downstairs if they had a *connection* with one of the inmates assigned there. But the major inducement was our office as an oasis. There, our clerks found autonomy and freedom from as many of Warden Ragen's rules as we could manage, along with mutual respect. This arrangement worked to protect our clerks, and to protect me from my own curiosity.

There was nothing in my experience to prepare me for the prison. And because I had never studied criminology, I had no perspective. My initial reactions were shock, fascination, and bewilderment. Because all my friends and acquaintances in Chicago were liberals, I felt repugnance at Warden Ragen. After I achieved some psychic balance, I became fascinated with the question: How did the place run? Did Warden Ragen really control it? I could easily have blundered into being fired without guidance from my clerks. Over the years I became acclimatized, and carried out the research which led to this study. But I was a busy bureaucrat, not an academic paid to stand above it all and observe.

I had an ideal perch, for no one cared what I did as long as the Parole Board's reports were done. The Board itself was comprised of part-time political appointees who spent one day a month at the prison; I almost never saw them. My ostensible supervisor, whose office was 300 some miles south at the Menard Penitentiary, visited me perhaps twice. Our supervision was transferred in 1961 to the State Criminologist five miles away in Joliet; still, this was only nominal oversight. Warden Ragen had no interest in my work.

In my curiosity, I accumulated research projects, none of which were required of me. Some were of practical use, such as updating the actuarial parole prediction tables we used in our reports for the Parole Board, or developing an administrative statistics program. Others were of interest only to me, but permitted by Warden Ragen: tabulating 19th century Joliet admission rates from the old ledgers; administering a questionnaire based on a psychological projective test to men on parole dockets; a linguistic survey as part of research in the summers of 1960, 1961, and 1962 using volunteers from the Television College. Chicago's Community College had a program of college credits by television, and had arranged with Warden Ragen to allow Stateville inmates to participate. They met in the basement of a cellhouse during the school year where television sets and chairs were set up. Summers, many volunteered to work for me. Some of them carried out the statistical data entry for my Ph.D. dissertation.

Each project in its own way introduced me to corners of the prison world, and some were surprises. I remember when I was using the 19th century ledgers in a front office where inmate clerks and civilian women worked together, and I happened to feel the voices, eyes, and electricity between an inmate and a woman clerk. It was mutual attraction; unrequited, I believe. I realized then there was no way to introduce women into a male maximum security prison and not add another complication to its existing cauldron of emotion. Also sexual attraction existed among employees. I remember hearing of two lieutenants who began competing for the affection of a young woman switchboard operator. It got tense before the warden fired the young woman.

The place of women employees in maximum security prisons is a difficult one to assess. My question is do they create problems in the control of the institution, and if so, are there solutions. Much of what appears in the academic literature, such as Zimmer (1986) or Feinman (1994), is nothing more than special pleading in the guise of scholarship. While I have reservations about women as guards in male maximum security prisons, I do not mean to suggest they should not be correctional officers, civilian employees, or volunteers elsewhere, even in selected areas of maximum security prisons. There were no women guards at Stateville during my tenure there, and the research that exists on women in maximum security prisons does not inspire confidence. Nor do newspapers or the media provide much insight. The reality of sexual attraction between inmates and guards in prisons is reported only if someone is fired. Such an incident was reported in the January 31, 1988 *New York Times* in an article about New York's Sing Sing prison where women guards were providing sex to inmates.

We find some description of women employees in prison in the book by Pete Earley. His journalism is based on two years he spent during 1987-89 interviewing in the United States Penitentiary in Leavenworth. His stories must have some basis in fact since the book was praised in a 1992 review by no less than Norman Carlson, the retired Director of the United States Bureau of Prisons. Earley, like any journalist, recounts one dramatic human interest story after another, creating exaggerations. But the substance holds: he created a picture of one of the Bureau's maximum security prisons in which inmates controlled their day-to-day lives, and did as they wished so long as they did not openly defy the guards. In effect, Leavenworth was little more under its warden's control than are most state prisons dominated by inmate gangs: stabbings, assaults, and extortion were routine. For the most part, Earley's book consists of dramatic human interest stories similar to Hollywood movies or other journalists. If you have reservations about accepting a journalist's account of a prison, I recommend you read Fleisher's (1989) ethnography based on more than a year of fieldwork as a corrections officer at the Lompoc prison, a federal maximum security institution. Professor Fleisher, an established academic with years of experience in corrections, was hired by the United States Bureau of Prisons to study the prison and the result is an excellent study of what it means to be a corrections officer. Its only flaw is Fleisher's misapprehension that Lompoc was a well-run institution. It was a virtual duplicate of Earley's Leavenworth, from the *macho* world of corrections officers and inmates, to the prestige of hand-to-hand combat, and the endemic violence throughout. After you read how Warden Ragen ran Stateville you will understand what prison control really means. Another excellent academic study of the psychic world of guards, an interview study rather than ethnography, is Kaufman's 1985 Ph.D. dissertation for Harvard University. Earley's work focusses on inmates, but he portrays the *macho* guards and the prison world just as well.

Earley's work uses journalistic conventions and is replete with sensational-ism, but intellectually it is the equal of these first rate academic reports. If you believe that academics provide a higher form of knowledge about prisons than do journalists, you should ask what intellectual superiority or greater integrity they demonstrate. Moreover, several of Earley's stories are unique, as in Chapter 20, where he produced dramatic examples of the problems of women employees in prison. There were no women correctional officers at Leavenworth for Earley to write about, as there were none during my time at Stateville. He focusses on Leavenworth's civilian women employees, with examples of how rapes and murders took place. Moreover, he raised the issue of seduction in the case of a beautiful and voluptuous young woman secretary who used the Bureau's lack of proscriptions to walk by herself in the prison, spreading erections among inmates and apprehension among guards. He makes this young woman sound more naive than calculating when he recounts the process of how a sophisticated convict was courting her and she was falling under his spell. She was fired before the convict achieved his aim of manipulating her to bring in the means of escape.

Other than that, believable accounts of women employees in prisons surface only occasionally. One story occurs in the 1994 autobiographical account by Nathan McCall, a young thief who became a professional journalist, and who graphically recounted his reaction to a young woman school teacher in his prison: *"She has to know she drives us crazy."* (His italics, p.191). McCall's story raises some important questions because another woman school teacher did not have this effect on the prisoners. The sex goddess in question seemed to be a young, buxom woman who felt she was attractive so she dressed and acted that way, no differently than if she were teaching school outside the prison.

There are problems of sexuality when women corrections officers, civilians, or volunteers work in a male maximum security prison. Some of these are problems of how to control the institution. These are not unique because problems may arise from men employees in women's prisons, and perhaps homosexual guards in male prisons. In Chapter 8, I recount how I gained an insight into modern day maximum security prisons adaptations to women guards when I toured Stateville in 1991 and 1994.

While I learned about Stateville from my work with the prisoners as clerks, I also learned about Stateville from my interviews for the Parole Board. These were usually brief, superficial, and ritualistic, for the convicts told me what they thought I wanted to hear. But not always, as in the account of the guard who was punished for his supervision of the machine shop which I recount in Chapter 7, "Control of Guards." This came from an inmate from that assignment whom I happened to interview for parole just after the guard was punished. Over six years, I learned to see the prison through the eyes of the convicts who lived there because they were my major daily encounters.

I learned less about the guards, for I had no routine business with them, although the stormy winter nights when I stayed overnight in the guards' dormitory provided times to talk. I rarely probed when talking with the guards, for they were more fearful than the inmates and, I learned, with good reason.

Finally, in the natural course of events, I saw men at work at their assignments: my car was repainted at the Vocational School, or I had to see someone at the Isolation-Segregation building. It was happenstance, but I did visit many (though not most) assignments. Sometimes I was part of assignments in the *yard*, and in one case this led me to understood what I have called the "Potemkin Village effect" upon visitors to a prison.

In the days of Catherine the Great, legend has it that the Governor of the Crimea, Grigori Potemkin, built sham villages to indicate prosperity along the route of the Czarina's inspection tour of 1787. Earley's Chapter 36 is an account of how the warden at Leavenworth created the equivalent of a Potemkin Village for a visit by the Director of the Federal Bureau of Prisons. A tour line of inspection was developed with its sites freshly cleaned and painted to perfection, and its scenes scripted. It worked perfectly. The Director and his entourage were led by the nose step-by-step through the charade, and left none the wiser. The story illustrates the perils of inspection by outside experts such as academics. There is an inherent limitation for outsiders studying prisons, where both guards and inmates cooperate to play their "proper" roles. This response is an extreme version of the problem of anyone doing fieldwork in a school or factory, for example. But in a maximum security prison there are steel bars on real cages, which keep the "outsider" at a distance as well.

An example of the Potemkin Village effect occurred while I was administering questionnaires to men who were to appear before the Parole Board in the coming month. These were self-administered questionnaires based on a psychological projective test, (Sargent, 1953), which took about two hours to complete. Once each month the approximately 100 Stateville inmates who were to appear on the next month's Parole Docket were called to the prison high school where they filled out the questionnaire on a Saturday morning when the school was not in use. Only some of these inmates knew one another, so it was not a cohesive group, and rarely would any of the inmates know the guards, who were themselves *relief screws* filling in on episodic assignments.

The school itself was a one-story building designed for control. It was shaped like an +, with a very large square at the intersect of the stubby legs; the guards' post was at this intersect, so they could see into each of the classrooms in each of the 3 legs of the +. (The fourth leg was used for offices). Each classroom had windows along one wall and a blackboard at the foot of the leg so students faced away from the intersect, while a partition formed the other wall. (On the other side of the partition was a similar classroom). Since no classroom had back walls or doors, they were open to the observation point at the intersect.

I had been administering these questionnaires for two years, so the process had become an accepted part of the prison routine. I ran a loose ship, and we all knew it. I brought in cigarettes and candy for the inmates—theoretically, I was smuggling, but no one ever questioned me; they could go to the toilet, talk and "visit" with one another as much as they wished.

On this particular morning, the inmates were sitting in the classrooms quietly filling out the questionnaires; my ground rules were that the classrooms were to be quiet, and all socializing was to be done in the intersect. I was sitting at a desk to one side of intersect, and it was the normal scene when no lieutenants were present. It was relaxed and noisy: some inmates were wandering around, some to the toilet (which was open so guards could observe); some were taking a break from filling out the questionnaire and gossiping. Old friends were getting together, some with horse-play and joshing. The two guards themselves were lounging back in their chairs at the intersect. They were sitting next to one another so they could chat, and were paying little attention to the convicts.

Suddenly, an inmate appeared at the door of the high school and yelled something like "Visitors!" I did not really hear him, for I was busy, it was noisy, and the scene was so normal I was not even aware of it. (I had to reconstruct the next 2 or 3 seconds, after the event).

Visitors were almost always preceded by some inmate heralds, with Warden Ragen's approval if they were outsiders. This also occurred without his blessing—inmate runners, or telephone code words were used—if it were Warden Ragen, his assistant wardens or captains. Lieutenants were the greatest fear because there were so many constantly circulating they could come up on a group unawares.

Instantly, the scene was transformed: I sat up, startled by the hush. The guards and inmates acted automatically; the guards gave no commands, for it seemed that everyone was galvanized simultaneously. Literally, quiet descended in seconds: convicts at the toilet quickly buttoned their trousers and strode to nearby benches, while others hurried back to the classrooms; the school's porters faded into the background, looking busy with wastepaper baskets and mops; all the inmates put out their cigarettes, as did the guards, even though smoking was permitted.

Both guards jumped to their feet, taking a "parade rest" stance (hands clasped behind the back, feet spread apart, while standing rigidly erect). One overlooked one classroom, the other determinedly peered into another. Of course by doing this neither could observe the other classrooms or the intersect. Silence reigned.

Then a chaplain came in accompanied by a man and a woman. They stood to one side while the chaplain pointed and talked in a low tone of voice. After a few minutes they left. I watched this time. No sooner were they out the door than normalcy returned: the two guards returned to slouch in their chairs, the porters put down their waste paper baskets, cigarettes came out, the babble and yapping rose comfortably, convicts lounged around, and a few headed back to the toilet. Again this was automatic; the guards gave no orders beyond their physical relaxation, simultaneous with the convicts'.

I do not present this as a typical prison scene, for I set a relaxed tone compared with most work assignments, where a guard or industrial foreman was in charge. But all assignments developed small worlds, ever alert to intruders, whoever they might be. Naturally, this kind of Potemkin Village behavior will vary according to the situation. At one extreme might be a situation such as Earley described at the Leavenworth Penitentiary, where the warden needed to impress the Director of the Federal Bureau of Prisons with how well he controlled everything; at another are some prisons where there is no control, the guards are a slovenly rabble, and there is nothing anyone wishes to conceal. There are descriptions by awestruck visitors to Stateville of the robot-like organization they saw when Warden Ragen took them on tours. Ragen's Stateville was an impressive place, but it wasn't the Potemkin Village of the tours.

These are the ways in which I learned of Warden Ragen's prison during those six years. This book, then, is my understanding of his control of that intense and seething world. It is not an objective account, although I have used objective information such as guard and inmate punishment reports where I could. Many of my insights were autobiographical. I first learned the reality of control early in my employment from an incident which remains graven in my memory. The Officer's Kitchen (the dining room) had a spatial etiquette at lunch (different from breakfast and supper) in which all guards and most sergeants sat at a massive bank of tables. To one side were a few small tables where one found the male civilians (clerical and professional), the industrial foremen, and a few sergeants of long service—men of experience, functional importance, and no power: this is where we sociologists sat. Adjoining were two tables reserved for Captains and lieutenants, and for women civilians, the only ones with waiter service. Warden Ragen and the assistant wardens did not eat in the Officers' Kitchen.

One day, sitting down to lunch with some industrial foremen and sergeants, I made a careless joke about getting fired. I was startled by the reaction. It was not a response of laughter to a good joke, sick grins to a bad one, or irritation at one in bad taste. Rather, the response was one of frozen-faced men caught at mid-breath and jolted to their bowels, who then finished their meal rapidly and in silence. In Warden Ragen's despotic regime, preemptory firing was an ever present fear, not a joke.

However, there is a difference between the autobiographics of learning and the intellectual task of presenting evidence. When analyzing my material in 1969,

I was surprised to find that I had made no notes of several key incidents, including the latter one. In order to minimize the distortions of memory, I have used the following guidelines: all narratives and examples are based on notes made on the spot or incorporated in my 1969 and then 1976 manuscript, unless I indicate otherwise—usually by prefacing them by "I remember;" all my interview quotations without exception were written verbatim. Sometimes these are exact transcriptions of face-to-face interviews, or more often reconstructions or paraphrases, usually done from notes made within hours, but sometimes a day or two afterward.

Any number of personal anecdotes could illustrate power in Stateville. Two principles were sacrosanct: first, Warden Ragen brooked no criticism of his authority or his supervising officers; and second, whenever a mistake occurred, a guard was punished.

As a result, I did not criticize the regime to inmates I did not know and trust—it would get back to a lieutenant—I did not disagree with officers, particularly lieutenants or captains, and I was circumspect when speaking to others. If you were not, you could be sorry. One sociologist on the staff of the State Criminologist, a quiet and humble man, once disagreed with a captain of the guards, and for months afterwards was searched on admission to the prison and even had his pencils taken away: to interview a prisoner, he had to borrow one from the inmate. My co-worker, for a few years before he was fired or forced to resign—I never learned which—was openly critical of Warden Ragen, and sometimes was refused admission to the prison until he had gone through elaborate and time-consuming procedures.

Although working in such an environment was irritating, as long as I did not question authority, no one cared what I did. All the Parole Board wanted were their reports, and all the Warden wanted was a placid exterior. Everyone got what they wanted. The Parole Board docket required 125-150 reports a month from their two sociologists, a routine which continued for my 6 years. During the last few years, my interviewing was lightened so I might update the parole prediction tables and develop an administrative statistics program.

Warden Ragen never refused a request to carry out research projects. Moreover, after I had been employed a while, Warden Ragen unexpectedly called me into his office where he and Assistant Warden Pate suggested that I might wish to spend more time in the prison *yard*, thinking I might find it profitable to spend a few days observing each of the various assignments. I declined the invitation with thanks, and pointed out that at least for the present, I was over-burdened with routine interviewing and research commitments. I did not mention that while this was true, another reason was my belief that this kind of *carte blanche* would make me, in many inmates' eyes, a *pipeline* to the Warden. As it turned out, the normal routine of my work took me to many (though not most) of the work assignments and cellhouses, not as an observer, but as a prison bureaucrat doing his job. The difference was crucial: the observer with no business to transact raised everyone's eyebrows, and sometimes their hackles. During all those years, no one paid heed to me, perhaps a tribute of indifference to the comings and goings of a harmless drudge.

This freedom can be illustrated by my experience with two questionnaires I used with inmates. In one, I developed 24 situations of conflict in prison situations based on a psychological projective test, (Helen Sargent's 1953 "Insight Test"), to be administered to men on parole dockets; there were never objections from Warden Ragen. In another project, I developed a linguistic questionnaire searching for names which inmates had for inmates and guards. There were many questions he could have objected to, but it is interesting that he did so only once, and it was on one of the most sensitive issues in prison control, guards using physical coercion against inmates. In Chapter 12 I discuss how I had only to make some minor changes to satisfy his objection.

Except for asking for his clearance at the beginning of a project, the only other material I sent him were copies of completed reports. In part, some of this latitude stemmed from his complete control; again, an anecdote illustrates this. In the summer of 1960, I began carrying out statistical research using volunteers from inmates assigned to the Chicago Community College's Television College program; these were the men who became a crucial part of my linguistic fieldwork two years later. Since my project was new and would last only for their summer vacation, I had to organize quickly. I had long since learned that no one below the Warden himself could make any decisions. So I made informal inquiries of the civilian supervisors of education to insure they had no objection, then I made my usual polite obeisance to the assistant wardens, and finally, I waited on Warden Ragen; I made an appointment through his secretary, and personally asked permission.

Then the waters parted. He gave permission and authority to request of numerous subordinates items of equipment such as trestles and planks to make temporary work tables. (I submitted a list of necessaries in advance). However, on the first day, I discovered an oversight on my part: I needed larger light bulbs in the cellhouse basement. Those in use during the school year were small so that the inmates could see the television screen comfortably, but I needed bigger ones. But light bulbs were not on the list Warden Ragen had initially approved, and neither the cellhouse sergeant, nor any lieutenant, captain, or assistant warden had authority to add them. Only when I made a direct request to Warden Ragen— an appointment through his secretary, and an appearance before him in his office—were the light bulbs changed.

You might dismiss this system as a lumbering dinosaur, but consider another example. Once, my office had trouble bringing inmates up for interview because our "call tickets" were not being answered. My inmate clerks were quite vocal in pointing out the bad service and the incompetence of the Warden's staff. My office received a copy of the prison's official notice every time an inmate changed assignment or cellhouse, and from this we maintained a file which listed every inmate's current assignment and cellhouse, so call tickets sent *via* runners to one of these hubs would be relayed to his exact location. This was the theory, but there were 3,500 inmates who could be anywhere in the prison's 64 acres, and changes in assignments were continuous.

After one particularly bad day, I sent a note to the Warden listing a dozen of these cases, and asked if the situation could be improved. The next day, a very polite lieutenant of the guards came to see me with every inmate's location the previous day, shown hour-by-hour. He went over my list, pointing out inmates who could not respond to my call tickets because at the time they were on other call tickets; I had no means of knowing this, but he did. He also pointed out several of my call tickets which had been addressed to the wrong place because my own office file was in error. When I discussed this afterwards with my clerks, they sang a different tune. They agreed that the Warden's records were better than ours, and he really did know every inmate's location every hour of every day.

This incident illustrates another aspect of Warden Ragen's control, for how can a warden really know where every inmate is every hour? In reality, most wardens probably don't. Once out of a cellhouse, there are hundreds of places to be, and it constantly changes. This complexity of inmates constantly circulating is the reason prisons are like beehives. But lack of knowledge of location means lack of control, and enables inmates to relax away from the average warden's grip. It also provides the means for inmate leaders to create gangs, control assignments, and if they wish, extort, intimidate, beat, or rape.

We can end this autobiographical account with some events which accidentally caught me in a conflict over power, and which marked the beginning of the end of my employment in Illinois prisons. Moreover, it illustrates one of Warden Ragen's techniques: all employees were potential informers.

February 1962 marked nearly five years since I began my employment and a little more than one year since the conservative Republican Governor William Stratton was replaced by the liberal Democrat Otto Kerner. Among Governor Kerner's appointments was Warden Ragen as Director of the Illinois Department of Public Safety, with authority over prisons, state troopers, and other functions.

The newly appointed Director Ragen was now a major player in Illinois politics, and he began imposing his stamp on the Department. The dust jacket of his book, written with the reporter Charles Finston in 1962, proclaimed that his appointment, "resulted in the advancement of approximately thirty people into higher ranking and more responsible positions." This is probably an understatement. Numbers of wardens, assistant wardens, captains of the guard, and other executives in Illinois prisons were his protegés; I expect he had a similar influence on the state police and the other agencies under his command.

All through State government this Jacksonian process continued as people were fired and others hired in partisan politics and personal payoffs. It followed the aphorism of Paul Powell, the dean of Illinois Democrats in the state legislature: when Adlai Stevenson's election as Democratic Governor of Illinois in 1948 ended years of Republican rule, Powell crowed that, "The Democrats of Illinois can smell the meat a-cookin' on the stove."[1]

Although none of the actual conflict reached those of us in the lower depths, there were Parole Board echoes as Governor Kerner began to replace the Republicans on the Parole Board with Democrats. For example, the practice had been that while inmates were being punished because of infractions of prison rules, they were refused a Parole Board hearing; some of the new members—I assume liberal Democrats—contested this. This of course locked them in a power play with Director Ragen, for it diminished the wardens' leverage over their convicts.

Thus, I was not happy when on February 28, 1962, during a Parole Board hearing day at Stateville, one of the new Parole Board members (whom I had never met), Mr. Charlie, telephoned to ask me to have lunch with him. Hitherto, members of the Parole Board barely acknowledged my existence, and in fact, the custom was that they dined with the Warden. Moreover, by our leaving through the gates of the prison it became a conspicuous public event; if he had wanted my opinions he could have met me anonymously in Chicago. We drove to a nearby restaurant, and all the while Mr. Charlie fulminated against Director Ragen's expectations, including that he dine with the Warden. The lunch consisted of Mr. Charlie criticizing a number of Parole Board practices and inviting my comments, while I pleaded ignorance about policy matters, and nattered on about how we could improve our reports for the Board. It was a case of an aggressive, ambitious politician trying, with no success, to embroil a cautious bureaucrat in controversy.

The next day, I saw my supervisor, the State Criminologist, on routine business. I expected that he knew of my luncheon with Mr. Charlie, so in good bureaucratic fashion, I cleared myself. That is, I spoke only truths, but vague and partial ones: that Mr. Charlie had asked if I had any opinions, but I had demurred and had forcefully enunciated our need for more staff, and similar bromides. My supervisor, Mr. Able, then surprised me by launching into an attack on Mr. Charlie as someone who was causing problems on the Parole Board, had irritated even the Governor, and was unsuccessfully seeking an appointment as a judge. I knew that Mr. Able was one of Director Ragen's protegés, but I had not known the antagonisms ran so deep.

I worked late at the prison that evening, and when I reached home my wife informed me that Mr. Able had telephoned, and finding I was not home yet, had left his unlisted home telephone number with a request that I return his call. When I did, Mr. Able asked to see me in his office the next morning.

The next morning, when I entered his office, Mr. Able closed the door and said:

> I would like you to prepare a subsumption of the luncheon conversation that you had with Mr. Charlie. It doesn't have to be addressed to anyone, and there is no need for you to sign it, just a statement of what happened.

He then went on to tell me that after I left his office the day before, he had telephoned Director Ragen and reported our conversation, after which Mr. Ragen had instructed him to have me write up an informer's report.

Fortunately, I had anticipated this was coming; driving out to the prison that morning, I realized all these unusual goings on might lead to something of the sort. My wife later told me she suspected something of the sort the previous evening, but thought she was being over-imaginative, and so had said nothing. Consequently, I already had my shock and explosion of anger in the privacy of my car, and I met Mr. Able with the calm and thoughtful reply that I did not think I would write his "subsumption," but that I needed some time to think about it. It was Friday, so I would return to see him Monday. As I left Mr. Able emphasized his polite command by telling me that Mr. Charlie had been "snooping around," and Director Ragen had a right to this.

I never had any intention of writing anything, but I needed time to have my inmate clerks clear the office of any contraband should Warden Pate (Director Ragen's successor at Stateville) order a *shakedown*. As a measure of how untrusting (or perhaps paranoid) I was, I moved my prison notes from my apartment to a friend's house. My clerks and I spent the day cleaning our office of anything embarrassing.

I had already seen the Warden's abrupt *storm trooper* tactics first hand several months earlier when my co-worker of several years was fired (or forced to resign). I was completely ignorant that anything was brewing when, over a weekend, my colleague was escorted into our office by a lieutenant in the evening to collect his personal belongings. When I arrived on Monday to find myself locked out of my office, I was directed by a guard to see Warden Pate. After a pleasant but firm avuncular chat in which he assured me that none of this involved me personally, I was permitted back in my office. It resembled the consequences of a whirlwind. Several lieutenants had cleared the center of the floor, and then, as everything from pictures to garments on hooks on the walls to the contents of drawers were inspected, they were discarded on the growing pile at the center of the floor. Fortunately, they had only rummaged the thousands of inmate files, but had not dumped them; that was about the only exception. Thorough for them, but a mess for me.

This tempest with my supervisor, Mr. Able, was Director Ragen expanding his system from Stateville prison to all of Illinois corrections, so all employees were potential informers. When I returned to see Mr. Able on Monday, to give him my "No" as softly as possible, the result was dramatic. He was quite equanimous as he listened to my answer. And then, before my eyes, last Friday's stern alter ego of Director Ragen metamorphosed into a noble idealist! My newfound friend and supporter said:

> I told the Director I didn't think it was ethical and I didn't think you would do it. I told him that if the Parole Board Chairman asked him to report a conversation with me I don't think he would do it, and I don't think you should do it now.

After a few more pleasantries I left, expecting the worst, perhaps to be locked out of the prison, certainly to be harassed. But nothing happened, and for aught I remember now, I may have been disappointed. But whatever my reaction, everything went on as before and no one thought further of the occasion.

Except in some of my responsibilities, I began getting no response. For example, I was to devise a statistics program. But now, memoranda were answered vaguely or not at all. Then, the resources necessary for the program shrank. That summer "financial exigency" forced the Department to reverse its commitment to pay my expenses to present a paper at a professional meeting. So it went, and after a decent interval for reality to sink in and to find a new job, so did I.

Postscript

As you read this long essay you may ask why do I expound so on how I came to understand Warden Ragen's prison? Part of my aim is to persuade you that the writings on the control of maximum security prisons have been by academic researchers who have had little understanding of the matter. I claim no superiority, for had I not seen Warden Ragen's regime, I would not have known better. It may be a measure of my own limitations that in Chapter 12 I suggest the lessons to be learned are modelled after Warden Ragen's regime. If other wardens create equivalents in control that are different in nature from Warden Ragen's, and someone describes them accurately, we may learn something.

But meanwhile we have to contend with existing academic research, and it is woefully lacking for several reasons. Two are referred to throughout this book: (1) the secretive nature of the prison world and (2) the mistaken view of academic researchers that they bring a higher form of knowledge to the investigation. Another limitation may be that they have a limited comprehension of lower class life. One example of this is in Jacobs (1977:47), an academic's study of Warden Ragen's regime in which he goes on at length over what he called the "poignant" reaction of a young inmate assigned to pushing a wheelbarrow on the "coal pile." The young man found it torturous, for it was heavy, dirty work of a sort he had not done as a thief, and the guards were unsympathetic. Jacobs quotes the young man's travails in detail, and make no mistake it was a tough job. But the reality was there was too little work and too many inmates so those assigned to the coal pile worked half a day, about three hours in the morning, and in a few months were assigned elsewhere.

However, anyone acquainted with working class life or who has watched a construction project realizes that ordinary construction laborers work hard, and push wheelbarrows. But they do it for full working days, day after day and year after year, often until they are 40 or 50 years old. Only a prison observer who had led a sheltered life could feel sorry for the young men on Warden Ragen's coal pile.

Endnotes

1. Illinois politics of my time can be illustrated by Paul Powell, Democratic legislator from a poverty-stricken small town area of Southern Illinois, and one of the dominant politicians of the State. He lived in a hotel in Springfield, the state capital. Upon his death on October 10, 1970, his personal secretary, who shared his suite, showed investigators what she said was his personal wealth: $800,000 ($3.1 million in 1995 dollars) in cash, stashed in his hotel room. This was accumulated from a lifetime in politics in which his highest salary was $30,000 ($118,000 in 1995 dollars). It is not clear how much wealth Powell possessed; one estimate was that his personal fortune amounted to $3 million ($11.8 million in 1995 dollars). He willed much of his fortune to the Johnson County Historical Society in Vienna, Illinois, to preserve his home as a museum and shrine. He stipulated that his gravestone bear the inscription that he was a "Life-long Democrat." (See the *New York Times* in 1971, stories in January, May, August, September, November).

   Not to be outdone by the Legislature, both Governors I served under were indicted by Federal Grand Juries. In 1965, ex-Governor Stratton, a conservative Republican, was indicted for income tax evasion, but was acquitted upon trial (Kenney 1990). Ex-Governor Kerner, a liberal Democrat who had been subsequently appointed a federal judge, was indicted in 1971 for conspiracy, bribery, perjury, and income tax evasion, all committed while he was Governor. He was convicted (*New York Times*, July 19, 1974:39).

   Supporters of both men suggested political motivations lay behind the United States Attorney General seeking these indictments, and indeed Stratton was indicted with a Democratic President in the White House and Kerner with a Republican there. They have a point. The fact is that prosecutions for complex white collar crimes have many grey areas, and points that one prosecutor may see as criminal or prosecutable, another may not. A sympathetic United States Attorney General is an invaluable asset.

2

Chicago's Criminals, Politicians, and Joseph Ragen's Career

Introduction

TO LEARN from Joseph Ragen's accomplishment, we need some understanding of who he was. I can only provide a sketch, because no one has written a realistic biography. He accomplished something unique as a prison warden; he was also part of an era in history But the basis of what he did lies elsewhere: he was, before all else, a politician.[1]

This county politician was a determined man who climbed the greasy pole of success in Illinois State politics, a cut-throat profession. He began as a Democratic Party elected rural county sheriff and treasurer and became a power in state politics as Director of Public Safety (prisons, state police and similar agencies). His first move out of county to state politics was as a prison warden appointed by the Democratic party in 1933, when he was 36 years old. Then he lost out when the 1940 election brought in a Republican Governor. Ironically, that loss turned out to be the lucky break that saved his career. Nearly two years later, he seized the moment: in 1942 the famous Chicago gangster Roger Touhy, along with several confederates, firing guns which had been smuggled into prison, scaled the walls of Stateville and escaped. In the uproar that followed, the man who was warden at the time of the escape (Ragen's 1940 replacement) was fired, and Ragen had his old job back, this time by Republican appointment.

Then, over the next 20 years he transformed himself into a power to be reckoned with in Illinois corrections and politics. I saw this when I worked in his prison during 1957-63, at the height of his power. That power was based on the bedrock of his considerable talents as a politician, and something underrated, the importance to Chicago politicians of keeping Roger Touhy under wraps and out of the public eye.

To recount all this would be a book itself, with others for those whose lives touched Ragen's: the gangster Roger Touhy; the swindler John "Jake the Barber" Factor; not to mention the wars between the Irish and Italian hoodlums during the "Roaring Twenties" and the Depression of the 30s, recounted in the media as the era of the Al Capone gang. I do include essays on Roger Touhy and Chicago crime of the Prohibition era, both because Touhy's prison escape brought Ragen's job back, and because the frame-up that put Touhy in prison in the first place highlights the interplay of crime and politics of that day. That interplay formed the bedrock from which Ragen negotiated with other politicians the power to run his prison.

Although this essay does not attempt to understand Joseph Ragen as a person, I should mention I was astonished when I read Mike Royko's *Boss*, the biography of the late Richard J. Daly, Mayor of Chicago, Ragen's contemporary and fellow conservative Democrat. The quality of Daly the man, portrayed in Royko's book, radiates the qualities I remember of Ragen, the man. Taken together with Erickson's (1957) picture of Ragen, I think it safe to say both were ruthless men of tremendous energy, ego, and the will to dominate, who combined intelligence, and the shrewdness to select protégés to mold remarkable organizations, one a prison, the other a city. And while I can only speculate, I think it no accident that both were Irish Catholic, a people who have repeatedly shown their mastery of American politics.

Warden Ragen has become a myth in corrections, and we shall not see his kind again. But his power rested on the fear that Chicago's politicians had for Roger Touhy—or what Touhy represented. Nor shall we see that again. I have based this essay on readily available sources, and since no Chicago newspapers of the time had indexes, there are many gaps over which I have speculated.

His Early Career

Joseph Ragen was born November 22, 1897 in Trenton, near Carlyle, Illinois, the county seat of Clinton County, in the southern part of the state. Illinois, with its great metropolis of Chicago, is one of the larger states of the United States. Its ten million inhabitants in 1960 (the time of this study) made it the fourth most populous in the nation; since 1970, its population has stabilized a bit higher. They live in 56 thousand square miles within boundaries which meander 500 miles, (as the crow flies, perhaps 400 miles), along its western border, the Mississippi River, as it runs from Wisconsin in the north to Kentucky in the south. In comparison, the entire United Kingdom in 1961 contained five times the population (53 million people) in less than twice the area (94 thousand square miles), with just over 300 air miles between London and Edinborough, or almost 600 air miles from London to Berlin.

Even today, and more so when Joseph Ragen was born at the end of the 19th century, the people divided geographically and culturally. Northern, central, and southern Illinois held different kinds of people, particularly, the "Yankee" northerners who were indistinguishable from people in Wisconsin, in striking contrast to those in the south, who were no different from the people of Missouri or Kentucky.

Joseph Ragen was born to a successful Clinton County political family. His father, William, was elected to three terms as sheriff and one term as judge. Joseph, following in his father's footsteps, was later elected county Sheriff, and then treasurer in the late 1920s. Since the 1920 Illinois *Historical Encyclopedia* (Bateman) notes that Carlyle, the county seat, had both public and parochial schools, there must have been a substantial Roman Catholic population to serve as their voting base.

We think of that day at the turn of the 20th century as the end of the American "Gilded Age," but this southern part of Illinois, known as "Little Egypt," was poor, rural, and small town, a hardscrabble world of dirt roads running between mines and farms being pulled into the automobile and radio age from the world of outhouses and kerosene lanterns. It was southern border country, where men carried guns and used them—usually for hunting, but if necessary on each other (Angle 1952; Erwin 1876).

An example of this occurred in 1922, the "Herrin Massacre," which occurred in nearby Williamson County when Joseph Ragen was a young man (Tingley:106). William Lester of Cleveland, Ohio, who owned the Southern Illinois Coal Company, solved a dispute with its union by firing the union members and hiring 50 strikebreakers and armed guards. After an armed confrontation took place, the strikebreakers surrendered to the miners upon getting a guarantee of safe passage. During the march out of the county while under an armed guard of miners, there was an explosion of gunfire near the town of Herrin, and 19 of the strikebreakers were killed; a number of the miners were brought to trial, but all were acquitted.

Such violence was part of the society. A decade later, history repeated itself (Littlewood:5):

> Troops manned machine guns behind sandbags piled at a church corner in Taylorville. The National Guard had been on duty for months to prevent open warfare between members of the United Mineworkers of America and the Progressive Mine Workers of America. These days when there was a knock on the door after sunset, the cautious miner darkened his lights and went for his shotgun before answering. Patrols of snipers roamed the alleys at night. Men were gunned to death while taking out the garbage.

And these were *law abiding* working men asserting their rights; those who became criminals were even more headstrong and violent. (Remember this the next time you read how today's criminals are so much more violent and uncontrollable than those of yesteryear). This was Joseph Ragen's world as a young man and as sheriff, the police chief for Clinton County's rural areas and small towns. It was no job for someone of delicate sensibilities.

Joseph Ragen and his father before him were important politicians in that world, for criminal justice was, and still is, profoundly a matter of county politics. Illinois is a typical state: while the United States Constitution sets the parameters, the Illinois Constitution organizes the justice system, a state responsibility decentralized to the county level. The state legislature defines crime and provides for a state penitentiary for felons, but the state does not maintain courts of trial. Rather, each of its 102 counties (and to some extent, municipalities within counties) elects and maintains its own police, prosecutors, and courts of trial. The state courts exist only as courts of appeal. The counties also imprison those awaiting trial or convicted of misdemeanors.

The politicians of Joseph Ragen's world spanned a galaxy of players whose power was based on their ability to win elections. Usually the most powerful figure was the county's states attorney who was elected county-wide. He made the basic decision whether to investigate on his own, or prosecute someone who the police brought before him. He decided whether to consider the case a misdemeanor or felony. The grand jury, a group of citizens summoned by the judiciary (also elected) voted the decision to indict or not, but the real power rested with the states attorney who decided what evidence they saw. A decision of the states attorney not to prosecute or to present evidence in a flawed way meant the suspect was let off scot free. If the states attorney did decide to prosecute, then it was his job to investigate and try the case in court.

This was, and still is, an astonishing power for a local politician, virtually unknown in other Western societies. In everyday reality this county politician had supreme power of prosecution, with no practical checks or balances by other branches of state or federal government. (The United States has more than 3,000 counties). True, there were checks and balances, theoretically. But the majesty of judicial review or the checks and balances of legislative oversight rarely intruded into routine larcenies, burglaries, and assaults, the workaday world of everyday criminal justice.

Political campaigns for nominations and votes were waged in conjunction with other politicians in criminal justice agencies. The county sheriff was another major player. Elected county-wide, he was the police commissioner for parts of the county, usually the rural areas, and he ran the county jail. He and his corps of deputies decided which crimes would be thoroughly investigated, who would be arrested, and all too often, who would be protected to run the county's booze, sex, and gambling rackets. Similarly, judges were elected in an array of jurisdictions, and made the critical decisions of freedom or prison.

All these politicians, some with law degrees, some without, had to cooperate or fight among themselves. Some were in criminal justice, some not; some were elected from the towns and cities of their county; some were in state or even national politics. Further, other politicians or politically connected friends, such as police chiefs, were in appointed office, and some were in outside business such as lawyers, bondsmen, insurance brokers, or municipal finance bankers. This was the world in which Joseph Ragen grew up, a politician and the son of a politician.

Then in 1933 he moved from his base in Clinton County to enter the wider arena of Illinois state politics as Warden of the Menard Penitentiary, some 60 miles southwest of his hometown, Carlyle. I do not know how this came about, but prison jobs then, sometimes down to the guard level, were political appointments. The prison itself is located near Chester, a little town by the eastern (Illinois) bank of the Mississippi River. Across the river, some 60 miles to the north on the western bank, is St. Louis, Missouri, then very much a border south city. It was later in time, but still the same part of the river, with elements of the same world in which Samuel Clemens lived as a young man, when he worked on the riverboats of the Mississippi almost a century earlier.

Ragen at the Menard prison was in his home region; its convicts came from the counties south of the state capital in Springfield. Further north, the State was more Yankee and included the great metropolis of Chicago, where convicts tended to go to nearby Joliet-Stateville prison.

At Menard we have a first outside evaluation of Warden Ragen. Donald Clemmer's *Prison Community* (1940), was based primarily on his work experience as a Sociologist for the State Criminologist at Menard in the early 1930's, with some input from his Joliet-Stateville work a few years later. Clemmer gave high marks to the "reform" warden. That warden was Joseph Ragen during his tenure at Menard. (See also Jacobs 1977:250). It is ironic that Clemmer's pioneering study, which created the sociological study of prisons, included a cameo of the young Warden Ragen as a humanitarian reformer in 1933. A generation later, Ragen was reviled by liberals as a reactionary.

Ragen certainly had the approval of major politicians, for in 1935 he was appointed Warden at the Joliet and Stateville prisons to the North. At first he knew little of prison control. This is illustrated by an escape which occurred on his watch and could have ended his career. To give him the greatest benefit of doubt I use Erickson's description, since her biography is almost embarrassing in the way it inflated his accomplishments and minimized his flaws.

In October 1935, just at the cusp of change as Ragen was driving north to Joliet, Basil "The Owl" Banghart and three other convicts escaped from Menard by commandeering an outside truck making a delivery inside the prison, and driving it out through a flimsy fence. Banghart and two others were captured soon after. By the standards of the game, Ragen should have been fired, just as was Warden Stubblefield of Stateville when Roger Touhy escaped seven years later in 1942. After all, the Menard escape exposed security far more lax than at Stateville.

Banghart was as daring and reckless a gunman as Dillinger, albeit without the media and Hollywood movie coverage. My guess is his *moniker* "The Owl" came from his eyes: I knew him only when he was about 60 years old, and the earlier newspaper photographs never did him justice. I remember a slender man of average size, of receding hair, and slightly stooped, with a handsome, angular face whose dominant feature was eyes with large eyelids, like hoods. He worked across the hall from my office and I remember a courteous and friendly but distant man who kept his own counsel.

"The Owl" was a dangerous gunman. He had been on the FBI "Most Wanted" list as "Public Enemy Number 1" in the 1920s. Erickson noted that he had already escaped the federal penitentiary in Atlanta, and shot his way out of a South Bend, Indiana jail. Then in 1934 he was convicted with Roger Touhy on a kidnapping frame up. After his 1935 escape from Menard, Banghart was sent to Stateville, where he again escaped—this time with Touhy in 1942. At that point, the federal authorities stepped in with a previous robbery conviction, and shipped him off to Alcatraz. In 1954 he completed his federal sentence, and was returned to Stateville until he was paroled around 1960.

I remember he gained his freedom for health reasons, and sometime later called me at home. He was working in my neighborhood as a janitor at one of the old and elegant but fading Grand Hotels of Hyde Park on Lake Shore Drive. He was helping raise money for St. Dismas House or one of the other charities for ex-convicts. I mentioned this later to David Maurer, who was then doing field work in the prostitution *rackets* in Chicago. Dave was amused; he said Basil was more than just a janitor. Banghart's hotel was the home of the South Side's most expensive call girls, and they valued him highly. He was a man they could trust for advice, with their confidences, and with their money.

Despite Basil's spectacular escape from Menard, Joseph Ragen's luck or political connections prevailed; he was not fired. He took up the Joliet-Stateville wardenship. This job was a major challenge, for these prisons were not only the immense cesspools of more sophisticated convicts from Chicago, but they had been uncontrollable, and on at least one occasion the National Guard was called in to subdue them.

That prison violence was part of a society more violent than we see today. Virgil Peterson recounted (1952:179) one 1937 episode of Chicago's labor history at the Republic Steel Corporation plant:

> Chicago police officers met the strikers in force at this point and ordered them to disperse. Suddenly a shower of bricks and clubs was hurled at the police and the crowd started to surge forward. Clubs were swinging wildly on both sides. Some of the strikers were armed with short pieces of pipe and two-by-four boards. The onward movement of the strikers was brought to an abrupt halt as the air was pierced with the sharp cracking of pistol shots. Men fell with streaming wounds. Others were clubbed to the ground.
> Chicago was witnessing one of the bloodiest labor battles in its history. Ten pickets shot by the police during the encounter died from their wounds. Twenty-six policemen were injured and required hospital care.

And the criminal violence of that day made labor strife look mild. In comparison, no one today can imagine the Chicago police killing ten labor union strikers; even in the riot of the Chicago police at the 1968 Democratic National Convention, there were no deaths.

Such was the vineyard in which Warden Ragen labored from 1935 through 1940, with I believe, minor results. The claque of newspaper reporters who trumpeted his later years sweep over these early ones as the beginnings of a victory march, but the facts suggest otherwise. For one thing, how could he discipline guards for mistakes or corruption? Those were the terrible Depression years, when any job, especially a steady government one, was a treasure. Supervisory officers and guards had political sponsors, as Warden Ragen himself must have had. His staff could call on their political connections just as he could, so he probably thought twice before drawing on his political credit. Added to this, the inmates, certainly those at Stateville, really did run the place, and in the worst possible way. We know that entrenched gangs in any prison are difficult to tame, so how could Ragen do it with such limited authority over the custodial staff? He was also limited in his ability to transfer gang leaders out of Stateville, for he had only the Menard prison to send them. It is doubtful that the Menard warden, with his own political clout, would burden himself with many of Warden Ragen's worst problems.

Another indication of Warden Ragen's limited stature occured when the newly elected Republican Governor Dwight Green took office in early 1941. Democrat Joseph Ragen resigned, the normal workings of the political patronage system. This was the lucky break that ultimately made Ragen, for had he stayed I am sure Roger Touhy would have escaped the prison just the same. Ragen did not go on to greener pastures, so his departure was that of a minor politician who jumped before he was pushed.

His career showed little promise. According to the Chicago *Tribune*, he went on to some unspecified federal government job in "the registration of aliens," part of the new war effort. It is not likely this was much of a job or he was a success because he soon left. He was found in October 1942, less than two years after leaving the wardenship, the superintendent of security at a factory, the Pressed Steel Car Company, where he reported to a Vice President. This is hardly the track record of a ball of fire, to go from a Wardenship to a short-term government job, and then to being the security chief of a factory. This job must have been a humiliation. This is suggested by its omission from Gladys Erickson's biography, a book embarrassing in its fawning. She puffed up his most minor deeds but made no mention of Ragen's factory job, presumably because it was so great a fall.

The Main Chance: Warden Joseph Ragen Returns

Then in autumn 1942, chance changed everything: Roger Touhy and six confederates scaled the walls of Stateville Prison on Friday afternoon, October 9, 1942. This electrified Chicago, as we see from the Chicago *Tribune*'s headlines. Before the escape, the Second World War dominated the front page. For example, the Chicago *Tribune*'s banner headline the morning of the escape read, "US Carrier Force Hits Japs," with a story of a great U.S. Naval victory in the Pacific; other front page news covered the U.S. Marines landing in Guadalcanal, while the Russians and Germans were locked in death's embrace at Stalingrad.

That afternoon, Touhy and his six confederates escaped. It was spectacular. With guns that had been smuggled in, they shot their way out. The next day, the *Tribune*'s October 10 headline was, "Hunt Seven In Touhy Escape," and only gradually did Roger Touhy depart the headlines and the concerns of the world return.

Then, 10 days after the escape, on October 19th, the *Tribune* reported Stateville's Warden Stubblefield had resigned. During this interval there was no mention of Joseph Ragen. The next day a small story on the bottom half of the front page was headlined "Ragen One of 3 Listed As New Prison Warden." Ragen was on the short list with the Joliet City police chief, and the warden of the Pontiac prison. The next day another small story on page 1 announced he had the job. The final appearance of Warden Ragen was on October 23, when a small editorial a few inches long toward the bottom of the editorial page (about half the size of its surrounding editorials) captioned "A Good Appointment," crowned him with some praise. Coverage in the other Chicago newspapers was on a par. The *Daily News* had one story of his appointment on October 21 and a lead editorial of praise on October 22nd. The praise in both editorials was probably deserved, and it is important that both strongly defended Republican Governor Green for appointing a Democrat, so entrenched was the expectation that Wardenships were part of party spoils. The strength of Illinois pork-barrel politics of the time can hardly be imagined by people today. Neither the *Herald American* nor the *Daily Times* ran stories or editorials, though the *Daily Times* ran his picture on October 23rd.

From this inauspicious point, Joseph Ragen began his transformation into a power in Illinois politics, the man who broke one of the nation's most violent prisons to his yoke. How he did it over the next decade must be accorded to his own abilities and the lessons he learned during his 1933-1940 wardenships. But the basis by which he leveraged power must have been the grip which the Roger Touhy legend had on the imagination of the people of the midwest. Illinois politicians, anxious to store Roger Touhy safely out of the public eye, were probably ripe for concessions when negotiating with Ragen, then a seasoned politician 46 years old who had tasted the bitter fruit of being cast aside. And, I think the politicians of Illinois were willing to pay Ragen's price to keep Touhy out of the headlines and safe in prison: enough power, particularly over the guards to put him really in charge. I remember one of my clerks telling me that Warden Ragen assigned a guard whose job was to know where Roger Touhy was every minute of the day. Touhy worked in cellhouse help, a housekeeping assignment to keep cellhouses clean, so he stayed in his cellhouse all day. At the time, I did not note it because it seemed pointless. But on reflection, I have concluded it was true and important: it had meant Ragen's career.

From then on Warden Ragen's prison received only favorable publicity. When Adlai Stevenson, Governor of Illinois, interrupted his 1952 campaign for the presidency because of Illinois prison riots, none were at Warden Ragen's prison. There were never any embarrassments, disturbances, or riots at Warden Ragen's prison. I don't think it was for any lack of trying on the part of some of his inmates. I was never able to track down anything specific, but there were inmate attempts to start riots and build bombs. I also heard of one attempt to embarrass Warden Ragen over money, probably commissary funds. (See also Jacobs, 1977:252). None ever came to anything.

The two possible embarrassments which occurred during my tenure were sidestepped. In one case, inmates had subverted the cellhouse "deadlock" mechanism and were poised to break out of their cells, and either take over the cellhouse or make an escape attempt. It must have taken months or years to secretly re-engineer the mechanical and hydraulic mechanism, and they were caught just on the brink of success. It was an incredibly ingenious breach of a major security system. An accurate report would have made a laughing stock of Warden Ragen, but what appeared in the press was a garbled story which made him look vigilant. In another case, a white convict killed a black convict, the only inmate murder which took place during my time at Stateville. There were no witnesses, so all we had was the white killer's statement that he resisted a homosexual attack. The county grand jury did not indict the killer, and what came out in the media was that two inmates fought over cigarettes, nothing about sex or race.

I remember hearing inmate stories about ongoing official conniving, some of which may have been true. Favored banks handled the prison money, favored businesses were its suppliers, and the politically connected bought prison manufactures for personal benefit. But I saw no evidence, and there were no public embarrassments.

As a result Warden Ragen was on the best of terms with the media. The Chicago *Tribune* put out a series of glowing articles in 1955; Gladys Erickson published her hagiography in 1957; in 1962, the journalist Charles Finston prepared an official version of how Stateville was managed. I learned how closely Warden Ragen was connected to conservative political forces when I saw some of the correspondence with the Chicago Police Department's Censorship Board which approved all movies shown to inmates, and guaranteed they were wholesome and free from communist influence.

Since Warden Ragen was firmly ensconced as a power among political conservatives, it must have been all the sweeter when in 1961 the newly elected liberal Democratic Governor Otto Kerner appointed him Director of Public Safety—prisons, the state police and more. Ragen had more patronage to dispense than ever; his proteges assumed high positions throughout the State, beginning with his Assistant Warden Frank Pate, who became Stateville's new warden.

Then in 1965 it ended, when newly re-elected Governor Kerner eased him out of office. The political tide shifted, and in 1970 Ragen's protegé Frank Pate was forced out as warden when political liberals took over the prison system. Joseph Ragen died at the age of 74 on September 22, 1971, in the city of Joliet, Illinois.

The Criminal Era

Why was Roger Touhy's escape so crucially important to Illinois politicians that they gave Warden Ragen unparalleled leverage over his prison? I must rely on conjecture based on the obtainable facts; as with Ragen, biographies as yet unwritten would provide the necessary corrections. Roger Touhy was a folk hero in Chicago, similar in stature to one of his contemporaries, John Dillinger, the bank robber. Touhy was the last of Chicago's Irish gang lords, destroyed by the Italian thugs who are usually hyped by the media as the Al Capone gang. But Touhy's destruction was more than a colorful footnote to Chicago's history: it was an unusually public example of government officials in business with organized crime.

THE CHICAGO RACKETS

Chicago criminals during the 19th century already had links to the police and politicians; together with prostitutes, entertainers, gamblers, the sporting world, and rich businessmen, they created a demi-monde. They even had a great celebration. For years, two Aldermen, "Hinky Dink" Michael Kenna and "Bathhouse" John Coughlin, sponsored the New Year's Ball of Ward 1, which ended in 1910. But with Prohibition enacted in 1919, a new dimension was added in which Americans formed a mass market for illicit goods: bootleg liquor. This phenomenally lucrative market spun the dance into a new step in which the money available to criminals expanded so much that the old relationships changed. Politicians and police previously took payoffs to look the other way, but now they and others in criminal justice agencies became partners and employees of the criminals, who in turn became more businesslike to cope with their new responsibilities as manufacturers, marketers and distributors. The criminals now organized syndicates—independent gangs meshed into a hierarchy, with a gang lord at the top who coordinated and controlled them—and relied on murder to enforce decisions.

At the beginning of this century, Chicago businessmen, alarmed by criminal power and violence, had formed the Chicago Crime Commission. In 1929, John Landesco, a research sociologist and criminologist in their employ, published a landmark report on organized crime in Chicago (primarily since the first World War). Since then a procession of books on Chicago crime has rolled off the presses, often with the magic names "Al Capone" or "Dillinger" in their titles. Many are junk, but some seem reliable, although always subordinate to Landesco (dates and details of facts sometimes vary) for two reasons: few lay claim to any original authority; and second, more contemporary works rarely correct Landesco.

The 19th century world of thieves continued into the 20th, with pickpockets, confidence men, and racketeers such as the Mont Tennes who controlled gambling in over 20 cities. Among Chicago's south side gang bosses, "Big Jim" Colosimo headed the dominant Italian gang, which had co-existed with other ethnic gangs, at least since 1909.

Then changes began in the Italian gangs: around 1918, Johnny Torrio came from New York to work under Colosimo. He was followed a year later by Al Capone to do the same, followed a year later by Colosimo's murder. By then Prohibition was in force. Torrio, a born organizer, became the gang boss and began molding the powerful syndicate of later years. Landesco lists, as of 1929, a dozen gang leaders of varying ethnicities as his allies or lieutenants. Torrio made crime a business, and killed (or had the police kill) other gang leaders who did not cooperate.

As a measure of Torrio's ability, Landesco—either repeating or corroborating a 1924 newspaper story—explained how an unnamed young businessman, one of four brothers from a wealthy family of brewers, became Torrio's partner. He taught Torrio how to run a business, knowledge which Torrio added to his criminal rackets: gunmen, and fixes with the police, politicians, and probably everyone else, from newspaper reporters to prosecutors. Landesco estimated that after 1920, this young businessman pocketed $12 million per year ($91 million in 1995 dollars).[2]

After he was wounded by an assassination attempt in 1924, Torrio retired from the Chicago rackets, and different hoodlums vied to take his place. Landesco, writing in 1929, considered Al Capone a leading contender but by no means in charge. Since Landesco's report was published five years after Torrio left the scene, it suggests there was no dominant crime boss in Chicago at the time. Landesco never mentioned Roger Touhy in his report.

Then came a defining moment: in 1929, the year of Landesco's report, organized crime became a national business. The story of this is in Dennis Hoffman's (1993), account of how the "Secret Six," a small group of Chicago businessmen, funded counter-measures to the growing power of Al Capone. In 1929, the first national conference of mobsters from cities across the United States convened at the Presidential Hotel, in Atlantic City, New Jersey. It was chaired by Johnny Torrio, and the names of the attendees were overwhelmingly Italian, with some German, Jewish, or English-sounding names, but none distinctly Irish. Naturally, few Americans of Italian, German, English, Jewish, or Irish ancestry became criminals, but by this point, those who were recruited their own, and over the years those of Italian ancestry dominated, with numbers of

Jewish subordinates; the Irish seem to have been marginalized or killed off.

Shortly after the 1929 national crime conference, Capone became the gang lord of Chicago. He reveled in media attention, and became an embarrassment to the Chicago rich, not the least because they were planning to make Chicago respectable with a World's Fair in 1933. The Secret Six succeeded in getting the Republican White House to go after Al Capone, and he was imprisoned in 1931.

Along the way the Secret Six accumulated material about Chicago's rackets. They estimated that more than half of Chicago's 6,000 policemen took bribes from Capone's gangs. My calculations from Hoffman's figures suggest that the annual gross profit from bootleg beer and liquor in the Chicago area approximated $270 million ($2.5 billion in 1995 dollars) around 1930.

It was during this period that Al Capone consolidated his place as the dominant gang lord of Chicago, and because he was such good copy, the media inflated his considerable talents and accomplishments beyond all bounds. But Capone was imprisoned after only a few years of absolute power; in 1929 Landesco considered him only a leading contender to take over Torrio's mantle, and he was gone after 1931. He had built well on John Torrio's foundation. After him, Paul Nitti took over the Italian syndicate which dominated crime in the city.

During Capone's heyday and continuing into the Nitti reign, a small cloud growing on the criminal horizon started to rain on the Italian syndicate's parade. In the 1920's, a group of four Irish brothers (of five brothers and two sisters), offspring of a Chicago policeman, had developed their gang based in suburban Des Plaines, northwest of the city, near where O'Hare Airport is now. Led by one brother, Roger, the Touhy gang recruited members, mostly Irish, and took over the bootleg (and presumably other) criminal businesses in the northern suburbs, reaching into Chicago's north side. (According to the Chicago *Tribune*, from Irving Park Road north). It was no tea party: in the gangland battles of the time, two of Touhy's brothers were killed, as was one of Capone's.

Those who claim that criminals of today are unparalleled in their violence simply suffer historical amnesia. The Senate Subcommittee on Organized Crime in Chicago (1983:12) tabulated 1,081 gangland slayings in the 65 years from 1919 to 1983. But Landesco, writing in 1929 had already written that in just four of those years (1922 to 1926) there were 215 gangland murders. In effect, 20 percent of those killings occurred in just four of the 65 years. And this omits Landesco's tabulation that in the same four years the police killed another 116 gangsters. Landesco also recounted how the turf wars to control the gambling rackets caused incessant bombings across the metropolis, year after year.

The violence continued unabated as the Roaring Twenties crashed into the Depression of the 1930's. But then disaster struck at the end of 1933, soon after Franklin D. Roosevelt was elected president, when the Prohibition amendment to the Constitution was repealed. The bootleg booze market collapsed, and the criminal groups depending on it—along with other staples such as stealing, extortion, gambling, the sex trade and other necessities of urban life—were faced with retrenchment and collapse. Many gangsters accelerated existing gambits such as kidnapping or preying on the expanding labor unions. But all faced hard times.

Some writers on organized crime have portrayed the ascendance of the Italian syndicates as a kind of hoodlum sporting event, like an old John Wayne movie—only with all bad guys. Purportedly, they went at each other until the baddest guys won. But there is a missing piece in this script: Chicago's politicians and police. This fact has been reiterated time and time again by reform groups, such as the Citizen's Police Committee (1934:3):

> Over all hangs the judgement of Cook County grand juries. In 1928 a special grand jury declared the Chicago Police Department to be "rotten to the core," and another more recently has announced that its investigations disclosed the existence of a well-established, three cornered alliance between the Police Department, the corrupt politicians, and the criminal element. The natural and inevitable results of that alliance take the form of hoodlum gangs, and rackets, with organized prostitution, syndicated gambling, beer wars, bomb terrorism, kidnaping and extortion, the exploitation of legitimate business, and control over the ballot box and the agencies of criminal justice-all linked together in one vast conspiracy. The distinguishing mark of this alliance is murder on a large scale.

Testimony before the U.S. Senate Subcommittee on Organized Crime in Chicago (1983) suggested that nothing had changed. And the *New York Times* of January 18, 1996 noted, in a story about the conviction of a Chicago City Council alderman, that the United States Attorney General convicted 18 local judges during the 1980's, and 18 Chicago City Council aldermen since 1973.

We have a problem of nomenclature to clarify here. Chicago was run by criminal syndicates dominated by Italians in partnership with the police, other criminal justice agencies, and politicians who were dominated by the Irish. The wealthy businessmen who were neither Italian nor Irish sometimes acquiesced and sometimes supported this arrangement. The criminals and the police and criminal justice agencies were the businessmen's allies in suppressing or corrupting labor unions. I will refer to this interlocking arrangement as "The Criminal-Political Complex," or simply, "The Syndicate."

ROGER TOUHY

My guess is that The Syndicate met its match in Roger Touhy. Part of his edge was his base in the northwestern suburbs, where he was the one who had the police in his employ. According to Touhy, Al Capone tried to sucker him into a business collaboration in the late 1920's, and he rejected the offer. This unrequited courtship led to an all-out war in which Touhy gave as good as he got. By the early 1930's it was a standoff, and Touhy had achieved an aura with Chicagoans, both as an outlaw (like Capone or Dillinger) against the proper society which had brought them the Depression, and also as David against the Goliath of The Syndicate.

Perhaps an accommodation could have been reached over time, but I doubt it. First was the difference in moral values, strange as it may seem. Touhy the gangster promoted liquor and gambling, but he was a devoted husband and father who would not tolerate organized prostitution which was promoted by The Syndicate. In this he solidified his alliances with suburban politicians who shared his values. Perhaps this disapproval was an expression of Irish Catholicism.

Certainly the Criminal-Political Complex could have tolerated this eccentricity, but Touhy's protection of labor unions was a direct attack on their incomes. Today when racketeer dominated labor unions are seen as a regrettable but common part of the political landscape, it may come as a shock that it was not always so.

Some of this forgotten history has been preserved in a decision by federal District Judge John Barnes of the Northern District of Illinois. We know little about this remarkable man because no one has written his biography.

In this instance he did something I had never seen before: he transformed a post-conviction appeal into a documented re-creation of past injustice. It began in 1948 when Roger Touhy filed an application for a writ of *habeas corpus* in federal court contesting his Illinois 1942 escape and 1934 kidnapping convictions. During the next five years these appeals lumbered all the way to the U.S. Supreme Court, where his appeals were finally denied. Touhy had to wait until 1959 when Governor Stratton used the power of executive clemency to let him out.

Judge Barnes used the occasion of Touhy's application for a writ to recreate the 1934 trial. He required the assemblage of over 3,300 pages of documents, affidavits, and testimony, and he wrote a 600 page decision analyzing the trial and the corrupt political world of Illinois justice.

In his decision (1954), Judge Barnes described how the Syndicate saw the union treasuries as ripe for picking. They surmounted their enmity to Touhy to make a good-faith offer to divide the spoils (478):

> When the Capone syndicate started moving into the unions their representative brought a list of the unions with the amounts in their treasuries around and showed it to Roger Touhy's brother Tommy. They asked Tommy which union he wanted, and Tommy said he wasn't interested. Roger Touhy said he wasn't interested either.

The Syndicate at that time was moving to begin the process of looting the labor union treasuries of the Teamsters, Building Service Employees, Bartenders, Moving Picture Operators, Janitors, Laundry, Cleaning, and Dying industries. Judge Barnes discussed how Touhy tried to help the unions in his territory (479):

> Roger Touhy's brother Tommy warned his union acquaintances that the syndicate was going to move in on them, and they banded together for protection in Park Ridge. These men included: Paddy Burrell, Vice President, International Teamsters; James Lynch, Head of Maywood Teamsters; Eddie McFadden, Material Drivers Union; Art Wallace, Painters

Union; Jerry Horan, Building Janitors and Building Service Employees.

From the names, it seems this was primarily an Irish Catholic coalition, ironic since The Syndicate itself was a criminal enterprise dominated by Italian gangsters and Irish politicians. Judge Barnes recounted (479):

> These men got together a fund of $125,000 [$1.25 million in 1995 dollars] to resist the syndicate. Roger Touhy took charge of this money for them.

It all came to naught as Judge Barnes noted how one, then another of the union heads either sold out or capitulated to The Syndicate. But the important point is, if Judge Barnes' conclusions are correct, there was a moral gulf separating The Syndicate from Roger Touhy's gang. Touhy actively organized the politicians in his territory to oppose organized prostitution, and he organized the union leaders to maintain the integrity of their unions, all against the racketeers and politicians who finally prevailed after he was framed and imprisoned.

The final aspect of Touhy's conflict with The Syndicate requires us to leave the security of Judge Barnes' evaluations and enter the paranoid world of conspiracy theories which center about the assassination of Mayor Anton Cermak of Chicago in 1933. Like the paranoid world of conspiracy theories which evolved from President John Kennedy's assassination in 1963, some of those theories may be true—we shall never know.

Anton Cermak, who had won the mayoralty in 1931, was assassinated in February 1933 while conversing with President-Elect Franklin Roosevelt at a rally in Miami, Florida. The accepted belief is the six people who were shot by the deranged gunman Giussepe Zangara were accidental casualties near the intended target, Franklin Roosevelt. Most writers report that Zangara was deranged and he really did want to shoot President-Elect Roosevelt.

After that, there is a wide range of interpretations. One by Allsop (1961:177-8) is intriguing. He states that after Roger Touhy's murder in 1959, Saul Alinsky, the political organizer who had been a sociologist employed at the Joliet prison at the time Touhy was incarcerated in 1934, made public a story that involved two points: Mayor Cermak had enlisted Touhy to kill off Al Capone's gang; and a Capone gang member in the crowd that day in Miami shot Mayor Cermak with a .45 caliber pistol while Zangara was wildly firing a .32 caliber gun. It is not clear from Allsop who Alinsky is supposed to have told this to, or whether Alinsky claimed to have heard this directly from Touhy, but given Saul Alinsky's importance as a community activist, writer, and ally of the Roman Catholic hierarchy, such a claim cannot be dismissed out of hand.

Leaving aside issues of the assassination, there is independent testimony by John Lyle of Anton Cermak's hostility to The Syndicate and his acquaintance with Roger Touhy. John Lyle was a prominent Republican politician of the 1920's and 1930's, and in his memoirs (1960:260-1) he recounts a meeting with Cermak before the mayoral nominations were in:

We talked for about an hour. Cermak expressed the hope that I would win the [Republican] nomination. "That's the only sure way to wipe out the mafia," he said. "Whichever one of us is Mayor will go after them."

He was vehement in his denunciation of Capone and the Blackhand society. But in the same breath he said, "They don't know how I feel about them. I think I can get some support from the mob in the campaign. I'll take it. But after the election I'll boot them out of town."

In effect, he was announcing his intention to double cross the Capone mob. It was, I reflected, a dangerous game to play with cutthroats.

Lyle then continued:

Cermak spoke of the suburban beer gang headed by Roger Touhy. They operated in an area supervised by Cermak as county board president. "I get along fine with Touhy," Cermak said.

This raised a question in my mind and I voiced it. Did he intend to stamp out all gangs or just the Capone crowd? Cermak replied, "I'll go after all of them. None of them are any good. It'll be the popular thing to drive them out of town."

This is not a blueprint for a Cermak-Touhy collaboration, but Touhy was the only gangster accorded such status. And Lyle was a shrewd observer: he liked Cermak but he skewered Cermak's profusions of affection for him, and he discussed some of Cermak's shady deals. All the more reason to take seriously his (p.265) recounting of some hearsay:

Belonging here chronologically, is a statement made years later by Roger Touhy. He said that Cermak had urged him to war on the Capone mob with the understanding that the territory thus vacated would be made available to the Touhy gang.

Touhy, according to his story, told the mayor he did not have the manpower. He quoted Cermak as replying, "You can have the entire police department."

What are we to make of these straws in the wind? First, there was a distinct moral chasm between Touhy and the Criminal-Political Complex which ran Chicago. Touhy would not tolerate organized prostitution and he tried his best to protect the working men of the labor unions. Even more threatening, Touhy probably did make some alliance or *laissez faire* arrangement with Mayor Cermak which was at the least detrimental to The Syndicate. Cermak was not squeamish. Alex Gottfried, in a sober academic biography of Mayor Cermak, suggests (1962: 316ff) that the police detective who shot and nearly killed Nitti, Al Capone's successor as head of the Criminal Syndicate, was one of Mayor Cermak's personal police guard, and the shooting itself was a botched assassination attempt. With Mayor Cermak's death, the old Criminal-Political Complex ascended again. But Roger Touhy remained a problem to be eliminated, and he was more than a match over the barrel of a gun.

A way out of the impasse presented itself to The Syndicate in the person of John "Jake The Barber" Factor. It was alleged that he had swindled English investors in the 1920's out of $1.5 million ($11 million in 1995 dollars), and on another occasion in 1926, of $20 million ($172 million in 1995 dollars). Factor then fled to the United States at which time the British government filed to have him extradited back to England to stand trial.

In 1933, Factor came forward with the claim that he had been kidnapped and held for ransom, a plausible charge, for in 1933 the nation was in the midst of a wave of kidnappings. Criminal gangs began to kidnap gamblers and other shady types as a kind of extortion racket, and then graduated to doing the same to the rich. Roger Touhy was charged with the crime, but his first trial in 1934 ended with a hung jury. In his second trial, Touhy and two associates were convicted in Chicago Criminal Court of kidnapping John Factor. The newspaper coverage was enormous. For example, on February 16, 1934, the Chicago *Tribune's* front page banner headline (printed in capitals several inches high across the entire page) was "Touhy Kidnap Jury Chosen." From then on, it was almost all front page stories or banner headlines until February 23rd, when the banner read "99 Years For Three Touhys" (Roger Touhy and two associates). After they were transferred to the Joliet Penitentiary, feature stories dwindled, and soon Touhy was forgotten.

A federal Appeals Court summarized Judge Barnes (U.S. v. Ragen, 224 F.2D 611z): "The alleged kidnapping of Factor was a hoax, planned by Factor himself to prevent his extradition to Great Britain."

And further, as summarized in the Chicago *Tribune* of December 17, 1959, p.6:

> Barnes also ruled that Touhy's conviction had been obtained on perjured testimony with the full knowledge of Daniel Gilbert, former Chicago Police Captain and States Attorney's Chief Investigator, and presumably with the knowledge of Thomas J. Courtney, then States Attorney and now a Circuit Court Judge.

The Chicago *Tribune's* coverage of both 1934 trials was astonishing: Roger Touhy was a ravening beast, the Capone gang was only a tattered remnant of its former self, and John Factor was a respectable businessman. Judge Barnes recounted how Touhy could not retain the lawyer he wanted and his witnesses were harassed by the Cook County States Attorney—and by the FBI, if one includes an earlier case in Minnesota in which he was acquitted—while witnesses for the prosecution committed wholesale perjury. Newspapers described how the trial judge had the courts ringed with squads of Chicago police.

Judge Barnes in his 1954 decision did not deal with the Syndicate's control of Chicago, but its involvement is now part of conventional wisdom. As Girardin states (1994:294): "Touhy was...later framed by Al Capone for a bogus kidnapping that removed him as competition."

The last and most mysterious chapter of Roger Touhy's life was his murder. The Republican Governor of Illinois, William Stratton, reduced Touhy's sentences so that he was paroled from Stateville in 1959, a man of 61, his brothers dead, his confederates dead or enfeebled. On December 16th, 23 days later, he was killed in a professional gangland execution, gunned down at the doorstep of his sister's house in Chicago. As usual, the Chicago police made no arrests. His murder remains a mystery.

"Jake The Barber" Factor

Another revelation of the relationships between criminals and politicians surfaced with John Factor's ties to the Democratic Party. Judge Barnes recounted how Thomas Courtney, the States Attorney of Cook County who was prosecuting Roger Touhy, went to Washington D.C. and had a personal interview with President Franklin Roosevelt, urging the president to refuse the British government's extradition quest and keep "Jake the Barber" in the U.S. for the kidnapping trial.

On the face of it, this is incredible. The issue of an alleged swindler's extradition would normally be decided on some under-secretary level and then ratified by cabinet officers, the Secretary of State and the Attorney General, for the president's pro forma approval. The president's appointment calendar must have been set by a staff bedeviled to ration his time during those first frantic days of the New Deal, for the nation was at risk. I can only guess at the political leverage applied by Chicago politicians to get this interview. It worked.

Factor's extradition was delayed for the Touhy trial, and shortly after the guilty verdict in February 1934, the British government received unwelcome news from Franklin Roosevelt's administration: the United States would not honor their extradition request. John Factor never had to stand trial for fraud in England. He remained in the United States, where in 1943 he was convicted of fraud and sentenced to serve ten years in federal prison. He served six years and then vanished from the newspapers until 1962.

John Factor was a fascinating character, for nothing could be believed. He was actually born Jacob Factorovitz in Warsaw, Poland—not Hull, England as he told the newspapers. Even this may be wrong, for as Judge Barnes noted (p.333):

> John Factor has an extraordinarily agile mind—certainly the most agile mind of anyone the court has observed in connection with the case. He has had very little formal education—none in this country—but he has nevertheless had an exceeding [sic] broad and thorough education. He has learned all that a boy and man can learn as a bootblack, wash room attendant, newsboy, barber, high pressure stock salesman, Florida land salesman, bucket shop operator, and confidence man—except to be honest. So far as so-called business morals are concerned he is completely amoral.

Just 12 years after his prison release, Factor appeared in the newspapers as a rich man. The August 31, 1962 *New York Times* noted he and his wife were principal shareholders in the Stardust Hotel, Las Vegas, Nevada, and were selling it for $14 million ($71 million in 1995 dollars). Another reference to the Stardust (for the same time period) now called a "Casino" appeared in testimony to the U.S. Senate Subcommittee on Organized Crime (1983:531), where Angelo

Lonardo, a member of the Cleveland, Ohio Mob testified that in the late 1940's the Cleveland and Chicago La Cosa Nostra obtained interests in the Stardust Casino, and sometime in the early 1960's, a "sitdown" over their mutual interests occurred. Nothing appeared in the newspapers to explain this apparent overlap in investments by Factor and organized criminals.

Another reason Factor appeared in the 1962 newspapers was that President John Kennedy issued him a Presidential Pardon on Christmas Eve 1962 for his 1943 felony conviction, paving the way for Factor to be free of a renewed U.S. Immigration and Naturalization Service attempt to deport him, which in turn enabled Factor to reach safe haven with U.S. citizenship awarded in 1963. In the coverage of those events, the *Times* of December 29, 1962 revealed that Factor had contributed $22,000 ($113,000 in 1995 dollars) to then candidate John Kennedy's 1960 presidential campaign. Other generosity alleged in the *Times* was $25,000 ($127,000 in 1995 dollars) to a fund to help the Cubans marooned by President Kennedy's Bay of Pigs fiasco, and $250,000 ($1.3 million in 1995 dollars) to clinics for mentally retarded children supported by the Kennedy family. Factor disputed any favoritism, claiming as evidence of his evenhanded-ness a $5,000 ($26,000 in 1995 dollars) contribution to the Republican Richard Nixon's 1960 presidential campaign.

The last evidence of Factor's public spiritedness surfaced years later when it was disclosed that he had supplied $100,000 ($437,000 in 1995 dollars) in cash and $250,000 ($1.1 million in 1995 dollars) in "loans" to Democratic party nominee Vice President Hubert Humphrey's 1968 presidential campaign.

John Factor died in January 1984 in Los Angeles, at the age of 90, described in his obituary as a "millionaire investor" and honored for his many contributions.

Conclusion

Much of the reason for Joseph Ragen's accomplishment must be accorded to his own genius on the small stage of the Joliet-Stateville Penitentiary. And something in his nature must have drawn him into the world of politics and prisons.

Illinois politics provided his vehicle to move from the county to the state level as a warden appointed by the Democratic Party's politicians. As a minor politician, he lost the throw of the electoral dice when a Republican governor won, eight years later. As a warden he had accomplished little because he had little power over his guards, a reflection of his lightweight political standing.

But he had learned much during those eight years about the power he needed to run a prison, and how to operate in Illinois state politics. After two years of declining fortune outside of political office, he was shrewd enough to seize the moment when the gangster Roger Touhy's escape gave him another chance at the brass ring—he was rehired as warden. Anyone who thinks Ragen's negotiations to return to the prison with real power was some sort of above-board rehiring with a boy-scout pledge by the governor betrays an ignorance of politics. It took all of Ragen's wiles as a 45 year old experienced politician to navigate that dog-eat-dog world. He'd had a lifelong tutorial, so he bore the scars of experience.

Ragen's renegotiated power was unprecedented, and the Chicago *Tribune*'s editorial defending the Republican governor for rehiring a Democrat reflected this. But Joseph Ragen was necessary to keep Roger Touhy out of public consciousness. Touhy's frame-up sealed the Faustian bargain between Chicago's Irish politicians and police, and the Italian criminals. With Touhy gone, their Syndicate ran the metropolis as a fiefdom of corruption and crime, and, with businessmen's cooperation, turned Chicago's labor unions into cash cows for racketeers. Ironically, Touhy's persecution may have contributed to the success of the next generation of some Irish youth, who with no future as gunmen in organized crime, saw banking and business as their future.

Endnotes

1. I use the term "politician" both for those who make their livelihood by running for office, and those who live by their connections with those who do. Occasionally I do use terms such as "politically astute" or "politically connected" as synonyms. Abstractly, greater precision might be called for, but the lesser is adequate for the purpose. A case in point was a public college president recently in the New York newspapers who was called a "politician" by reporters. He protested he belonged to no political club, he had never run for office, and he preferred "politically astute." The reporters relied on his lifelong friendships with important politicians, the extensive use of the college's physical facilities by politicians, his generosity in hiring spouses and family of politicians, and, of course, the generous funding the college received from politicians.

2. The dollars of earlier years have been adjusted to equal 1995 dollars using the U.S. Bureau of Labor Statistics' Consumer Price Index, All Urban Consumers, U.S. City Average, All Items (1982-84=100).

3

The Round of Life:
Controlling Time and Space
An Overview

Introduction

PRISON control really begins with the fact that every day inmates must eat, sleep, and be clothed—in addition to other necessities such as medical care or religious services. Thus, Warden Ragen, like any other warden, had to manage such things as buying food, transporting it into the prison, storing it until it was used, cooking it, and serving it. Every day and every week, he provided most of the goods and services of a small city, but, unlike a city, the prison's residents were ever alert to steal or wrest control from him. Because all this existed in the cramped time and space of the prison, the contest for control was never ending, minute by minute, inch by inch. But before providing a picture of how Warden Ragen controlled the Stateville Penitentiary, I begin with a critique of the material which now exists about his regime. This review provides a background for my subsequent narrative and should enable you to gain a perspective.

The Literature on Warden Ragen's Stateville

Over the years several inmates wrote about their experiences in Warden Ragen's Stateville[1]. Warren's 1953 memoir of his incarceration from 1940 to 1944 described a young thief who entered Stateville at the end of Warden Ragen's first tour, (before Ragen was eased out by a newly elected Republican governor), and who was released after Ragen got his job back. I know nothing of the author, but the story seems authentic. Because Ragen was warden for only the beginning and end of this convict's incarceration, and because the inmate spent some time away from Stateville in the Menard prison, his experience has limited relevance to Warden Ragen's regime. But we can infer from this autobiography that Ragen did not control Stateville during this early period: ordinary guards beat inmates with clubs, inmates falsified records, and the psychiatric detention hospital was an inmate–run resort for *hooch*, sex, and card games.

Other autobiographical accounts are less informative. Nathan Leopold's (1958) autobiography was part of his campaign to be paroled after a lifetime of incarceration. Leopold was the surviving half of the Loeb–Leopold murderers of Bobby Franks in Chicago in 1924. (Richard Loeb was killed in the prison by another inmate). Leopold included little about how Warden Ragen ran Stateville, and he can be discounted for several reasons. In the first place, Warden Ragen allowed him to write and publish his book, a privilege accorded to no other inmate. Obviously, this required Leopold to walk a fine line. Also, no inmate I knew trusted Leopold. I had no way of verifying their suspicions, but in order to keep my own contacts with inmates open, I kept my distance from him. Leopold was a relatively short stocky man, perhaps 5'5", pleasant to talk with, and with intelligent critical comments about Stateville. But he did not publish any comments about the prison after his release.

Roger Touhy, the Chicago gangster, published his autobiography in 1959, which included some material on Stateville. As I remember, Touhy smuggled his manuscript out typed on carbon paper included with papers for his lawyer. Touhy was no friend of Warden Ragen, and did not need to placate him, but his enmity limits the usefulness of his comments about Stateville in the book. I could not reach him because of the watch Warden Ragen kept on him. I talked with Touhy once or twice because one of my clerks was his good friend. Touhy was a short, stocky man with thinning silver hair who spoke in a voice so low I could hardly hear him. But I was able to see him only when I had an excuse to call him up because he was applying for executive clemency from the governor. Otherwise my clerks would never have dared send a call ticket for Touhy: the cellhouse sergeant would have immediately alerted the captain's office and then Warden Ragen. I can only conjecture, but Touhy's description of his escape in 1942, in conjunction with Warren's description of his life as an inmate during 1940–44, indicate to me that Touhy and his confederates would have escaped in 1942 whether or not Ragen had remained the warden. Had that happened, Ragen would have been the warden banished to a decent obscurity in 1942.

By the early 1950's (perhaps a bit earlier) Warden Ragen had achieved control of Stateville, and the attention of journalists followed. All the reports were varieties of hero worship. There were a spate of riots in the early 1950's in American prisons, but Stateville was not among them. John Martin (1954), reporting on the causes of the riot at the Jackson prison in Michigan, compared that prison with Warden Ragen's Stateville. Martin caught the fact that Ragen controlled his prison, but the report is unrealistic, a Potemkin Village version of Stateville.

Other reports by local journalists were just as exaggerated in their hero worship of Warden Ragen, but they are treasures of facts and old photographs of the prison during his regime. From July 2 to 12, 1955, George Wright and Chesly Manly published a series of articles in the *Chicago Daily Tribune,* later reprinted as a pamphlet by the John Howard Association, with a long introduction by Warden Ragen. Then in 1957, Gladys Erickson wrote a biography of Warden Ragen. Needless to say, neither provide the slightest hint of how the prison was run or controlled. For example, Warden Ragen's cultivation of informers is never mentioned.

During this period, Warden Ragen began to write about Stateville. He did this when he acted as a consultant to other states and analyzed their prisons. One such typescript exists at the New York Public Library, his May 1963 report on Georgia prisons. In 1962, he and the reporter Charles Finston published a tome on Stateville. All of Ragen's writings are valuable for conveying the tone of his overbearing righteousness, a plethora of factual material and photographs of the prison, and in his book with Finston, photocopies of many of his bureaucratic forms. But they are largely boiler plate reprints of his memos, guard training manuals, and reports on the prison. They provide little help in understanding how he controlled his prison. He does not discuss his use of informers, for example, his control of the guards by merciless punishment, or his use of physical violence—which I wish to emphasize was not brutality—to control the inmates.

If you believe academic research provides a higher form of knowledge about prison operation, those about Warden Ragen's Stateville will disappoint you. There were no such attempts during Ragen's lifetime, and only one serious attempt since. In this Jacobs (1977) was handicapped by the fact that his investigation began long after the Ragen era was past. Jacobs' book was his Ph.D. dissertation in sociology, a report on the entire history of the prison since it opened in 1925. His thesis was the result of three years of research during 1972–1975. Jacobs' actual field research in Stateville was limited to two sessions. First, he spent four months in 1972 studying the inmates. During these months, he was accepted by some Latino gang leaders, and treated warily or rejected by everyone else. Jacobs' second field work session allocated six months to study the staff and ended in February 1975. His methodological appendix, which is a detailed discussion of his first field session with inmates, is an excellent essay reflecting his ability as an observer. He is silent about his fieldwork studying the staff.

Perhaps one–tenth of Jacobs' book is a description of the Ragen regime, an essay of about 12,000 words covering the 30 years from 1936 to 1965. Since my own work covers only 1957–1963, when Warden Ragen's system was most fully developed, disagreement may exist because something was true only at an earlier time. Thus, it is not easy to fairly summarize the essentials of what Jacobs has to say about control in Warden Ragen's regime without creating an interminable laundry–list of odds and ends.

Fortunately an objective summary exists. In 1989 Useem and Kimball published an analysis of prison riots in which they provided descriptions of many prisons. They based their account on existing studies. They relied primarily on Jacobs' account for Stateville, so we can take their sketch of Warden Ragen's Stateville as a fair summary of Jacobs essential points (p.66–67):

> From 1936 to 1961, Warden Joseph Ragen ruled Stateville–Joliet with an iron grip. Strict rules governed every aspect of inmate life. Inmates were not allowed to talk in the dining hall or while marching from one assignment to another, which they did in precise formation. Inmates could speak to guards only in answer to questions. Not even the slightest infraction of the rules went unpunished.

Useem and Kimball attribute this summary to Erickson and Jacobs. It is a reasonable summary of what can be found at various points in both sources, and conveys Jacobs' account of the aura of Ragen's Stateville. Unfortunately, it is nonsense.[2] After convicts became acclimatized, they violated many of Warden Ragen's trivial rules. For example, they conversed among themselves while walking in line, or in places like the dining room, but they had to watch out for lieutenants, *fish screws* (new officers just out of guard training), and the occasional vindictive guard. They had to keep their voices and body language low. Inmates certainly did not "march" in "precise formation;" they walked, side–by–side, in a slow shamble. There *was* a great social distance between the castes, but numbers of inmates made superficial small talk with guards, particularly about sports, and particularly on assignment.

Useem and Kimball continue on page 67:

> Inmates who dared openly challenge the regime—by attempting to escape, defying a direct order from an officer, or organizing collective resistance—could expect a beating by a captain or an inmate helper, and then years in segregation.

This is a paraphrase of Jacobs (1977:50). It is not true. It is no accident that Useem and Kimball pick this one short paragraph of Jacobs', for violence is the core of control in any maximum security prison. Violence by guards against inmates is a key issue which goes to the heart of prison control; the other side of the same coin is violence between inmates. Chapter 9 explains the basis for my conclusion that Stateville inmates were sure to be beaten only when they hit guards. I believe that on occasion inmates who were already placed in segregation were beaten by lieutenants, but only when they persisted in aggravating the staff by such activities as throwing feces or urine at guards. Very few inmates spent years in segregation. Further, with regard to "inmate helpers," force was used by inmates on other inmates when the Psychiatric (Detention) inmate nurses subdued a convict who was considered to be psychologically unbalanced, or a *bug*. But this was done without beating the inmate. Chapter 9 provides my detailed evidence for these conclusions, since the control of face–to–face violence is at the heart of Warden Ragen's control—and indeed, the control of all maximum security prisons. Without begging the question, you must realize that Warden Ragen's prison was a male, working class environment, not a kinder, gentler place. So a sock in the jaw by an aggravated lieutenant was not considered a beating.

It is understandable that Jacobs accepted so much misinformation from his informants, for it stems from the nature of his dissertation research. My criticism of his description of Warden Ragen's regime should be taken in this context: Ragen's rule was long in the past when Jacobs came on the scene, so he had to rely on the memories of those he found to interview. And he makes a major contribution to the study of Ragen's Stateville with the many tables of statistical information which he created from administrative records. His book is a major source of factual information about the prison, and I have mined it for information to which I had no access.

But in orientation, Jacobs chronicled and justified the ideological liberalism which had dismantled Ragen's conservative regime.[3] The liberal basis of his research is implied in his acknowledgements, and is explicitly mentioned in the book. Some of it is unspoken, perhaps unconscious. For example, he suggests on pages 44–45 that Warden Ragen's system drove men mad. This is plausible, for Ragen's style was of such an overbearing self–righteousness that even now, 30 years later, I wince. Jacobs' hypothesis is based on an observation by Roger Touhy, an inmate who was no friend of Ragen, and Jacobs' compilation of statistics of alternate year's transfers from Stateville to the Menard Psychiatric Prison during 1954 to 1972. But in later chapters where Jacobs reported the chaos and brutality inflicted upon the Stateville prisoners by the liberal reforms after Ragen, he omitted any discussion of this topic. Therein lies the rub. By Jacobs' intellectual sleight of hand, readers are left to infer that Ragen's rigid, predictable and safe environment drove men mad, but the liberal reforms which created anarchy and brutality did not. Perhaps unintentionally, Jacobs' discussion served as a rationale for the liberal changes.

Another way in which his treatment is ideological lies in his discussion of individuals who clashed with Ragen. Some of those he portrayed as professionals were also practical politicians or their proteges in the liberal faction of the Democratic party. For example, he accurately described the nastiness with which Hans Mattick, a sociologist for the Parole Board, was harassed, and how Joseph Lohman, the Parole Board chairman, had to threaten Warden Ragen with legal action on one occasion. But Jacobs omitted Illinois politics. Mattick was Lohman's student and protegé, and was later appointed by him to be assistant warden of the Cook County jail. Within the Democratic party, Lohman was a dynamic liberal politician in opposition to Ragen's conservative wing. The liberal Governor Adlai Stevenson appointed Lohman as Chairman of the Parole and Pardon Board. In turn, that position provided Lohman with the base from which he was elected Sheriff of Cook County, a powerful local office. That elected office was his next base to vault into statewide politics when he was elected Illinois State Treasurer. Lohman also had an association with the sociology faculty of the University of Chicago, his allies as an academic entrepreneur: he resigned the State Treasurer position in mid–term to become the dean of the new School of Criminology at the University of California at Berkeley.

Joseph Lohman did not win his appointments in Illinois corrections or California academia by some abstract professionalism, but by being a consummate politician. In addition, he and Hans Mattick were intelligent and hard working professionals—of liberal ideology. More of their caliber would be good for American corrections. Jacobs' comments that Warden Ragen kept partisan politics out of his operation of Stateville is half right: he kept *other politicians* out, until a liberal political tide swept him away.

I should emphasize that because my book focusses on Warden Ragen's regime, it ends in 1963 when I left the prison. A few years after I left, political liberals ascended and chaos ensued. But their era has long since ended in Illinois, and the rise of the "super max" prison grew out of the inability of conservatives to control the prisons. It is a sad truth that incompetence in prison control has been an equal opportunity failure for both liberals and conservatives.

Finally, Jacobs' sociological jargon about Warden Ragen's "charisma" and his condescending treatment of Frank Pate as Ragen's successor illustrate another misunderstanding of Ragen's regime and of prison control. The concept of "charisma" stems from the idea of the personal magnetism of a leader who inspires followers in a way suggestive of Jesus of Nazareth. Joseph Ragen did indeed inspire protegés like Frank Pate, but not by charisma. This can be illustrated by my memory of Warden Ragen's emergency store of canned beans in case the food for a meal was ruined. Inability to provide a meal, especially breakfast, where the men had not been fed in 15 hours, could spell an uncontrollable riot. Warren (1953:210) describes a near riot in the dining room when he was an inmate during the early 1940's, and dessert ran short midway through its serving.

But emergency rations were no small item, for just one meal required enough industrial size cans of beans to feed 3,500 men. Not only did Warden Ragen have to bring these cans into the prison, but he had to secure them near the kitchen. Many inmates would have given anything to have the opportunity to puncture these cans and ruin their contents, something which might not be discovered until they were needed in an emergency. A screwdriver or a weapon as small as a nail or scrap steel and some minutes of opportunity would do the trick. This opportunity could come when inmates were unloading the cans from the truck delivering them, in transit to inventory in the general store, or when moved to storage convenient to the general kitchen. Opportunities for sabotage could come repeatedly during many months or years. Warden Ragen inspired and developed subordinates like Frank Pate who could attend to minute detail with eternal vigilance. This was not charisma: it was motivating staff to pay close attention to a massive inventory of cans of beans. Academics may be taken with grandiose concepts but prisons are controlled by variations on bean counting.

This misunderstanding of what it took for Warden Ragen's system to work goes beyond the charisma nostrum to the infatuation Jacobs and others have with colorful gestures. With Jacobs, it came with highlighting a good idea, Warden Ragen's walks in the prison yard, usually with two guard dogs. I can only speak from memory, but I doubt the inmates were impressed. I saw Ragen going on some of these walks in the late afternoon after the men were locked in their cells.

When prison activity was at its height, Warden Ragen was busy at the front end of the prison in the center of his web of control. He had Frank Pate and the other assistant wardens, captains and lieutenants as his diligent alter egos prowling the prison and conveying information to him. That incessant energy was crucial for control, but he himself was too old and fat to be very active during my time at Stateville. By 1960 he was 63 years old, and I remember him in shirtsleeves in the guard hall. He was a tall man, with a round face, a bald pate, his chin an apostrophe in a roll of flesh rounding over his shirt collar; then, below, narrow shoulders and a torso sloping outward to an enormous waist. I remember Assistant Warden Frank Pate, a man in his middle years, slightly above average height, and medium build, wiry and energetic.

It took tremendous energy to control the prison, and Warden Ragen had it— —in his subordinates. In fact, Ragen also ran the old Joliet prison of 1,500 convicts which was located five miles away, with its Diagnostic Depot reception center across the street, and the two thousand acre farm outside Stateville's walls with the same iron fist, even though he rarely set foot there. He created this iron control with his uniformed staff. He also had informal confidants like the business office manager, a husband and wife who worked in the record office, and one chaplain. These were people whose judgements he valued after years of working with them. The infatuation with colorful gestures (which infects academics and journalists alike) leads to such homilies as the need for prison wardens to constantly "walk around" and not be desk bound. On the contrary, what a warden needs is a staff to be his ever–alert eyes and ears. Jacobs is not alone in this error; we see it in descriptions of how George Beto ran the Texas prisons during 1962–1972.

Jacobs confused style with substance. Frank Pate knew what was needed to control Stateville, a knowledge I discuss in Chapter 11 where I describe how he bankrupted the inmate economy to bring it further under control. His major limitation was the fact that he was only the protegé of Warden Ragen. He lacked the political standing or ability to shape the forces of ascendant liberalism. It was Ragen's retirement which left Warden Frank Pate to sink beneath the incoming liberal tide.

A Comparison: Director George Beto and Texas Prisons, 1962–1972

George Beto, director of the Texas prison system from 1962 to 1972, is known for running a system in which all the prisons of his state were rigidly controlled. Beto was in some ways a disciple of Warden Ragen's. It is essential for us to discuss Director Beto's regime because it is erroneously believed to be an extension of Ragen's Stateville system, something it was not. This error is of interest in understanding misconceptions about prison control: Jacobs and others provided the initial misinformation about Ragen's regime, and then writers on Beto's Texas system compounded the error.

We now have a fundamental choice to make: let me call it the Ragen model versus the Beto model. My study of Warden Ragen's regime leads to the conclusion that the warden of a prison is the key figure in prison control. The warden is engaged in a daily battle, minute by minute and inch by inch, over who is in control: either he is, or his guards and inmates are. The Beto model on the other hand leads to the conclusion that the state director of corrections is the key figure, while the wardens of the individual prisons can be nonentities. I cannot provide an authoritative description of Beto's control of Texas prisons because I must rely on the research of others. But I do argue that Beto's method was not based on Ragen's regime, and that it was not a viable alternative to the Ragen model.

Three major books include a discussion of Director Beto's Texas prison system. In 1987 John DiIulio published *Prison Governance*, and Steve Martin and Sheldon Eckland–Olson (to whom I will refer as "Martin") published *The Walls Came Tumbling Down*, a history of Texas prisons written by political liberals. DiIulio and Martin agree on some things, but concerning prison control, they provide an illustration of how a historical fact (Beto's Texas prisons) can be portrayed in diametrically opposite ways by conservatives and liberals. Two years later, in 1989, Ben M. Crouch and James W. Marquart (to whom I will refer as "Crouch") published *An Appeal To Justice*, a history of the court fights which transformed the Texas prisons after Beto's retirement. None of these books focus just on George Beto's regime, but all discuss it at length.

All agree that Director Beto exercised rigid control over the entire system and that he was greatly influenced by Warden Ragen. Beto certainly adapted some of Ragen's ideas. All three writers show Beto was a shrewd politician, decisive in action, and authoritarian in temperament. These are hardly characteristics Beto was likely to learn in middle age from Joseph Ragen.

Crouch (pp.38–39) is the only writer who provides details of Beto's decade–long friendship with Ragen before he became the Texas director. All three accounts agree Beto learned from his service as a member of the Illinois Parole Board. Certainly board members did learn something about prisons, but not a great deal. Beto was appointed to the Illinois Parole Board in 1961 by the newly elected Governor Otto Kerner. He left Illinois to head the Texas prison system nine months later.

Illinois Parole Board members had part–time political appointments which required about one week per month of work. At Joliet-Stateville, the Board appeared one day during the month to interview inmates on that month's docket. This involved reading the inmate's folder, interviewing him, and then dictating a recommendation. Board members would interview all day, breaking for lunch with the Warden. Joliet-Stateville was the state's largest prison complex, housing nearly half of Illinois' convicts, so the workload at the other prisons was smaller. Each prison in the state had its parole hearing day during the month. This meant a few days work scattered through the month. Then, one day per month the board met in Springfield, the state capital, to formalize their recommendations, socialize, and politic.

It is important to realize that Beto organized a system of control which was different from Ragen's: Ragen controlled one prison complex while Beto controlled all the prisons in Texas. Ragen probably spent a decade from 1942 onward developing his system and identifying and training his protegés before he really had it under his thumb by around 1950. And he was close at hand, with a daily noon conference in his office. At least for the first few years that Ragen was director of the prisons of Illinois (until I left in 1963), he did not have all of Illinois prisons under the kind of control portrayed for Beto in Texas. DiIulio implies that Beto worked some kind of magic: Beto was in office for only ten years, but gained control of all prisons almost instantly. Even if Beto built on the foundation laid by his predecessor, it was a remarkable accomplishment that all three writers assert but do not document.

We have limited information about Beto's system. Wardens under Beto were such nonentities that DiIulio and Crouch only mention one or two. DiIulio never mentions how many prisons Texas had or how far away they were located. Crouch (p.xi) provides a map of Texas, (presumably for some date after Beto retired), with perhaps a dozen locations of correctional institutions, each of which may have had several prisons. DiIulio and Crouch indicate that Beto left his office at the state capital and descended upon his prisons unexpectedly, knowing exactly what was wrong and who was to blame, righting the situation, and then riding (or flying) off into the sunset. But from whence to where? Were there two prisons or twelve? Five miles away or five hundred? (Texas is a big state.) Most puzzling, how did Beto know what, who, why, when, and where something was wrong? DiIulio reports only that inmates mailed letters, Beto interviewed selected prisoners upon release, and he made frequent and unannounced visits to the prisons. Crouch (p.40) reports that Beto visited all farms, "at least once every ten days to two weeks." This means about three visits to each farm every month. Crouch's map indicates about a dozen locations of correctional institutions, and I assume each of these locations had at least one farm. If there were only one farm in each of a dozen locations, and Beto made three visits per month, he visited 36 farms per month. Each of these farms were probably thousands of acres, with building complexes to match. If Beto visited more than one location per farm, or if there were more than a dozen farms, or if Beto visited Texas correctional institutions other than farms, his visits would increase exponentially. Since Beto was also Chief of Chaplains of the Texas prisons, I imagine he used Sundays for those duties, leaving 24 days per month for his visits. All of this suggests that Beto visited two different farms every day, in addition to directing his central office and maintaining his well known ties with the politicians and important business-men in the state capital, all the while supervising at least a dozen prison wardens who are so anonymous that none of the authors discuss them. Crouch (p.40) mentions that on one occasion Beto called from his airplane when he learned that one of his wardens was seeking a veterinarian for a sick cow. Beto instructed the warden how to proceed. With such microscopic interest and, I imagine, tens of thousands of livestock, Beto must have been a busy man. Apparently Texas prison wardens needed guidance to find veterinarians for sick cows, and were so lacking in self–respect that they were not humiliated by having that fact broadcast. I do not have a clear picture of Director Beto's system of control of Texas prisons, but I suspect a number of academics have been taken in by tall Texas tales.

Beyond this, whether Director Beto's system could be duplicated rests on a single issue: how were the inmates controlled? After all, maximum security prisons house violent and desperate men, and Warden Ragen's system rested on a bedrock of coercion. (See Chapter 9.) Paradoxically, Warden Ragen's State-eville had very little actual violence because his system of coercion was so effective. But how about violence and coercion in Director Beto's Texas? Here the conservative DiIulio and the liberal Martin portray two different prisons which have nothing in common; Crouch—like DiIulio an admirer of Beto—suggests control methods more like Martin's description.

DiIulio portrays Beto as a philosopher king: an ordained Lutheran minister, formerly president of a Lutheran college, who prayed daily and read Greek. DiIulio never mentions coercion or violence of staff against inmates. Punishment is referred to only in passing as solitary confinement with a bland diet, or extra work assignments. The only suggestion of coercion is DiIulio's discussion of "building tenders," inmates referred to by DiIulio as "super trustees." According to DiIulio there was a three way system between a prison's warden, its "building tenders," and Director Beto. This system was corrupted to brutality after Beto retired, but until then Beto kept it pure and effective. But DiIulio never tells us how it operated.

But if we turn to Martin, the ideological liberal, we can hardly recognize DiIulio's description. Martin agreed with DiIulio on the rigidity of Beto's system. For example, inmates "were required to remain silent in the hallways and while eating." But Martin's account of how this was enforced bears no resemblance to DiIulio's. Martin reports (p.23–24):

> Punishments were swift and severe. Special sessions for "attitude tune ups" or "ass–whippings" were sometimes held in staff offices for disrespectful or threatening inmates.

In effect, verbal disrespect, or threatening body language which stopped short of physical violence were grounds for beatings. And since Martin uses the plural—"staff offices"—he implies that these beatings were carried out by various staff members in different prison offices. He does not define what he means by a beating. For reasons you will see in Chapter 9, this is distinctly antithetical to Warden Ragen's Stateville system, where beatings took place only in Isolation–Segregation and only by certain officers when an inmate hit a guard Inmates were not beaten for disrespectful speech or threatening body language.

For more trivial rule violations, Martin states that inmates were humiliated and degraded (p.23):

> Often punishments were administered in a fashion so as to humiliate the inmate. Offending prisoners were berated with personal, family, and racial epithets and sometimes required to "stand the wall" [stand with his nose pressed against the wall] in the main corridor for days.

I have no way to choose between DiIulio's and Martin's accounts of Director Beto's system, but neither corresponds to Warden Ragen's Stateville, where ordinary guards just wrote tickets, and the captains sent the inmates to isolation, segregation, or recommended revocation of "good time." Social distance tended to prevail. It precluded a lot of interaction, which prevented a lot of degradation. If the ideologically conservative DiIulio never met a Texas warden he didn't admire, the liberal Martin's account reads like the script for a Hollywood movie.

But Martin has more (p.24):

> Control was further enhanced by the use of inmates as both informants and enforcers. Carefully selected inmates called "building tenders," "turnkeys," and "bookkeepers" were routinely placed in key positions on the unit and expected to remain absolutely loyal to the staff. Often prisoners who were management problems ("inmate toughs") were placed in these key positions, much like Ragen had done in Stateville.

The reference to Warden Ragen's Stateville is interesting because it is not true. Warden Ragen didn't need or use them. The closest thing was his use of informants, for he did have *society stool pigeons* who reported on the "tone" or presence of tension on assignments. For example, Warden Ragen's personal barber slept in a regular cell and kept him apprised of whether there was tension or unrest in that cellhouse. Inmate work gangs had *gaffers*, or inmate foremen. I had one for my summer project using inmate volunteers from Stateville's Television College, because I needed to coordinate the work of a couple of dozen convicts. Inmates working in the isolation or segregation buildings were janitors and porters, but they were probably expected to help if a fight exploded in their presence and the officer was getting the worst of it. But these are hardly Director Beto's "building tenders."

Crouch narrates one incident, which since it is in Director Beto's own words, probably summarizes the reality of his system of control. Crouch reports (p.39):

> Shortly after he [Beto] took over, the inmates at the Harlem farm staged a work strike ... He drove to the prison and went straight to the field to talk with the prisoners, which proved unproductive. Beto wanted to avoid anything that looked like a draw. He had to win to demonstrate to the guards and inmates that he and the guards were in control.

Then Crouch quotes Beto:

> I put four or five of those wardens on horseback armed with wet rope, or

rubber hoses, or some device of that nature, whatever was available, and instructed them to go out and put number one hoe squad to work which they did, and there was a flurry of excitement and number one went back to work in a hurry.

Since Crouch provides no explanation, I can only infer that a small (but unknown) number of convicts on foot in an open field of the prison farm (and thus surrounded by armed riflemen) were ridden down by horsemen and were threatened or whipped into submission.

Is this how Warden Ragen handled Stateville? There was no worker strike while I worked there. However, I remember one occasion that had some equivalence. A large group of inmates at a bank of tables in the dining room "booed" an officer, in a mass action. As I explain in Chapter 4, the dining room was the most dangerous place for a disturbance at Stateville.

All these inmates were immediately ordered into isolation, packed perhaps six or eight to a cell. Listening posts were set up, including some guards with their ears to the wall outside the isolation building. This continued around the clock to try to identify any leaders. Punishments followed, presumably placement in segregation, loss of accumulated "good time," reduction in conduct grades, or transfer to an unpleasant assignment such as the coal pile. I never heard that any inmates were beaten.

All this discussion of control in Director Beto's Texas prison system comes down to an accepted belief that the Texas prisons were rigidly controlled during 1962–1972. But the tale of how they were controlled and by whom tells us less about the tale and more about the teller of the tale. Looking on in 1996, we really don't know how Texas prisons were controlled during 1962–1972. But I believe it is a fallacy that Texas prisons resembled Stateville under Warden Ragen. You will see this as we begin to describe how Warden Ragen really controlled his prison.

Warden Ragen's Stateville

THE INMATE'S SCHEDULE

The most immediate and dramatic way to see how Warden Ragen ran his prison is to consider the day of a Stateville prisoner. This is the way journalists attack the subject. At specified times, a first bell and then a "wake up" bell rang; after a specified time during which the prisoner washed, made his bed, and was counted by the guards, the prisoner lined up and under the supervision of guards went to the dining room where he ate breakfast. Then, guards led his line to his work assignment. At a specified time he left his assignment, lined up and was marched to lunch, after which he lined up and a guard led the line back to the work assignment. In the afternoon he stopped work, and had the option of either going to recreation yard, or back to his cellhouse to stay in his cell until the specified time for supper arrived. On a line led by a guard, he went to the dining room, ate and then lined up for the guard to lead the line back to the cellhouse, where he remained in the cell until the first bell the following morning.

During the week, at specified times he lined up to take a shower, be shaved, go to the commissary where he could purchase sundries, and on weekends attend a movie (winters) or a ball game (summers). As the year passed, other variations entered such as later meals as the days grew longer, and the specified privileges on holidays. Furthermore, he learned that the official schedule was broken by special rules for routine things like sick call, or replacing worn out clothing at the clothing room, and for personal business such as visits from his family.

Official sanctions were controlled by Warden Ragen operating a line of authority downward from assistant wardens to captains to the officers, any of whom could write reports on any inmate they caught breaking any rule of the institution. Moreover, the officials controlled the basic framework of real power within the prison: no prisoner could go from one place to another unless he was in a line of prisoners directed by a guard, or unless he had a "ticket" signed by the official requesting his presence, counterstamped by a captain of the guards, "timed out" by a guard when he left his place of origin, timed "in" and then "out" at his destination, and then timed back "in" again when he finally returned. The prisoner was routinely searched or shook down several times a day at prescribed times and places. All job assignments were made by a captain of the guards. Assignment determined cellhouse, and cell placement was made by the lieutenant of the guards in charge of the cellhouse.

THE PRISON'S SCHEDULE AS AN ORGANIZING PRINCIPLE

But this focus on the inmate himself, while it dramatizes his day–to–day life, actually obscures the system by which Warden Ragen controlled the institution.[4] To understand this, we must focus on time and space in the institution itself—more exactly, the yard where the prisoners lived—and on such mundane details as the number of custodial officers and the length of their working day, the sequence in which prisoners ate and worked, and the locations of these places.

One of Warden Ragen's major difficulties was a lack of time in the day and having enough guards on duty to allow flexibility. Some things had to be done: for example, men must be fed. But Warden Ragen added other "desirable" activities such as factories and schools. These made control more difficult for Warden Ragen and perhaps impossible for the average warden. Thus, a central point of prison control is to simplify time and space. If there were no factories or schools, each of the three meals and the guard force necessary for supervision could be spread over a simpler schedule in time and space, giving average wardens more hope for control.

To understand this, we should first outline Warden Ragen's system. While the heart of the face–to–face world in which convicts lived came from their interaction with other convicts, Warden Ragen's deputies set the parameters. For example, a convict had little freedom to choose his assignment. A captain did this largely on the basis of requests put in by the custodial officers or civilians responsible for operating the assignments. Of course, convicts had some room to maneuver, for each month saw hundreds of assignment changes caused by numbers of new inmates received and old ones released. Someone had to fill the jobs. Once this decision was made, the convict automatically took up his residence within the bank of cells in the cellhouse where convicts on this assignment were quartered. Even more, the specific cell in which he lived was decided by the lieutenant responsible for the cellhouse. Unlike Stateville, inmate clerks in many prisons control assignments and cell placements through an informal accommodation with the custodial staff.

Once a Stateville prisoner was assigned to a cell in one of the round cellhouses, (rectangular B cellhouse had one man per cell), he found himself with at least one, and often two cell partners. Maintenance of this cramped and overused space was a feat, from repair of toilet valves and faucet washers, to extermination of roaches––especially when many of the Warden's unwilling guests would have gladly destroyed their accommodations. In a space just over 6 X 10 feet, hardly larger than many bathrooms, the inmate subculture had its focus, for inmates lived in their cells about 15 hours of every day. Nor did they escape those effects during the remaining nine hours, as one inmate reflected:

> Your cellie shares your life because he is locked up with you, works on the same assignment you do, eats with you, goes to the barber shop, commissary, bath [shower room], movies, ball games with you, and usually shares his possessions, conversation, and expectations with you.

We do not deal with the inmate subculture in this book, but it is obvious that its parameters were set by Warden Ragen's system of control. And this control took place, not in the metaphysics of attitudes and motives, but in a limited prison space one–tenth of a square mile (64 acres) in area, bounded by concrete walls 33 feet high, equivalent in height to a two or three story building. The density of population of these 3,500 inmates was thus the equivalent of 35,000 persons per square mile, far beyond the density of any American city.

Within these walls, the warden kept the prisoners alive and in good health – – and under control — until such time as the courts or Parole Board ordered them released, or their sentence expired. To accomplish this — particularly their control — the warden deployed and controlled his guards. But this control of the guard force accommodated itself not only to the architecture of the prison, but also to the limited number of guards on the staff, and the fact that each guard worked eight hours per day. Consequently, the warden had to schedule the prison so that the busy times of the prison coincided with the availability of the largest number of guards and the eight hour working day; in fact, full activity inside the prison rapidly built up after 7:00 am, and rapidly dropped off after 3:00 pm, eight hours later.

THE PRISON'S SCHEDULE IN OUTLINE

Although it is somewhat arbitrary , we can break the custodial staff's routine on a weekday in spring into three major parts: 7:00 am to 3:00 pm, 3:00 pm to 6:00 pm, and 6:00 pm to the next day's 7:00 am. Before we plunge into detail, we may best see it in broader perspective. The quiescent period of midnight gradually became more and more broken by the stirring of activities in preparation for the day as dawn approached. For the sake of discussion however, we begin at 7:00 am when the main day–shift formally came on duty. Shortly thereafter, the main activity of the day began, with its primary concerns of food (breakfast and lunch), work, and recreation (yard). This first period ended at 3:00 pm, eight hours after it began. It had to: the guards went home.

The second period was one of decreased activity, which lasted the next three hours: the men returned from recreation to their cellhouses, marched to the dining room for supper, back to their cellhouses, and finally were locked in their cells for the night, at about 6:00 pm.

Activity was minimal during the third period: although a few prisoners with specialized jobs remained out of their cells until 10 o'clock at night, lights went out and the prison radio turned off before midnight. Then in the small hours of the morning, special assignments of prisoners again began work, growing in activity with the end of this third period, at seven o'clock in the morning.

FIGURE 3.1
Major Inmate Movement During the Day, In Sequence

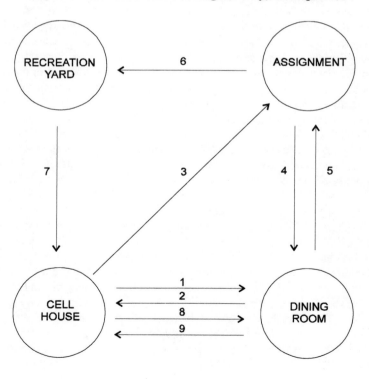

If we consider the first two periods, when the prisoners were actually out of their cells, we can now look at their timing. The daily round of inmate activities is shown in Figure 3.1. Here we see the sequence of the inmate day: cellhouse to breakfast in the dining room, and return; from cellhouse to work assignment; from work assignment to lunch in the dining room, and return; from assignment to recreation yard; from recreation yard to the cellhouse; and finally, from cellhouse to dining room for supper, and return. It would be much easier for an average warden to control a prison if steps 3-6, movement back and forth between the assignments, were eliminated. A warden has to continue assignments essential to maintain the prison, but many programs could be dropped.

The nine steps shown in Figure 3.1 were not of equal importance. On the contrary, the steps early in the day—particularly those encompassing the dining room—were most critical. Consider step one: if it were delayed, Warden Ragen had to control 3,500 hungry men who had their last meal 15 hours ago; moreover, the entire day's activities might be disjointed — and he had still to slow down the day after 3:00 pm when the eight-hour day ended for the guards, regardless of what had transpired. Similarly, step 2, the return to the cellhouse had to be carried out smoothly, for although now the convicts had full stomachs, they were out of their cells in a compact mass in a large dining room. Each of the succeeding steps became somewhat less critical, but the Warden always had to control large numbers of convicts outside their cells. Of course he had extra guards available for emergencies, but this meant mobilizing guards in a large physical space of 64 acres broken up by a complex architecture (Figure 3.2).

On first inspection, the pictorial outline of the prison's layout in this Figure is a jumble, but it is actually a grossly oversimplified representation, for only the major locations are shown. For example, not shown in one of the circular cellhouses is its basement, the assignment workplace for inmates (22 in 1960, 60 in 1962) who were enrolled in a two–year Junior College program operated by the city of Chicago, and beamed by television cameras throughout the metropolitan area. The inmates who were assigned there sat all day in front of television sets in the cellhouse basement listening to lectures, and did their homework in their cells in the evening.

It is clear from Figure 3.2 that the dining room sequence of steps 1 and 2, 8 and 9, in Figure 3.1, took place in a compact spatial area; all cellhouses closely ringed the dining room, each connected by a roofed–over concrete walk. What is less discernable from Figure3. 2 is the spatial arrangement of Figure 3.1's steps 3, 6, and 7, a triangle from cellhouse to assignment, from assignment to recreation yard, and from recreation yard back to cellhouse. I have outlined this in Figure 3.3, which can be illustrated by the pattern for cellhouse B. The majority of work assignments for these inmates were in the front part of the institution, shown with arrow 3. From these assignments they went to their recreation yard (arrow 6), and afterwards returned to the cellhouse (arrow 7). Figure 3.3 also illustrates that cellhouses E and F had similar clusters of locations, indicating the men of these

FIGURE 3.2
Structures and Outline of the Stateville Penitentiary
(Not Drawn to Scale)

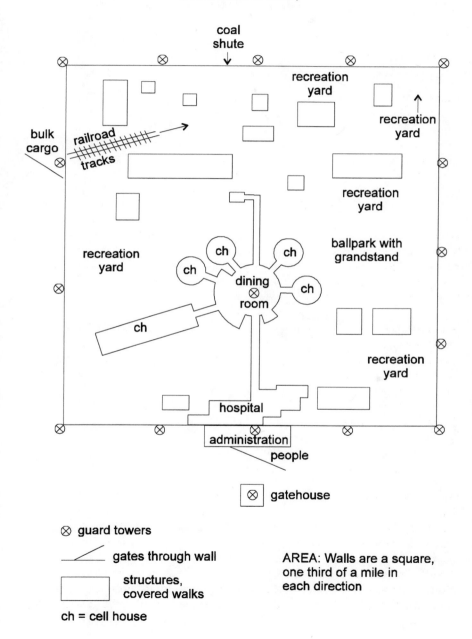

coal
shute

recreation
yard

recreation
yard

bulk
cargo

railroad
tracks

recreation
yard

recreation
yard

ballpark with
grandstand

ch   ch

ch

dining
room

ch

ch

recreation
yard

hospital

administration

people

⊗ gatehouse

⊗ guard towers

⟋ gates through wall

[ ] structures,
     covered walks

ch = cell house

AREA: Walls are a square,
one third of a mile in
each direction

FIGURE 3.3
Major Inmate Movement During the Day
by Spatial Direction, for Cellhouses B, E, and F
(Not Drawn to Scale)

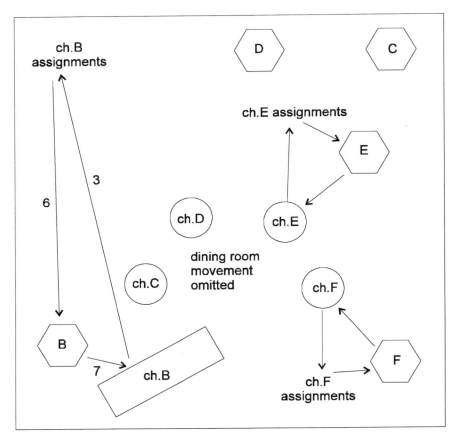

ch.= cellhouse. e.g., cellhouse B

 recreation yard

NOTE: Architecture and construction prevented simple spatial presentation for ch.C and ch.D.

three cellhouses had almost no opportunity for daily contact, except in the dining room. Although the assignments and recreation yards for the men of cellhouses C and D were not so compactly clustered, it is clear that the interlaced activity of the prison was controlled by timing and spatial separation.

With this understanding of the basic sequence of the day in mind, we can turn to a finely detailed description of its appearance, timing, and spatial organization, to see the system of control on its most meaningful — microscopic — level of activity.

Endnotes

1. For example, Jacobs (1977:254) cites a novel about Stateville: J.E. Webb, *Four Steps To The Wall*, New York: Bantam Books, 1948.

2. Although an extended analysis of these points would come only with a book on the inmate subculture, I have touched on reality in several places in my analysis, particularly in this chapter as well as Chapters 1 and 4.

3. I use "conservative" and "liberal" as labels for political or ideological outlooks. Using contemporary American politics to define these terms by example, we can say broadly that Democrats are more liberal, while Republicans are more conservative. Or using a British example, we may say the Labour Party is more liberal than are the more conservative Tories. As a rule, conservatives tend to be supportive of wardens and correctional authorities, while liberals tend to be skeptical.

    Defining by example in this way conveys an intuitive but imprecise meaning. We have not tried to be more precise in meaning, which would involve creating abstract axiomatics, or finer shadings, such as moderate, extreme, radical, or reactionary; nor of specifying adjectives such as say, a fiscal conservative or social liberal.

4. Jacobs (1977, Appendix 2) provides original demographic information about Stateville during my tenure. The population ranged from a low of 2,987 in 1957 to 3,616 in 1961; that of the entire Joliet–Stateville complex ranged from a low of 4,322 in 1957 to 5,102 in 1961. I have used the higher numbers. Of the racial distribution between black and white inmates, the Joliet–Stateville percentage black (there were no separate Hispanic numbers) increased from 53 percent in 1957 to 57 percent in 1963. The percentage of men aged 20–29 at admission to Stateville was 54.0 percent in 1957 and 50.9 in 1963.

    The distribution of offenses committed by inmates admitted to the Joliet Diagnostic Depot in 1957 were robbery 31.6 percent, burglary 22.5 percent, larceny 12.7 percent, fraud 6.4 percent, murder 9.6 percent, sex offenses 9.4 percent, miscellaneous 1.3 percent, narcotics 6.5 percent. In 1957, 75.0 percent of admissions were from Cook County (which contains Chicago).

    In 1960 (the earliest year shown in Jacobs' Appendix Table 5) Warden Ragen hired 335 correctional officers and 340 were "separated." From 1943 to 1962, the earliest years shown in Jacobs' Appendix Table 18, Warden Ragen hired a total of 30 guards who were black.

    Additional information is found in Warden Ragen's 1963 consultant's report (p.89–95 and lviii). During 1961–2 the Joliet–Stateville complex had 403 guards, 57 sergeants, 28 lieutenants, 1 captain, 3 assistant wardens, and himself as warden. Since there had to be about a half–dozen captains, this list must include them as lieutenants, perhaps because of formal civil service rules. In this report Ragen indicates the complex had 1,826 inmates received and 1,865 discharged or paroled. Jacobs (1977:Appendix A, Table 7) provides higher turnover: for 1961 it was 2,909 admissions and 2,611 discharges. Ragen indicates an average inmate population during 1961–62 of 5,177, so total inmate populations are about equal in both sources.

4

The Round of Life: Controlling Time and Space Stateville's Schedule in Detail

Introduction

I F YOU drove round the curve on Highway 66A (Highway 53 today), 35 miles southeast of Chicago in 1960, you would have seen the walls of Stateville Prison looking very much as they look today. Set off from the highway by a broad sweep of lawn, marigolds, and poplar trees, it was bounded on the other three sides by its 2,200 acre farm with hay and peas, and hogs. Its 33 foot walls stretched a third of a mile to form a concrete square, tan in color, broken by 15 evenly spaced gun towers that overlooked the prison yard inside. Nearby was a State Police barracks. The front of the prison faced the highway. On one side wall was the "sally port," a truck and railroad freight car entrance, through which bulk merchandise entered and left.

A second opening in the wall was at the front of the prison. It began by a gate house with an observation tower at the end of the long drive sweeping from the highway through the park. Here an armed guard surveyed the drive (past this point, no guard carried firearms). The visitor was searched and relieved of such items as money, identification cards, and pencils. After this, the visitor signed in, walked to the administration building, and then upstairs to the long guard hall, surveyed by the gun ports of the prison armory. The two widely spaced and massive barred Gates 1 and 2 (which might never be simultaneously open) led to a Gate 3, the sole entrance to the prison compound – the Yard — itself.

It was Warden Ragen's responsibility to confine 3,500 prisoners within

Stateville's one–tenth of a square mile, and keep them in good health until they were released. According to my inmate sources, he relied on a staff of nearly 300 hundred custodial officers spread over four overlapping daily shifts, and also on 100 civilian clerks and industrial foremen. Overall, this meant about 12 inmates per guard. These guards effectively controlled the prison, but the number on duty at any one time varied from a high of 187 at noon to a low of 55 at midnight. Table 4.1 illustrates how during the day, when prisoners worked and ate, they averaged 19 per officer, but at night when locked in their cells the average rose to a high of 64 per officer.

Table 4.1
Average Number of Prisoners Per Custodial Officer By Hour of the Day

Hour of the day	Ratio
7:00 am - 9:59 am	23
10:00 am - 2:59 pm	19
3:00 pm - 5:59 pm	40
6:00 pm - 9:59 pm	60
10:00 pm - 6:59 am	64

Less than three fourths of the custodial officers on duty at any time were available to supervise prisoners. 17 percent were supervisors — sergeants, lieutenants, and captains — who watched the keepers. Moreover, many guards did not watch over inmates because they carried out the necessary chores of the prison one or a few at a time. They were in dozens of offices, cubicles, and rooms, such as the armory, mail room, gun towers, or information desks. Each remaining guard supervised an average of 30 or 40 prisoners during the day as they circulated through thousands of buildings, sheds, cells, rooms, closets, storage areas, hallways, nooks and crannies in an interlocking schedule of meals and commissary, work and recreation, medical care and bathing.

In order to know if any prisoner escaped during this closely organized schedule, Warden Ragen had to know where each prisoner was during each part of the day. This required that several times each day the entire schedule halted while every prisoner was counted. The count was then compared with a system of tallies throughout the prison in an elaborate series of sum checks, in which the subtotals of body counts had to agree with one another, and sum to the exact total of all prisoners in the prison. If there was a discrepancy of even one body, the prison schedule halted. These counts and tallies, location and movements slips all moved in a blizzard of paper forms. Every day, all 3,500 convicts ate and slept. Every week hundreds were transferred from one assignment to another, from one cellhouse to another, received punishments of loss of afternoon recreation for five days, loss of one Sunday movie, placement in isolation for one to fifteen days, loss of conduct "grades," or loss of statutory "good time." Every month one to two hundred inmates were legally processed into the prison — from the courts, other authorities, other prisons of the state, or from the parole authority; during the same month, one or two hundred other inmates were legally processed out of the prison — on discharge or parole, to the courts, or other prisons. For each man, daily, weekly, monthly, records were changed, and legal notifications were sent and received in dozens of offices of the prison and the state Capitol.

Throughout, the daily round of life continued. The men were fed, housed, and clothed; they worked, they received medical care, family visits and mail; they saw chaplains. Everything was recorded, scheduled in time and space, and watched. Each day the schedule continued. It varied with the season. It varied during the weekend; half a day Saturday, all day Sundays (and holidays) the schedule was relaxed. It varied on days of heavy fog, when all convicts were locked in their cells as long as the fog continued.

The Day Begins: The Count

If we consider our typical weekday in the spring, it began for most prisoners at 6:40 am, when the sergeant in charge of the cellhouse pressed a buzzer and rang an electric bell. This was the first (warning) bell, the signal to get up for the day. But long before this, the preparation had begun, mainly in one cellhouse where nearly all special details were housed. From 2:00 to 4:00 am., the head cooks and bakers woke, washed, made their beds, and were led by a guard to the dining room to prepare breakfast. Except for a few men on special assignments, or men being called up for special reasons, no prisoner might move between buildings without a guard escort. Following this, from 4:00 to 6:40 am. other convicts on preparatory and early assignments went to their assignments: cooks and waiters and busboys, the warden's personal servants, mail room clerks, farm laborers.

Finally, the preparatory period drew to a close with the first morning light at 5:00 o'clock. The sergeant in charge of the cellhouse then carried out "bed check:" He turned on all the lights in the cellhouse, including those in the cells, and two or three guards walked the galleries, counting the sleeping convicts. Then the lights were turned off in four of the five cellhouses where there were no special details. Most convicts learned to sleep through this period of noise and lights turning on and off as part of their adjustment to life in the prison.

The day was now about to begin, but before the first cell doors opened at 7:15, the guard force had to be at their stations. By 6:00 am, the captains and lieutenants had passed through the main prison gates, checked the previous night's reports, and approved the coming day's schedule. At 6:45 am the guards arrived, walking downstairs from the bachelor dormitory, or driving in from nearby towns. The guards changed into their uniforms in the locker room, and passed through the prison gates to the captain's office (adjacent to the dining room) for roll call and

FIGURE 4.1
Diagram of a Round Cellhouse, About 250 Cells
(Not Drawn to Scale)

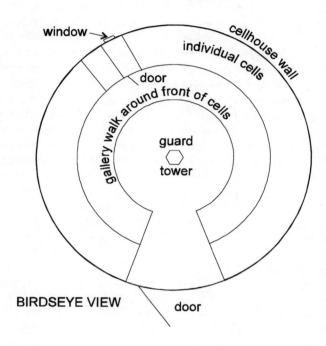

BIRDSEYE VIEW

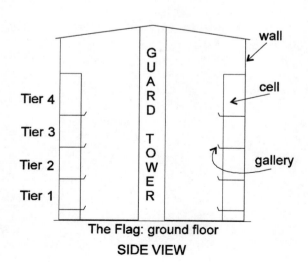

The Flag: ground floor
SIDE VIEW

any special orders of the day. They were almost always standing in front of their assignment when their shift formally started at 7:00 am., in uniforms neat and clean, including their shoes. Warden Ragen tolerated no dirt and little slovenliness. They had to prepare on their own time, with changes of uniform, getting orders, and walking to the assignment itself, before officially beginning work at 7:00 am. This could range from no problem at all for a guard assigned to the dining room to a time consuming journey for a watchtower guard. A watchtower guard had a physically uncomfortable assignment. He had to carry his own lunch and water, for he remained in the tower for his entire eight hour shift; he might have to walk over a quarter–mile from the front gate — not a pleasant commute during rain or a winter's night. Few towers had toilets, heat, or running water; in most, the guards stoked a coal stove and relieved themselves in a chamber pot.

At 7:00 am, the sergeant who had been in charge of the cellhouse during the night handed his keys to the day–time sergeant, and walked off duty with the two or three guards who had been under his command. The day shift sergeant, who supervised 5 guards who started duty with him, began the first count of the day. This count was the body count to determine if any prisoner escaped during the night. The sergeant went to his desk and pushed the button to ring the cellhouse "count" bell.

If we consider the count in one of the four round cellhouses, we will be in a cellhouse derived from the 19th century English philosopher Jeremy Bentham's design for a "panopticon" prison (Semple 1993). Here, two guards went together to the uppermost "4 gallery," while two went to the ground floor's "1 gallery." (The fifth guard was the "gate man" in charge of the cellhouse door). Each pair walked along their gallery, side by side, each guard counting convicts separately. As they reached each cell, the prisoners in that cell had to be on their feet standing directly in front of the cell door. When the two guards completed the circle of about 60 cells on the gallery, they checked with one another to see if their totals matched; if they did not they repeated their count. When the count matched, they called the number down to the sergeant who entered it in his "movement sheet." The two guards on 4 gallery then went down one flight to repeat this on 3 gallery, while the two originally on 1 gallery went up one flight to repeat the count for 2 gallery. Their counts done, all walked down the concrete "flag" where the sergeant held the movement sheet. This movement sheet listed the total number of prisoners which a captain of the guards had in a central ledger for each gallery of each cellhouse; if there were any mismatch of totals, the count had to be redone. Once the counts matched, each guard signed his name for each gallery count he had made. This signature was used to pinpoint and punish the guard who was responsible for any error, should one be discovered later. Then the cellhouse sergeant called the office of the captain of the guards to report the exact count.

Simultaneously, wherever there were convicts — in their cells, on special assignments, or on the prison farm — the count was carried out. As each officer in charge of each assignment made his tallies and found they matched the

FIGURE 4.2
Diagram of Cell House B, about 600 Cells
(Not Drawn to Scale)

cellhouse wall

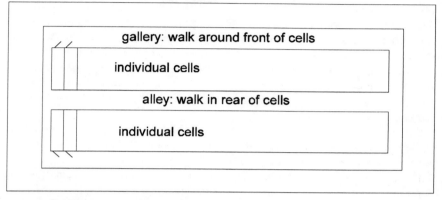

NOTE: All doors slide within walls

BIRDSEYE VIEW

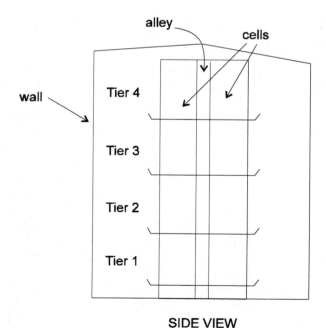

SIDE VIEW

movement sheet, he called in the number to the captain of the guards. As the captain of the guards received their counts, he checked them; until all totals checked exactly, the prison routine stopped. When the count checked he called the Warden (or deputy warden in charge that day) and notified him that the count checked. Then the Warden called the civilian switchboard operator to inform her that the count checked; only then might the switchboard operator call each assignment (and each convict night watchman alone in each part of each prison factory) and tell them that the count checked. Now the prison routine might begin again; it usually took 15 minutes to complete the entire count, a miracle in swift and exact human inventory, repeated several times a day, every day like clockwork. But pity the guard who made a mistake which held up the institutional schedule. Punishment was certain.

During these 15 minutes, each convict washed, dressed, made his bunk bed, and tidied up his cell. In the one rectangular cellhouse "B" men celled alone. In the four round cellhouses there were two or three men per cell. Figure 4.3 indicates, for a typical three–man cell in a round cellhouse, why coordination was important, for three men occupied space designed for one. The convict had to develop spatial meticulousness even on his straw mattress in bed. (There was one cotton mattress in the "show cell" to be shown to visitors near the cell house door.) From the mattress of the bottom bunk to the springs of the middle bunk was 19 inches; from the top bunk to the ceiling was 22 inches and only this man could read comfortably in bed by the light of the ceiling's 60 watt bulb. Once he arose, he had to coordinate his body movements to wash and dress at the same time as his cell partners: the total floor area of his cell was 68 square feet, but only about 18 of this was open and useable. All activities had to be synchronized: for example, the toilet and sink was one compact unit located in a corner with 18 inches clearance to the bunks; thus, if one man used the toilet, his cell partners could neither wash, nor easily walk around his legs to reach clothing hanging on pegs attached to the walls.

After the count checked, a cellhouse guard went to a central control panel where there were special levers (or "brakes"). These operated a complex locking system which functioned by hydraulic pressure, similar to that of an automobile braking system. The guard moved a brake (one for each gallery), from "deadlock" position to "key lock" position, releasing the pressure of the hydraulic system on the steel locking bars or "dogs" of each cell on a gallery. When the brake was on "key lock," it permitted a key to unlock a second steel bar and open the cell door. In this way a single inmate could be taken from his cell for a medical emergency in the middle of the night, while all other cells remained locked. Next all cells were unlocked at once when the guard put the brakes on a third, "open" position. This happened in all cellhouses at about the same time. The convicts were now about to walk out of their cells into their daily routine. It was visually a monotonous world dominated by the grey and tan of concrete and steel, often painted a modest green. It was modified by the dark blue of the inmate garb, the

FIGURE 4.3
Diagram of a Cell in a Round Cellhouse, with Three Occupants
(Not Drawn to Scale)

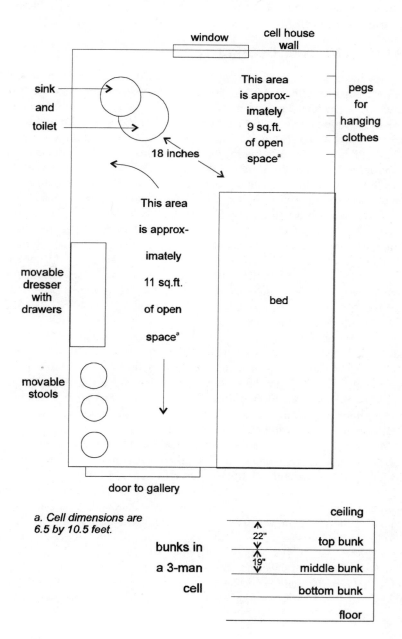

window   cell house
              wall

sink →

and

toilet →

This area
is approx-
imately
9 sq.ft.
of open
space[a]

pegs
for
hanging
clothes

18 inches

This area

is approx-

imately

11 sq.ft.

of open

space[a]

movable
dresser
with
drawers

bed

movable
stools

door to gallery

a. Cell dimensions are
6.5 by 10.5 feet.

ceiling

22"

top bunk

19"

middle bunk

bunks in

a 3-man

cell

bottom bunk

floor

pastel paint of a few cells, the sky, and in season by Warden Ragen's pride, the flower gardens. The prisoners were about to leave behind their cells which contained all their varied smells, depending upon the food they bought at the inmate commissary, and also their own perspiration and cleanliness, tobacco use, and bowel movements.

The Critical Moment: Breakfast

Now the prison's 3,500 men who had not eaten in 15 hours were ready for breakfast; any disruption to feeding these irritable, hungry men might destroy the entire day's schedule. They were fed in two seatings because the dining room could accommodate only half the inmates at a time. Prisoners might push open their cell doors. In our cellhouse, the noise of 500 men's voices, footsteps, and rustling of fabric blended and jarred with commands and steel clanging on steel, to echo across the glass, concrete and steel of this vast expanse. The sergeant rose above this to signal the first dining room line by yelling an assignment name, or "chow," or "one gallery," or by rapping on the metal railings of the appropriate tiers. Those men on the first chow line left their cells, closed the doors behind them, and lined up on the gallery outside their cells. Left behind in the cells were the men who wished to go on sick call and see the prison physician – these men missed breakfast. Each tier followed sequentially; beginning with the uppermost 4 gallery, they walked down the stairs to the concrete flag, ground floor, out the cellhouse door and along the concrete walk to the dining room. Each tier was spaced off from the next by a guard, while half a dozen guards were spaced along the few hundred feet of concrete walk to the dining room.

At this point, we quicken the complexity and the precision of the synchronization, for once the convicts left their cells, widespread activity was carried on simultaneously. For just one example, medical facilities were coordinated. The prison doctor usually completed sick call during the breakfast servings, to hospitalize the seriously ill, and dose those who were less so. The doctor had about an hour to screen everyone on sick call to make sure those with trivial ailments or those who were malingering did not miss going to work.

Meanwhile the first breakfast feeding had begun. There was no room for error. Newly awakened to another day in prison, the convicts were hungry from their long fast, and irritable. If 1,500 of them in a compact mass rioted, nothing could stop it. The men filed into the dining room, another great circle (much larger than a cellhouse) of concrete, glass and steel. It looked like a giant football field–sized dining room that was clean and looked clean. It smelled like an institutional food service but with no dirt or grunge or stink of grease or meals long forgotten. Inside, the dining room's outer rim was filled with windows and work areas — offices, kitchens, bakeries, dish washing machines, storage rooms. Within this rim, the seats and tables were spaced like a great pie cut into jagged wedges, and were lighted from skylights and strings of bare bulbs. At the circle's hub was a round steel tower rising over three stories to the ceiling, in which two to five riflemen (with the only firearms inside the walls) scanned the convicts from barred windows. Because no firearms were carried above ground, the prison had a subterranean tunnel which ran from the prison armory where these weapons were stored, directly to the dining room watchtower.

Facing the tower were 16 banks of terrazzo topped tables. Each bank of tables was shaped like a pie–wedge, with short tables near the central tower, longer ones toward the circumference of the dining room. Each narrow table had attached two to seven folding stools facing the central tower.

There was a slow swirling movement of long lines of inmates shuffling in from the cellhouses as they filed through the doors of the outer rim of the dining room. Then the minor noises of 1,500 men walking, talking, eating, serving food, echoed across the great chamber, jumbled into a low humming roar of a strangely non–human quality – like a muted, speeding railway train. Added to the noise and the movement of the long lines there now began an even more kaleidoscopic shifting as individual prisoners from all the long, massive lines broke ranks, and recreated new, smaller lines as they clustered around stands for special medical diets of high caloric, salt free, diabetic, or soft foods. All these varying lines now shuffled past large steam tables, or "stands."

To process all these men for a feeding, the distribution of food from large steam tables to individual plates had to be done quickly. A prisoner filed by a stand and picked up either a metal plate or a bowl (but never both for breakfast), then past a bread box where he took all the bread he wished, past the steam table where another prisoner (with a guard standing in back of him) doled out a portion of cereal or eggs. After this he walked down the aisle to the next table in sequence; turning to the table, he unclipped his personal metal cup from his belt, placed it at the end on the stone top (it would be filled by a waiter and passed down to him), and walked to his seat – the very next empty one to his cell partner, usually – where he found a spoon. Under the eyes of guards the prisoners filled up each seat in exact order. As the men ate, waiters dispensing bread, coffee, water and second helpings from the steam tables, walked up and down the aisles.

Eating was a busy social activity. Each prisoner as he ate was involved in filling orders for others. To get refills or second helpings, a prisoner passed his cup or plate and the word of what he wanted to the convict who sat in the seat at the end of the table on the aisle — and of course this meant that every inmate intermediate to our prisoner and the end man had to pass this along, in addition to his own chores. The end man was even busier, for he held up the correct number of fingers for slices of bread when the bread man came by, or pointed to the cup or plate when the other waiters came by. Then after the bread man with his immaculate white gloves gave the bread to the end man, it was passed from one bare hand of varying cleanliness to the next, till it reached the prisoner who asked. Similarly, the filled cups and plates were passed back. The prisoners seasoned their food with salt, the one seasoning on the table, and they stirred their coffee, ate their breakfast, and spread their margarine with their only utensil, a spoon.

After about 20 minutes, a guard in the central tower pressed a button and a first bell rang: all waiters left the aisles and assembled at the steam table stands. Then the tower guard rang a second bell: the prisoners stood, leaving their plates behind, and carried their cups and spoon, as seat following seat and table following table, they filed back out the aisles, past a guard who watched at the basket in which they dropped their spoon, and left the dining room. They washed their personal cup when they returned to the cellhouse.

Do not think this routine was carried out by robots. All during it, inmates violated the rules. They talked out of turn, *contacted* friends by swapping places in line, or exchanged contraband. If there was something especially good to eat, they cajoled the servers at the steam tables. In the dining room, few guards, except for the newly hired *fish screws*, enforced the Warden's more trivial rules. Inmates could talk as long it was kept discreet and there was no lieutenant nearby; similarly they swapped places on line, as long as every seat was filled in sequence without delay; contraband might be a few aspirins, a letter.

Episodically, enemies who could only get near one another in the dining room (because they were in separate assignments and cellhouses) flew at one another's throats. But it was usually small stuff, fist fights with no weapons. A typical incident was recounted by one guard:

> I saw a commotion between 1 & 2 stands and I ran to the scene. I saw about 5 officers trying to stop a fight. Inmate Able came flying out of the melee and I grabbed him around the waist and spun him to the front of the Dining Room. I told him to quiet down and he told me he would go with me quietly. Captain Smith then came over and said take him away. I led him to the extreme southwest corner of the Dining Room, where Captain Jones came and took him away. I did not see the fight start and the second I got there I had my hands full with Able.

The alertness and speed with which these half–dozen guards squelched this fight was par for the dining room, where anything would be tinder for a riot – something that never happened during my 6 years at Stateville.

If necessary, Warden Ragen's control could devolve from the barrel of a gun, as in the case where the guard in the dining room tower reported an inmate who worked in the dining room, "going into the inmates kitchen and getting a knife after he and inmate Baker, had been in a very heated argument. When I saw inmate Charlie have [sic] a knife I put the rifle out the window of the tower and told him to stop. Then I called and told Officer Smith that inmate Charlie had a knife and that he better get over there and get it from him."

I never heard of a shot fired in the dining room, probably because it was a credible threat. Although I did not know the guard, I am sure when that rifle pointed, there was no option: there was a live cartridge in the chamber, the safety was off, the hammer was cocked, and the rifle aimed by a guard who would not hesitate to shoot if disobeyed. And he would likely hit where he aimed.

Incidentally, Officer Smith, who was told to go after our inmate with the knife, did so. Immediately and without reinforcements. Ordinary working class men did this when they were Warden Ragen's guards. The inmate put the knife back without fuss.

Paradoxically, this iron control made for a certain calm in Ragen's Stateville. I cannot recall fearing for my life or serious injury, nor do I remember it of any inmates or guards. Guards and inmates were all held by an iron discipline directed by Warden Ragen, their room to maneuver limited to the edges of autonomy.

Except for those on special assignments, the convicts on the first feeding reversed their earlier path: back over the concrete walk to the cellhouse where they were counted through the cell house door up the stairs, to their galleries, and into their cells. The sergeant then called the men on second feeding out of their cells. It was now about 7:50 am. and the dining room crew was preparing for the second breakfast feeding: they washed spoons and dishes, cleaned the tables, finished cooking the food and replenished the steam table stands. In less than 10 minutes, the second feeding had begun, a duplicate of the first.

Warden Ragen's Stateville was tense for many reasons, not the least of which you have just seen: about 3,500 convicts fed in two sittings, all in about 60 minutes. For 3 meals a day, every day. And the food was not bad, within the limits of a massive institution; the food I ate in the Officers' Kitchen was adequate for a large institution, although the inmates' food was not as varied. But I still remember the Officers' Kitchen ate the same bread as the inmates; it was baked in the prison, and I could not buy bread that good where I lived in Chicago. I remember a friend of mine, a new MD, then an intern, who visited with a blood donation team. That small stipend (if I remember correctly, $5.00 every three months) was the only income for the poorest of inmates, almost all black men from Chicago. Thus, their diet was almost entirely from Warden Ragen's dining room. My friend remarked those prisoners were among the healthiest people imaginable.

The Full Complexity Unfolds

Now the day developed to its full complexity as men went to their work assignments. They moved between five cellhouses and about 50 buildings, crossing and crisscrossing their paths perhaps a dozen times from morning to afternoon — always with each convict searched, and counted. It was for the sake of these assignments that Warden Ragen made eating so clipped. He could do it because he enveloped his guards in a discipline that was effective, rigid—and as I will explain in Chapters 5, 6, and 7, nasty and punitive. His guards controlled the inmates. No warden today could duplicate Warden Ragen's discipline. Only by eliminating many of Warden Ragen's assignments such as industries and schools could today's wardens carry out centralized feeding. In contrast, on the tours I took of Stateville in 1991 and 1994, there was little control of eating; inmates straggled to and from the dining room, now shrunken to a few hundred seats, and food was served continuously all day. Eating was a giant fast–food service. And Warden Ragen's food staff of one to two hundred inmates and a few guards and sergeants, had been replaced by over 100 inmates and a substantial cadre of civilian food service workers. Illinois taxpayers must be footing a substantial food service cost compared with Warden Ragen's regime.

As soon as the second feeding line reached the dining room, the cellhouse sergeant began calling out assignments for the men of the first line who were now sitting in their cells. (Cell partners ate together and worked together). If the men on sick call who were not excused from work for the day had returned, they too filed downstairs and lined up on the flag to be escorted to work by a guard.

At this time there was another series of counts. The guard responsible for an assignment counted the number of prisoners in his line, and checked this with the slip made out by the inmate clerk assigned to the officer in charge of the cellhouse door — this slip had to equal the total number of men on the assignment, minus those men known to be absent for such reasons as sick call or isolation confinement. After the guard verified this count slip, the prisoners filed out the cellhouse door counted independently by the assignment guard on one side and the doorkeeper guard on the other. After the entire line passed, these two guards compared their figures; if their totals did not agree three ways — with each other and the count slip — the line had to stop on the concrete walk and wait while the entire counting process was repeated. This was not a minor matter, for a delay in one line at the cellhouse also delayed all other lines which were to follow. This in turn might cause further delays in the synchronization of the work at individual assignments. Moreover the prison was a collection of interdependent assign- ments — factories, schools, and maintenance operations — so ripples of disruption and irritation were ever–present, causing a premium to be placed on the routine and the simple. Any guard or inmate who caused delay would be punished.

One officer (or two, if it was an unusually long line of 100 or more) walked the men to their assignment which might be a few hundred feet or one–third of a mile away, a process which took one to fifteen minutes, for the lines of men moved slowly, at a rate of one or two miles an hour.

Variations complicated this schedule. Some might be for an individual inmate, to see a chaplain, sociologist, physician, or dentist, or receive a visit from family or friends; some might be for specific prison programs, such as an Alcoholics Anonymous meeting, or a school program; others might involve the custodial staff, such as the need to see a captain for a change of assignment, or to answer a guard's rule violation report.

The call ticket was an additional body count system, part of Warden Ragen's avalanche of forms. The staff member who wanted to see an inmate filled out a call ticket, writing down the prisoner's name, prison register number, assignment and cellhouse. Because there were hundreds of job and cellhouse transfers each week, a number of places, such as my office, maintained elaborate filing systems in order to know where each inmate was on any given day. The civilian or guard staff member signed the call slip and gave it to a runner, a convict assigned to carry messages and packages from one part of the prison to another. The runner then took the ticket to the assignment captain's office, a guard counterstamped it and sent it to the prisoner's actual location (either by the same or a different runner). The call ticket at its destination set another clerical system into operation. There, the guard in charge called the prisoner over, and carried out a shake down; on the back of the ticket, he then entered the time it was received, the time the prisoner left, his own signature, made an entry in his log for his own *count,* and then sent the prisoner on his way. Now the prisoner might walk by himself, but he was still controlled by the ticket: he might first go to his cellhouse (where he would be shaken down and again timed in and out). When he finished the business of his ticket, he might either return to the assignment, or wherever the men on his assignment had moved (where he would be shook down and timed in).

These individual call tickets raise a possibility of simplifying inmate movement in time and space. At Stateville, a visit from family really did require an inmate to meet them in a special space, the visiting room. This in turn required summoning the prisoner from his cellhouse or assignment, which in turn required Warden Ragen's call tickets. But sometimes this was a needless complication of habit. For example, when I interviewed convicts at Stateville, I summoned them to my office with a call ticket. But when I interviewed convicts outside Stateville — the Honor Farm, the Diagnostic Depot, or the old prison at Joliet — I went to the inmates. I used a spare office, an empty cell, a table in the dining room, or a couple of chairs in a quiet corner. Depending upon architecture, a prison might eliminate some offices by moving professionals and chaplains to inmates. Even congregate programs such as religious services might be moved to simplify the prison's operations.

In addition to the individual variations controlled by call tickets, the schedule of an assignment was complicated by institutional needs; for example, convicts had to take showers and they might buy candy and cigarettes. In this case, the prisoners on each assignment spent one morning or afternoon each week on their "bath–shave–commissary" line. After their breakfast or lunch, instead of being led from the cellhouse to their assignments, they first went to a shower room (once a week), then to be shaved at the barber shop (twice per week) and then to the commissary (once a week) where they might purchase sundries such as cigarettes, candy, or canned food. Even this single case could become more complicated, for if a convict had missed commissary (because, for example, he had a visit from his mother), there was a prison–wide *missout* line on Friday afternoon. Moreover, this list could be expanded to include other activities, such as the one half–day per month set aside for haircuts. While these minute variations were mind–boggling, Warden Ragen's ability to control it was even more so, the result of his rigidly controlled guard force and his avalanche of forms.

Throughout the prison, the cramped synchronization continued. By 8:30 in the morning, the second breakfast feeding was over, and the factories and schools were in operation. Other guards, and civilians — industrial foremen and office workers — were coming to work.

Large groups of prisoners were busy maintaining the institution: in the dining room, cooks and bakers were preparing for lunch; electricians, carpenters, and garbage collectors were at work; in the cellhouses, convicts were mopping and cleaning. The control of this cramped synchronization can be illustrated by the prison laundry. One day a week, prisoners had their one sheet washed. To accomplish this for more than 500 men in a cellhouse, each man draped his dirty sheet (stamped with his prison register number) over the gallery railing when he left for work in the morning. By the afternoon it had been picked up, taken to the prison laundry and washed, dried, ironed (in a device called a "mangle"), and returned to the cellhouse. On one other day of the week, this was repeated with one of each convict's two sets of heavy ("hickory") cotton shirts and denim trousers. The men washed towels, underwear, and socks in the sinks in their cells.

With this account of the laundry, we may become less detailed in our discussion. But first, we would like to use the laundry to emphasize how this microscopic level is where control was won or lost. We have seen by now that the realities of daily prison life were cramped in time, space, and synchronization. In the laundry for example, could delay be tolerated? Not in Warden Ragen's prison.

But who cares? Other prisons wash sheets and clothes for inmates. But the difference between other prisons and Ragen's Stateville was who was in control. In other prisons, whether the sheets and clothing were promptly and thoroughly laundered for every inmate became a detail which some custodial officer had made into a little enclave of power, which he in turn would share with (or even lose to) his inmate help. In such a case, how did the average inmate get clean sheets or shirts or trousers without tears and holes? By bargaining: perhaps cigarettes for the inmates assigned to the laundry. Those who were weak or poor would be dirty or ragged. In consequence, the picture one gets of other prisons is a federation of little baronies, each controlled by officers and inmates, with the prison warden functioning to orchestrate the whole lot. Whether or not this is true in other prisons, it was not so in Ragen's Stateville, where the image is better thought of as a pyramid of power controlled from the top, where the guards and inmates had little autonomy, and all were coordinated to serve Warden Ragen's purpose.

In Ragen's Stateville, guards were expendable, and this was his key to controlling the inmates. The guards in the laundry were no more diligent than they had to be. But they knew that if sheets and shirts and trousers were not laundered properly for all inmates, or if the inmates on their assignment were caught with a *stash* of contraband or engaging in illicit activity such as gambling, both inmate and guard would be punished. The inmates knew this too. Warden Ragen's lieutenants were aggressive, vigilant, and constantly checking informers tips. Consequently, the contraband the inmates did stash and the illicit activity they did engage in were pale versions of what might have been. A stash might be a few packs of cigarettes, but not a knife. Illicit activity might be some hurried consensual sex with a homosexual, but not rape. This extended all through the prison assignments. Thus, an inmate who wanted to use a knife to attack an enemy could only get one by the greatest of effort; a *shiv* was so hard to get that only a very well connected *right guy* could ever hope to obtain one. The consequence was that the fights that constantly erupted in the dining room and cellhouses were almost always fist fights, occasionally with some weapon of opportunity such as the leg ripped off a chair.

The convicts in the laundry could not determine who got new, clean, pressed sheets and thus, they could not charge for these services. Throughout the prison, inmates on other assignments had no say in who ate well, who got good medical or dental care, who had roaches exterminated in their cells. Warden Ragen determined these things. Guards and inmates alike did what he decided, where he decided, and when he decided they would do it.

The Inmate Transportation System

But there were limits to Warden Ragen's control. The inmates maintained a lively transportation system, but its importance was only a pale reflection of what occurs in the ordinary prison. Inmate distribution of goods varied from an easily concealed razor blade to a bulky, perishable sandwich. All required not only men to carry them, but also storage places where inventories could be warehoused adjacent to switching points where a pass could be made between carriers. Inmates had two major transportation systems, the Warden's and also their own. In the first, two clerks would send messages and contraband via the official within–prison mail, addressed to the guards in charge of their assignments or with some risk, they telephoned one another if they thought they could beat the civilian switchboard operator by making her believe guards were on the line. Rarely, they could time their call for when an inmate was on switchboard relief duty. The second was more complex. Letters moved within the pages of newspapers, magazines, on the library book cart. Small packages however, required individuals trained to avoid detection. In part, this was because of the ubiquitous shakedowns, but primarily because only actors or thieves were sensitized to the nuances of physical control of gait and stride, body tension and eye movement. As one convict explained:

> You take a man, unless he's a professional, he's very easy to detect. A con can spot another con when he's doing something dirty, like that, if he's hot. Some of these old– time officers can do that too... Just the way you look, you just look at a man you know when he's got something.

Most thieves develop some awareness of body movement in the course of their work. Consider an armed robber who aims for competence. He will avoid notice during the preliminaries while he is casing a job to study its architecture and time schedule, the topography or traffic pattern of its surrounding community, or contacting his *caser*, a legitimate employee of the firm, who although a *square john*, is not above selling information. Moreover until the critical moment of revealing himself, he wishes to avoid notice while engaging in split–second deployment and synchronization with his confederates. At this point, he must become highly visible and capitalize upon the shock inflicted by producing firearms, so that by movement, gesture and tone of voice he may control numbers of frightened spectators and employees during the few minutes he has in which to secure the money. Immediately following this, he must quickly leave and cease to be visible. Although few convicts are skilled thieves, they are aware of these factors, and have learned the rudiments of some. These are illustrated by one inmate who remembered:

> One time I had this package of 50 aspirins in the dining room, I had to bring it over to the commissary, it's a pretty big package... I had my mind on something else and I didn't notice when I sat down at my place there wasn't any spoon, and when we were going out I come by the screw counting the silverware and he asked me, "Where's your spoon?" Right away I realized I can't tell him I ain't got none, with those aspirins in my pocket, so I tell him "I must'a left it at the table," and I turned around and went back like I was going to look, even though I realized it wasn't there. I got back and took the aspirin package out of my pocket and held it in my hand put it up in my sleeve, just inside. When I come back, I told the screw, " I can't find it." So he tells me, "Stand over there, and after this line goes I'll shake you down," which is what I knew he'd do. So I stand on the side, and I drop my hand by a radiator and let the package drop behind. Naturally, when he shook me, I was clean... Later, I grabbed a runner and told him what happened. He went by and it was still there, so he picked it up and delivered it... the runners wheel around here and get to know when they can go in and when they can't... they gotta watch too and see no inmates sees them too, but the thing is to act average like, like you're not doin' anything, you don't look as if you're pullin' anything off...

How were these relatively delicate body movements noticed? They were no secret. Experienced custodial officers knew their rudiments in the sense that they noticed the absence of skill in order to pinch a con who was dirty. Inmates knew there was a characteristic pace of body movement in the prison, for although some men shambled and others strutted when they walked, the unnoticed inmate followed a slow measured pace either in a line or by themselves. Moreover the prison–wise ones learned to cooperate with their fellows, especially if they were message carriers or runners. For example, Gate 3 which separated the main prison yard from the hospital was glassed against the weather and screened against insects in the summer, and against inmate attempts to pass contraband through it in any season. However, authorized messages and small packages constantly streamed through, so to avoid having to open and close this gate constantly, a small door a few inches high and a few inches wide was placed shoulder–high in the gate. My notes describe a pass that I happened to observe only because I was accidently standing just to one side:

> On the Hospital side, the runner blocks the view of the guard [with his body], he has the message or whatever in his palm. The runner on the yard side steps up simultaneously. Now they're both in motion in the same direction. The hands lift, the pass is made in no more than a second. Only a momentary flash of paper shows, and then only if you're standing next to one of the passers. There's no facial expression, just the usual slow gait.

Because all inmates moved from one location to another, and inmate runners did so as part of their assignment, messages and small packages constantly moved with them.

Storage, a necessary adjunct of carrying and switching contraband, was, however, more difficult. Here, the *yard gang*, about 50 inmates who were assigned to keep the Yard clean and pick up garbage throughout the prison were crucial. They worked in small groups, going from place to place at a pace that could not be rigidly pre–scheduled. Because they could not be supervised closely, they transported and stored bulky items in their containers, or in some convenient nook or cranny of a factory, school, or shop. Also, small items stashed in cannisters were buried in the Warden's flower gardens by the inmate gardeners. Of course, once contraband reached a cell or an assignment, storage was easier.

But it was never safe, either in transit or storage. In transit, it was subject to search. Because of the constant inspections, storage in one's cell was only moderately safe, while on assignment it was more so. But there, unless one was a skilled workman or a clerk, opportunities tended to be limited. Production workers in the factories, or students in the schools, for example, did not have the individual desks or work areas that more autonomous workers had.

Warden Ragen was able to control transportation not because any of his precautions were unbeatable, but because each one created an obstacle, no matter how minor. To surmount any one of these took effort, and the cumulative nature of myriad obstacles diligently applied by his obedient staff controlled the inmates. I could always find examples of ways in which inmates "beat the system," but the difficulties and dangers restricted its incidence. For example, coffee was much prized, and some few still *scored* for it, but it was beyond the reach of nearly all. By centralizing its storage, the Warden insured that the inmate who wished to score faced considerable obstacles. For example, guards at checkpoints instantaneously scanned the underside of carts delivering merchandise with mirrors attached to poles. Further, by setting the punishment for detection as high as Merit Staff referral — perhaps a 27 month delay in seeing the Parole Board — he made it a *touch* that most inmates thought twice about, even if they had an *in* where the bean was stored, or where brewed coffee was available in the kitchens. Finally by putting instant coffee up for sale in the inmates' commissary, he permitted the wealthier convicts to forego stealing the institution's coffee.

You will learn just how inconsequential was inmate bargaining power when we discuss later how Warden Pate bankrupted the inmate economy by restricting commissary purchases. His ability to apply stringent sanctions, by punishing guard and inmate alike, weighted the process of competition for control in his favor. In addition, his control over money and barter squashed the inmates into an accommodation where their economy was fragmented to the point of inconsequence.

But in their daily lives, the guards and inmates were not some Orwellian robots. Inmates watched out for *fish screws* and lieutenants so they could talk in the dining room or on line as they walked to and from assignments and elsewhere. On assignments the socializing was even livlier.

The Pace Begins To Slow

Returning now in a more summary way to the institution schedule, the guards bore responsibility for surveillance and maintenance. Some of this was specialized as, for example caring for the elaborate hydraulic cell locking system in each cellhouse. Here, the routine simple adjustments — such as freeing a jammed locking bar in a particular cell — were actually carried out by convict mechanics. The inmates were nominally supervised by guards who usually had no idea of the mechanics of locks. Skilled civilians or officers were used for only the most difficult jobs. Most jobs carried out by the guards required little skill, but, at least theoretically, much diligence. For example, every day, a guard *rapped the bars*: he ran a steel bar, like a boy with a stick on a picket fence, across every section of bars of every cell door, listening for the changed ring which indicated the cut bar of an escape attempt. My guess is that for most guards, the diligence of such microscopic surveillance eroded over the years to bored ritual, enforced only by Warden Ragen's iron discipline.

The morning passed, and lunch time approached. But lunch in the prison began not at noon, but — to keep it within the guard manpower available — 10:00 am, when the short–line noon day meal line was fed. About 200 specialists from all over the institution such as important clerks or inmates assigned to the powerhouse, checked their tools, lined up, went through a *shakedown* and were walked by a guard to the dining room. The convicts then repeated the breakfast routine except that they might have a fork, or even a table knife if meat was served; when they finished they waited for a guard to return. This guard had even less time for lunch than the convicts, for after he dropped off his "short line," he proceeded to the Officers' Kitchen for his own lunch; he had the convicts' 20 minutes minus the five minutes it took to walk to and from the Officers' Kitchen. While he was not officially on such a schedule, the lieutenant of the guards who was watching the inmate short line eating would write a punishment report on any guard who did not pick up his short line in time. A guard who was tardy might delay the main line lunch and in turn the daily schedule of the prison. The guard and the short line walked back to the assignment, the line was shaken down, and the prisoners returned to work. This had to be completed by 10:30 am when the first of the lunch main lines began feeding.

When the two main lunch feedings began, the most complex traffic patterns of the day unfolded, for in two sittings, men from all over the prison compound converged on the dining room. And since they came by only a few main walks, they had to be synchronized to follow one another. This happened because of the spatial separation shown in Figure 3.3. On virtually all assignments, all men had to go to lunch whether they ate or not. The men stopped work, checked all tools, lined up, were shaken down, counted, and then escorted to the dining room. (A few assignments reported first to the cellhouse). Two guards would generally be responsible for escorting the line into the dining room, while two or three other guards walked along; as soon as this line reached the dining room, half these guards left and walked to the officer's kitchen for their own lunch while the remaining two or three guards watched the men eat. The first guards who had left for their own lunch again had about as much time to eat as the prisoners minus the five minutes it took them to walk to and from the Officers' Kitchen and the dining room. During the 20 minutes it took the prisoners to eat before the bell rang, the first guards would have eaten lunch and returned to pick up the line as it left the dining room, and escort it back to the assignment; this allowed the other guards to leave for their own lunch, and then back to the assignment. Then at 11:40 am, the first line had eaten, the dining room was cleaned, the dishes washed, stands set up again, and the second feeding followed. The men on the second feeding were usually back on their assignments by 12:15 pm.

While the average time for feeding was 20 minutes, there was no leisure allowed. If the lieutenant saw nearly all the inmates had finished early, he would have the bell rung and the men cleared out immediately, in which case the guards eating lunch would pick up the line along the way back to the assignment. At Sunday noon or holiday meals we can see what would be the hypothetical effect of abolishing assignments. Where there was no work and a more elaborate menu, dinner time might last as long as 40 minutes.

After lunch, some assignments, such as the coal gang, had finished, but most returned to work. The afternoon began with the same basic pattern overlaid with a thousand daily or occasional variations. At noon, the Warden met with his assistant wardens and captains in his office for their daily conference. Periodically, the tower guards had rifle practice, and the convicts would hear the crack of gunfire most of the afternoon. Warden Ragen believed that ordinary target practice on a rifle range was not sufficiently realistic, so the guards fired from their watchtowers at targets moved about outside the walls. Between 1:00 and 3:00 pm inmates went to the recreation yard for up to an hour. Men might go to Yard or not; those who did not, returned to the cellhouse. But all checked their tools, lined up, were counted, shaken down, and escorted by guards. A day's work on an assignment was three or four hours.

Toward the middle of the afternoon, the earlier morning arrivals among the guards began to go home, and the prison began to close down for the day. Supper consisted of an early short line (about 3:30 pm.) and two main lines (4:00 and 4:30 pm.). Then the men returned to their cells, and pulled their doors shut. Guards key–locked each cell door one by one; finally the brake was moved to deadlock, there to remain unless a lieutenant of the guards ordered it moved for such emergencies as illness or fights. The men would spend the next 14 hours locked in their cells. Evening came, and the last daytime activity shortly dwindled: between 5:30 and 6:00 pm, evening count check was carried out, and the powerhouse blew its steam whistle; after this, a few prisoners on special details went back and forth until 10:00 pm. By then only the night workers were up: the night shifts at the powerhouse; the night watchmen in the industries, guarding against fire till morning; emergency and special assignments, some with their own sleeping quarters (psychiatric nurses in the Detention Hospital, hospital help, punishment cell help). Except for emergency calls for plumbers or nurses, the routine quieted. Street lights went on, spotlights bathed the walls, and riflemen in the corner towers watched. The prison slept.

Until tomorrow.

A Note on Assignments and the Limits of my Research

I have not discussed control on assignments because there were so many and they varied so. At one extreme was my office where we did all we could to avoid the burden of Warden Ragen's system. At the other is the Inmate Commissary, discussed in Chapter 11, which was rigidly controlled. But for almost all assignments, little work was done by individual inmates, and further, there was no way to run assignments efficiently.

I judge that no more than half the inmates had assignments which required work, for there were too many convicts, too little work; of those who did work, most jobs required perhaps 3 or 4 hours a day. Simple arithmetic demonstrates that of the eight hours the prisoners were out of their cells, three or four had to be given over to personal needs. There was the dining hall, recreation yard, and the necessities of maintenance—showers, shaves, haircuts, commissary, plus visits from family, or appointments with chaplains, sociologists, and other functionaries. Even on assignments, time slipped by: a few minutes at a time for shakedowns, tools checked in or out, waiting for guards to give permission. The only way to add hours to the day and still control would be to hire more guards, something Warden Ragen's budget did not permit, just as it may not for today's wardens.

Space was the villain that prevented efficiency. This was easy to see in the factories where about 20 percent of the inmates were assigned. The prison had no space to spare. They could not warehouse much inventory at the factory, and with the security precautions at the Sally Port, they could not move supplies rapidly into the prison. Similarly, finished goods could not move rapidly out to customers through the Sally Port. Or cheaply. I remember hearing (it was probably true) that the sheet metal shop could not ship cabinets unassembled because convicts could not accompany the merchandise to assemble them on site. But the cabinets which were shipped assembled took up too much truck space to be profitable. So a "profit" was created by hiding the trucking costs somewhere else in the records.

As I discussed operations with the inmate clerks in the various factories, I was engulfed in a tidal wave of questions:

Were the purchased raw materials, services and equipment accurately described? For example, was the cloth delivered to the clothing factory really the first quality heavy weight as billed, or lesser quality or weight? Were there hidden discounts and kickbacks, or sweetheart deals between the suppliers and the sergeants or civilians in charge?

Were the finished products accurately entered in accounts receivable as they were sold, or were some shipped unrecorded, to be paid "off the books" to an employee, or laundered by a local banker? Did politicians take delivery of office furniture for their municipality to sell it for personal gain? What was the quality of the finished products?

In the factories, were the payrolls padded with inmates really working elsewhere, as I knew was true for the Inmate Commissary payroll? How often were time sheets and hours worked falsifed, or erroneous wage rates paid? What fringe benefits and perks accrued to the civilians and sergeants in charge?

To make up balance sheets, estimates had to be made to allocate overhead expenses, and anticipate future cash flows or orders, as it happens in any business. Who made them, how did they make them, where was the documentation, did anyone check? Indeed, what was the "true" market value of the factory? What were the "true" profits? If these were private businesses in Chicago: would an auditor conclude the books were honest? Would a financial analyst conclude the business was really profitable? Would an honest broker recommend investing your money?

These questions made me realize I could not study the factories. More important, I saw how Warden Ragen's control was eroded. Partially, it was because the guards could not see much. The factories held hundreds, perhaps thousands of rooms, closets, cabinets, nooks and crannies. Equally important, the civilians and sergeants in charge had the goal of production, while the guards' was control. Where they conflicted, both lost. The only elements that aided a controlled environment were Warden Ragen's lieutenants who enforced his rules as best they could, and the foremen who tried to live with them as best *they* could.

Perhaps the glossy annual reports of today's prison factories portray industrial systems which surmount the inadequacies of Warden Ragen's Stateville. Or perhaps like his, they are largely sound and fury, signifying nothing.

5

Control of the Guards:
An Overview

What do we Know of Correctional Officers and Prison Control?

THE question in this title begs another question: what does *who* know? College students? Average citizens? Journalists? Academics? Although I need to critique the academic scholarship, it behooves me to sketch out what "everyman"— the citizen, the journalist — knows.

This comparison is important because we assume that scholarship exists on a higher plane than journalism. This assumption stems from the idea that scholarship is part of "high culture," a modern development. Over the past few centuries, European societies developed the idea of "high" culture as opposed to "low" to differentiate the higher orders of intellect from the lower. Usually, although not always, this idea implies a social class difference, in which the upper classes were drawn to "high" culture. (With the democratization of society, the middle classes joined their betters.) Today in American society this difference is usually called "fine art" versus "popular" or "pop" culture—for example, a Verdi Opera versus The Beatles. It is important to compare and contrast the "high" and "pop" portraits of prison guards because it is a striking example of bizarre stereotypes clouding our view of an occupational group.

Hollywood Movies and Prison Guards

The prototype of pop culture is the Hollywood movie, as I realized when I saw *The Shawshank Redemption* (1994). I was absorbed into the drama. After I viewed it again a week later, I concluded I had been mesmerized by a cheap potboiler. Such is the power of film, for the moving image engulfs our senses.

Such is also the power of the prison. Whether we are academics or officials, journalists or media types, we all carry emotional baggage. Our fascination with that dark world is illustrated by the report (*New York Times,* February 18, 1996) that the now abandoned Alcatraz prison, the ancestor of today's "super max" prisons, is San Francisco's third most popular tourist attraction, surpassed only by its Golden Gate Bridge and cable cars.

My beginning point, *The Shawshank Redemption,* spans two decades of a maximum security prison in Maine after the end of World War II. The film has two inmate heroes, one black and the other white. Both heroes are noble in character, and the film presents a wide variation of convict stock characters, both "good guys" and "bad guys." Their world is an inmate-dominated prison replete with rape, assault, and smuggled contraband.

But the stock characters for the custodial staff are all bad guys, visually and otherwise, brutal and corrupt. The guards, silent and somber, are dressed in navy blue versions of U.S. Army dress uniforms, carry clubs, and sometimes guns. Their few spoken lines are often threats of beatings, with body language to match. The two major staff parts are the captain and the warden. The captain is a sadist who opens the movie by gratuitously clubbing a hapless convict to a pulp, a scene reminiscent of the famous eyewitness video of the 1991 beating of Rodney King by the Los Angeles police. Later the captain beats an inmate bad guy into a cripple, permanently wheelchair-bound. All this occurs with guards impassively looking on. The warden is a corrupt Bible quoting hypocrite and embezzler who supports the captain; as a team they carry out the cold blooded murder of an innocent inmate, the captain wielding a machine gun.

A number of movies confirm this basic pattern. Another recent film, *On The Yard* (1979), had the same formula. In a Pennsylvania maximum security prison there was an inmate hero, a range of inmate stock types from saints to sinners, and a custodial staff of bad guys. In this film however, the captain and warden are passive incompetents rather than sadists. Only on one occasion did the captain administer a brutal beating, and this was to an inmate bad guy. A 1967 film, *Cool Hand Luke*, about a southern chain gang, repeated the formula of brutal and sadistic guards. The convict types resembled college fraternity boys.

I did find two films with heroes who were guards. One was *The Glass House* (1972), about a maximum security prison in a northern state. Here an idealistic young man joins the custodial staff to find a brutal inmate-dominated prison, and a cynical custodial force from the warden down. At a point when the warden orders our hero to perjure himself to cover up a murder, the young guard quits, vowing to bring the truth to the American people. Another recent film, *Against The Wall*, was set in the Attica New York prison at the time of the 1971 riot. It shows an open-minded young man following his father's footsteps by joining the guard force, only to find a bitter lieutenant and captain directing a cynical guard force who gratuitously demean inmates. This leads to the Attica riot, our hero among the hostages, and the other guard hostages turning against him because he isn't like them. Thus, in a Hollywood movie, even when a guard is a hero, he is overwhelmed by a cynical or corrupt correctional staff.

An exception to this rule is the 1962 film *Birdman of Alcatraz*, which focusses on a single inmate who spent most of his life in solitary confinement. Beside the warden, who is stiff-necked and stern but just, the guard who watches over the hero befriends him.

I wondered if this negative portrayal of the custodial staff was the product of recent history. After all, so many heroes of the modern world have been prisoners: Ghandi in India, Nelson Mandela in South Africa, Martin Luther King, Jr. in the United States. And, of course, since the discovery of the German concentration camps of the Second World War, the very idea of a prison guard has been tainted by association. But this formula existed from the beginning. In the 1932 Hollywood movie, *I Am A Fugitive From A Chain Gang*, the prisoners were amiable, while the guards were a brusque and brutal lot who carried out whippings and worked prisoners to death. In another pre-World War II movie, *Each Dawn I Die* (1939), the formula of a brutal guard force was repeated.

The general rules for the Hollywood movie formula appear to be that prisons are dramatic and harsh, dominated by brutish inmate gangs, and replete with murders, beatings, rapes, and contraband. Allowing for dramatic license, this may conform with the reality of some prisons. The dramatic action usually focusses on inmate heroes and villains, with a range of stock characters from good guys to bad guys. Again allowing for dramatic license, this does not seem unduly at variance with the reality of human nature.

But the custodial staff is painted in a monotone ranging from foreboding and threatening to evil, while the occasional corrections officer hero is rejected by an immoral warden. And allowing for dramatic license, this does seem at variance with human nature, for correctional staff are working class men and women with as great a range of saints and sinners as convicts. Correctional officers are the only occupational group who are unfailingly portrayed in Hollywood movies as bad guys; there are good and bad policemen and judges, doctors and lawyers, professors and plumbers, even mothers and fathers, but only bad correctional officers.

Granted that Hollywood movies are simple-minded distortions of the reality of prisons, you will see that writings in the "higher culture" of scholarship have had their own limits. I have already alluded to some academic misinformation about the character of the custodial staff in Warden Ragen's Stateville, and in Director Beto's Texas prisons. We should look at the picture more broadly.

The Correctional Officer

To their credit, modern academic studies of prison guards reveal the unfairness of their caricature in Hollywood movies. But balanced studies of prison guards are only a recent phenomenon. Ironically, Donald Clemmer's

(1940) pioneering work which launched serious intellectual studies of the prison had no such animus against guards. Subsequently, academics and prison reformers stereotyped guards on a level with Hollywood movies. Jacobs and Crotty (1978) begin with a popular 1943 textbook by H.E. Barnes and N. Teeters which criticized the "lock psychosis" among guards (a fixation on numbering, counting, checking, and locking). Jacobs and Crotty continue (p.1):

> The assumption that prison guards are incompetent and psychologically, morally, and socially inferior has been reinforced by subsequent commentators. Richard McCleery's well-known study of a Hawaii prison portrayed the guards as reactionaries who were subverting the goals of the reform regime. The same charge is often repeated by prison administrators frustrated in their attempts to implement vaguely defined prison reforms. The commission that investigated the 1971 Attica rebellion labeled the guards as racists. Prison reform activist Herman Schwartz has referred to guards as "frightened, hostile people." The public also tends to stereotype the prison guard as brutal, racist, and dimwitted. ....Few studies are available to confirm or deny the public's negative stereotype. Some data indicates that, contrary to popular opinion, guards adhere to the basic tenets of liberal criminology.

Jacobs himself was a leader in creating a more balanced view of guards with a series of articles in the late 1970's based on his field work at Stateville prison earlier in that decade. Since then reasonable portrayals of guards as an occupational group encompassing a wide range of types of people has become standard in academic research.

But these more balanced reports have little to do with prison control. Typically, like Jacobs (1978b), they study guards in prisons which are poorly controlled (Kaufman 1985), where brutality is institutionalized (Marquart and Couch 1984, or Marquart 1986), or where power is shared between inmates and various staff (Fleisher 1989, Owen 1988).

One of the best studies of prison guards is Lombardo's original 1981 study—his Ph.D. dissertation—at the Auburn, New York prison, done while he worked in the institution as a school teacher. His updated, second edition of 1989 is interesting because it reveals the pitfalls of academics who visit prisons to study them.

In his original research, which was based on fieldwork done from 1974-1977, Lombardo provides a sympathetic picture of the guards as working class men in a laxly-controlled minimum or medium security prison. There was little in his book to indicate guard corruption except one mention on page 192. In answer to the question, "What sorts of behaviors can get an officer in trouble with other officials?" 14 of the 50 guards he interviewed answered, "Dealing in contraband." He gave no estimate of how many guards were corrupt. Guards had frustrations and tensions with inmates and with a purportedly incompetent upper administration, but on the whole it was a satisfying place to work. He did not discuss brutality of guards against inmates. While this was an omission, I expect violence between guards and inmates was rare, given Lombardo's apparent integrity as a researcher, his intimate involvement in the life of the prison, and the fact that it was a minimum or medium security institution.

His revised 1989 edition was based on two months of fieldwork done in 1986, a decade after his original research. Lombardo was by then an academic who returned from a distant university to a prison changed for the worse. Now it was a maximum security prison rife with violence and inmate gangs. Lombardo's Table 18 of Rule Violations 1976-1985 (p.239) shows a worsening situation, with inmate fights, drug possession and other failures gradually increasing over the years. However, an "Attacks on Officer" classification shows little change, which is noteworthy because he did not discuss this problem in his original edition.

Nor does he mention guard brutality toward inmates. Yet it is a matter of public record that something happened. It may or may not have been brutality, but since Lombardo omits the events, he distorts the reality of the world of guards, and deprives the reader of an understanding of how convicts were controlled. Prisoners Legal Services of New York (a state-funded legal services corporation) in 1995 still had the records of two 1979 and 1980 Auburn cases. It is possible that other cases had been filed with the United States District Court of the Northern District of New York prior to 1986 when Lombardo did his research.

Both cases charged guard brutality. In the 1979 case (Civil Complaint Number 79-CV-608), an inmate charged that seven corrections officers and four sergeants beat him. The suit was dropped after the Corrections Department agreed (i.e., a "stipulation") to pay the inmate $1,000 and transfer him to another prison. The 1980 case (Civil Complaint Number 80-CV-622) made a local newspaper, *The Citizen*, on July 28 and 31, 1980. It accused eight guards and one sergeant (a different cast of characters from the 1979 case) of beating another inmate, causing him a broken leg among other injuries. This suit was dropped after the Corrections Department signed a stipulation giving the inmate miscellaneous treatments and benefits. Since the Corrections Department did not admit guilt in these cases we have no evaluation of the reality of the claims. Lombardo did not discuss these cases. It appears that Lombardo carried out a thorough study in 1976, but did not update it a decade later.

But neither in Lombardo's nor other research do we learn how to closely control the custodial staff in a maximum security prison. Hence the importance of understanding Warden Ragen's regime.

Warden Ragen's Control of Guards

INTRODUCTION

Maintaining close control over a prison is simple in theory, for the warden controls the custodial staff so they in turn will control the prisoners. To this end, Warden Ragen created a labyrinth of rules and regulations, reports and forms. He then whipped his staff through this maze with a small carrot and big stick. The carrot was small, because he had few rewards to dispense. But he wielded a big stick, for the basis of his control was punishment of guards. We have arranged these punishments along a gradient which ranges from guard assignments which were crucial for preventing escapes to those which were irrelevant. He punished severely throughout. This was the keystone of his control: if a mistake occurred, a guard was punished.

What I describe is an iron discipline which I believe is necessary if today's prisons are to be controlled as Ragen's Stateville was. But I do not believe it ethical or possible for today's guards to be beaten down as his were. Modern control of guards might be based upon a model of military elite units such as the Marines or the Rangers, where *ésprit de corps* replaces Ragen's punitiveness.

My discussion of Warden Ragen's methods serves two purposes: first, it provides the believable evidence that Ragen really did control his guards; and second, it illustrates that the problems Ragen faced are universal. Today, the challenge will be the creation of a modern guard force with a discipline no less iron, but one based on self esteem.

The issue of believable evidence to prove a warden's control is no small matter, for the public has been badly served by academics, journalists, and officials whose reports often resemble those of press agents. Prisons are secretive societies where only a half-dozen wardens in the 20th century have claimed to control their prisons. But if we ask, "What is the evidence that this is so?" nothing is forthcoming, except in cases which make it clear that control was based on brutality, as it was in the Texas prisons of the 1970's and 1980's. My second point, that Ragen's problems are universal, remains for me to convince you. That turns on whether you believe my evidence.

The Definition of "Security" and Its Rules

Warden Ragen's goals began with his ideas of "security." For example, mimeographed material for the guard's training program warned of inmate skullduggery, and specified that:

> Security means many things — trying to escape, inciting riots, sex relationships, starting fires ... and other more common violations of the rules such as, pilfering, conniving, and agitating. Inmates who have been caught in the most serious of these violations will have been placed in grades and denied some of the privileges enjoyed by other inmates.[1]

Here, Ragen's definition includes almost anything that he objected to: escapes and riots, deviant sexual behavior, stealing (this means stealing anything — cigarettes from other inmates, or coffee from the kitchen), conniving (conspiring to violate rules), and "agitating" (saying anything to another inmate which might upset or irritate him). Some of this was necessary — escapes and riots were unacceptable, and even an innocent nut and bolt might be part of a homemade bar-spreader. But it also included anything one inmate might say to another, and indeed, even the unspoken: an inmate could be punished for "silent insolence," that is, giving a guard an unspoken "dirty look" of contempt or hatred.

A guard in training received a Handbook in which he learned he was responsible for knowing and enforcing 89 general rules and 1,222 specific ones (which varied according to assignment and special problems). Instead of trying to describe this mass of rules, their substance can be imagined from the very first one:

> [Guards] will not be permitted to associate with friends or relatives of any inmate presently confined in the institution, nor with parolees, discharges, or any of their friends or relatives.

The first general rule continued, to caution the guards that they:

> must conduct themselves in such a manner as not to bring discredit upon themselves or the authority under which they hold such position. Therefore, it will be regarded as cause for disciplinary action or dismissal if any employee (a) frequents or loiters about places of ill repute, (b) gambles or loiters about gambling houses, or (c) disregards his personal obligations so as to acquire an unsavory reputation.

And Ragen meant it. One incident which illustrates there was little escape from the Warden (at least locally), and that he meant the first rule (as he meant each of the others), was related to me by a guard who said:

> Smith [a guard] was in town, and I guess one of the cons followed him, Jones it was: he was out on discharge. He knowed Smith; I guess they were pretty well acquainted. He was going into Shorty's, I guess for coffee and a sandwich, and this here con was catching a train, going home. Well, they sat and talked. Finally this con, he got up, and he took both checks and he went over to the cashier and he paid them. Now there ain't nothing wrong there, is there? He was out on discharge...Well the next day the Warden calls the officer in and he has everything right out in detail, what happened, and, boy, he chewed his ass out!

This was told as an example of the perfidy of convicts, for the guard telling the story assumed it was the discharged convict who snitched to the Warden. But we don't know who told the Warden, and it is even possible (though not likely) that the story was apocryphal. But Warden Ragen would not tolerate even small touches of humanity between inmates (or ex-inmates) and his guards.

This concern for adherence to rules and moral rectitude, all delivered in an overbearing tone, was part of everything Ragen wrote. It was a grim, threatening seriousness from on high. It also pervades the image presented by his publicists, Finston (1962), Erickson (1957), and the 1955 Chicago *Tribune* articles.

Based upon my limited observations of his upper staff, I believe most shared the same concern, as did Assistant Warden Frank Pate who really ran the prison on a daily basis until Ragen made him warden in 1961. And this, I am convinced, is a major reason for Warden Ragen's success. He found young men like Frank Pate among his guards, generally poor, with limited schooling and prospects, and shaped their careers. It was part of Ragen's genius as a warden, executive, and leader to select men who really believed in him, and who were, in a sense, his disciples. Men like Frank Pate were not careerists, but true believers who had found careers. With a cadre such as this, Ragen could impose his vision on the large body of hapless young men who only wanted steady jobs as guards. The challenge for today is to forge something like this dedication by discipline and *ésprit de corps*, and for this someone must select modern wardens who have ability as leaders and give them the authority to do so.

The training program also required the new guards to absorb the handbook issued to each new inmate which listed the laws of the state which they might not violate, 34 general and 106 specific rules of the prison they must follow, eight specific actions they were permitted in prison and 155 they were not. It ends with 85 personal property items they were required or permitted to possess. By specifying only what was permitted, control was made simpler: because only these 85 were allowed, the myriad of other possible possessions automatically were forbidden. Observers have cited this as an example of Ragen's cleverness, and it was: there was no way for a *jailhouse lawyer* to argue with a guard over what was permitted. If the item in question was not on the list, it was prohibited.

These more than 1,500 guard and inmate rules were just part of a torrent. New ones constantly arose from new situations, while reminders were issued because the enforcement of existing ones grew lax. But it was one thing for Warden Ragen to organize a system of control, and another to implement it. Since in theory he could only know some percentage of an unknown number of guard derelictions and errors, it remains our burden to demonstrate (granted, by circumstantial evidence) the effectiveness of Ragen's control. To begin, we must consider whether the guards obeyed because they wished to, or because they had to. Let's first consider whether they wished to.

The Carrot: Personal Satisfaction and Material Reward

Some men liked the Warden's system. The guards were not some mass of the discontented, and some appreciable proportion of them looked upon the Warden's system as a wise one. For example, one sergeant of many years service recollected how Warden Ragen transformed the prison so the inmates obeyed orders by the guards:

> It used to be in the old days, before the Warden changed things, you'd start out with some cons to get a job done, you'd start out with ten, by the time you got down to the other end of the Yard, you'd be lucky if you had one. Those things don't happen no more.

Our sergeant appears more typical of the few who remained than of the many who began. Few of the younger guards appeared to relish the system, and the general pattern was a rapid turnover of the young. My own contact with one young guard illustrates this. I met him during one of my overnight stays in the guards' dormitory (upstairs in the Administration Building) when winter storms closed the roads. He had been employed at the prison for four weeks. There was nothing vicious about him but he thought the inmates were somehow treacherous and mysterious. The other guards in his trainee group were older and more mature, but otherwise similar men from the farms and small towns of southern Illinois, generally friendly, but suspicious of convicts. They commented: "If they're so smart, why are they in here? The inmates do not believe they've done wrong, but that society is wrong. The guards have to watch them all the time, or they'll get away with something." They asked me if there was something wrong with the inmates' minds; they made snide jokes about how so many of them knew law.

This particular young fellow had been working in a local factory for a year, was laid off, and then had applied for a job at the penitentiary. He told me the tricks of the inmates, and he spoke of one man who had concealed a knife in his shoe heel. He was quite impressed with this; in some unknown way an inmate had hollowed out his shoe heel to hold a knife. After he had gone on a while, I asked him to describe the knife. He stumbled over his words; all he could think to say was, "Like one of them strips from coffee cans." (A long thin strip steel from a tin can, perhaps one eighth to a quarter inch wide). I didn't dispute his description of the object as a "knife" but I asked him to tell me what would an inmate do with it. He was puzzled at this question. He didn't know, but the lieutenant in charge of new officers' training warned them of things like this. He then told me how glad he'd be to get his regular assignment. He was now relief man for various guards on vacation. He seemed obsessed with the idea of "not making any mistakes." I asked him if he had ever found anything amiss yet: he hadn't, although he said, "But I guess my time is coming."

Three or four months later we met again in a hallway, and I asked him how things were going. He seemed cheerful, and after he asked me to not say anything, he told me they were hiring back at the factory, and he expected his name to come up soon. He gave a furtive glance to the side to see if anyone was within hearing distance. There was a sneer in his voice as he said, "You know this is no job for a young man, this is a job for an old man." Then he parted; I wish I had the chance to find out what he meant by "a job for an old man." It was not a compliment.

Many guards who remained did feel the yoke. An officer of several year's service bitterly told me:

> You can never tell around here. It's a funny place. Guys get called up to the Warden's Office and they're just told to resign. When they go up there, they just sign a blank resignation and it's filled out later. They might not even know what's being put down there. Just now this guy, he was working here for five years. He did something wrong: he let some prisoner out of Isolation without a lieutenant being there. Some guys make a mistake and they get five days off, other guys get fired, you never know. Maybe a lieutenant's written a ticket on him for being friendly with an inmate, tickets you never see. He's [Warden Ragen] got them up there in his office, he just keeps them in the jacket and then he calls the man up. If you call a man up and tell him to resign, he doesn't have to resign, he can get fired and they can appeal to the Commission. One guy did that and he got reinstated. I think that happened about a year and a half ago. Maybe one in two hundred can do this, but if you resign you can get another job with the State; if you're fired, you're blackballed from the State. Of course, if he wants to, he knows everybody in the State, and can have you blackballed

> anyway. You never know why. He can get rid of anybody he wants to. We
> call him Little Caesar and his little world.

Other officers had more than the abstract fears of this guard. One officer who
had 20 years of service and was now an officer in the newly organized labor union
for guards was furious because, as he put it:

> You know, they're trying to get rid of me. I've got one of the most
> important jobs here. I've been here since 1941. I'm responsible for a lot of
> the maintenance. They shook me down [searched him for contraband]
> yesterday, trying to get me mad enough to quit. They want to squeeze out
> the last drop of blood and then get rid of you. The Warden don't like it
> because I'm active in the union.

These are, I think, accurate assessments of how Warden Ragen treated his
guards. His system is gone, and I shed no tears for it, for guards do have rights.
The difficulty is how to recognize these rights and still have a disciplined guard
force, for Ragen's system did protect the convicts. For example, one day I
overheard some fantasy by two white guards who were speaking of a black inmate
when one said:

> I'd like to get that god-damned black son-of-a-bitch: I'd give him a good
> one in the gut, and then when he bent over [silent pause]....That way it
> don't leave no marks and you can always deny it.

This was wishful thinking, for I don't think any ordinary guard would have
dared to strike an inmate. I have no notes or memory of any believable inmate
reporting such an incident.

Perhaps men conformed to the system because of its rewards? Consider who
became guards to see what they would consider a reward. Basically the guards
were relatively poor men who were likely to remain so. This can be simply
illustrated. In the late 1950's, semi-skilled factory workers in the Joliet area
usually earned a gross wage, before deductions, of $300 to $350 ($1,600 to $1,900
in 1995 dollars) per month for working a 40 hour (five day) week. A guard's salary
was $290 per month ($1,600 in 1995 dollars) for a 48 hour (six day) week.[2] Add
to this the factory workers' opportunity for overtime wages for work beyond an
eight hour day. (Guards might have to work overtime on occasion, but with no
recompense.) It is easy to see that the guards were poorly off. Warden Ragen's
main source of recruits were poor young men, primarily from the economically
declining farms and small towns of downstate Illinois. In times of prosperity he
had them for short periods while they sought better jobs in factories; in time of
unemployment he kept them longer, their ranks swollen by those in need of a
temporary job. Out of this he created a stable body of officers. But our concern
is not the social antecedents or the career of the custodial officer, but their
relationship to control. I wish only to emphasize that the average guard's
financial resources were slim, and his ability to seek alternative employment was
limited. Loss of pay or job was to be feared, and Warden Ragen made this fear
real and immediate.

Perhaps we might seek positive motivation in promotion and career, for the Warden had been responsible for the promotion of every member of his staff from deputy warden down to sergeant. Naturally, he needed his own genius in picking subordinates who possessed the necessary combinations of intelligence, energy, devotion to duty, and the character to embody that duty in the person of the Warden. One inmate, a clerk to a captain of the guards who had watched the sifting and sorting of the promotion process for many years, observed that the Warden:

> Picks them careful; there's not a lieutenant that don't think the Warden's God. He just made two new ones: Smith is a nothing, cold, but Jones's got a lot of humaneness to him, but he's all-state. When they get together, it's not like one of them alone: you get one, alone, maybe you can talk to him, make him see your side. But they get together and something happens, you can see them talking, they build each other up. They'll say, "So-and-so's up to something, we got to watch him," and then they'll wait and follow him and lay for him for two, three weeks, just till they catch him doing the same thing again.

This assessment by a convict who was a keen observer illustrates how a great executive is a leader who can pick, mold, and motivate subordinates. Ragen was a genius at this.

He was aided also by the development of the state's civil service "merit system," whose major goal was to eliminate the power of the political parties' influence on who would be hired, fired, and promoted. The goal was to substitute instead how well an individual performed his duties. Stripped of his ability to call on a politician for a sponsor and unable to draw any power from the embryonic labor union for guards, the guard could only look to the Warden for an evaluation of his efficiency. But no matter how efficient, there was no place to go, for the Warden had few promotional opportunities to offer. There were always vacancies for guards, but promotion opportunities were limited within the prison and transferability of skills elsewhere even more so. In Stateville, a guard who did well could really only hope to become one of the 35 sergeants, 15 lieutenants, three captains, or two assistant wardens.[3] The state's other wardens usually promoted from their own staffs. These limited promotion opportunities and a few dozen $25 awards ($130 in 1995 dollars) each year for extraordinary meritorious service were the Warden's only incentives. But it worked, at least for some guards. And for those not so motivated, there was the iron discipline imposed by Warden Ragen's captains and lieutenants; just how skilled and thorough they were is demonstrated by one incident in which I participated by accident.

How Sergeant Able was Fired

This incident involved firing the guard sergeant on day duty at Gate 3, perhaps 50 feet from my office. His was a very responsible position, for Gate 3 separated the main prison compound (the *yard*) from the Hospital Wing, the Visiting Room, and ultimately, Gates 1 and 2. During the day it was a busy and complex transportation and communication point. Inmates (each of whom had to be *shook down*) and staff passing through required him to open and close the gate constantly; also, small packages and *call tickets* for inmates coming to the *front end* (say, for family visits) were passed through a small window cut into the sheet glass or screening covering the steel bars. As I remember there were always several inmate *runners* on my side of the gate, plus a dozen more on the *yard* side who *wheeled* through the prison delivering official packages and messages (and, of course, surreptitiously, inmate packages and messages).

This was also the funnel through which all the hundreds of within-institution reports, notices, and orders flowed back and forth between the front (the wardens, the record and business offices) and the *yard*. It was where *front end* inmate mail (requests to staff or letters home awaiting censorship) was deposited.

Sergeant Able began to delay sending through large numbers of these within-institution envelopes, for no reason. Even more bizarrely, he began to rifle the inmate letters, and periodically—especially on his rest breaks—going over to the toilet in an alcove near his station (by my office) and flushing numbers of these letters down the toilet.

He had been eccentric as long as I knew him, and I suspect now that he was in need of psychotherapy. But no matter to the inmates who were affected; they just had to get rid of him, a matter in which their interests and the Warden's coalesced. In the beginning, as one of my clerks told me:

> I seen him about three weeks, maybe a month before this, he was probably doing it before...The next time I saw him there was a whole bunch of us [inmates] in the hall, so I woke them up to what he was doing ...He was standing in front of the toilet with his back to the door opening the envelopes and reading, tearing up some of it and flushing it, putting the rest back in his pocket. This was a procedure he was following every day before he went down to eat.

The next step was when one of the inmates who saw this told a lieutenant he was *connected* to. The result was one those contradictions that happen in real life, for I had seen this lieutenant behave in public and I would never have predicted the result:

> The next thing that happened was this *shine* [black inmate] told [Lieutenant] Smith about it, and he [Lieutenant Smith] wouldn't go up there and look because he didn't want to see it: if he didn't see it he didn't have to say nothing about it. Cause he's one of the rare ones: he doesn't want to *snitch* on another *screw*, or anyone else unless he has to.

Blocked in this direction, the next thought was to draw me in. My clerk arranged with another inmate on a nearby assignment to drop by my office while I was sitting around socializing, and *loudtalk* it to me. My clerk continued:

> So next came the day when [inmate] Baker brought it up when you were here. ...He was throwing the ball to you, to get you to *beef* on him [Sergeant Able] or something ... but you missed it.

It just never occurred to me to report this, just as my clerks had socialized me never to report anything to the Warden. The attempts so far would have allowed our inmates to pass their information on while remaining anonymous. Since that hadn't worked, they had to take some chances. Their next effort was to *loudtalk* it in front of an inmate, Jones, who was the clerk to one of the assistant wardens. Jones was a *square john* who so identified with the authorities that his nickname (behind his back) was "Warden Jones." This had to be handled carefully because none of the inmates wanted to be hauled before a captain or assistant warden and *grilled* to *snitch* on record.

So my clerk and a few of his friends staged the following event a week later when "Warden Jones" was waiting with them to go back to the *yard* at the end of the day:

> So somebody mentioned [Sergeant] Able, and we got to talking about how strong he must be. No one could touch him. So knowing [the inmate nicknamed "Warden"] Jones as I did, I just dropped that bit about these letters. I wasn't talking to Jones ... but I knew he was taking it in. I could tell by the way he looked when I first said it, he was interested, he got it. So then I didn't have to say much, because the other two picked it up....So then back and forth, he got the whole picture, a little bit here, a little bit there. .... You just *bullshit* every night. A half hour later, who remembers who said what.

It worked: "Warden Jones" *dropped* it up front. Then, Warden Ragen's captains and lieutenants swung into action. Their mission was to *nail* Sergeant Able with so much evidence that he would have no chance to appeal his innocence. My clerk continued, basing his knowledge, I believe, on plausible conjecture and information he was fed by his friends, the inmates who were the clerks to the captains and lieutenants involved:

> At the most five days later is when this gimmick with [Captain] Brown and [Lieutenant] White took place. One of them sent the other one something through the mail ...and whatever it was didn't happen as quick as it should have ... [Lieutenant] White started putting papers in envelopes and began marking it down on a sheet.

At this point, the captain had documented a pattern of needless delay in official mail. Next, they *nailed* our miscreant sergeant:

> [Lieutenant] White ... called [Sergeant] Able's relief and asked him what time he relieved him. He told him 10:20, that was it. So a few minutes before time for [Sergeant] Able to go to chow, [Lieutenants] White and Blue, and [Captain] Brown, they all came up to the front end.

This was a strange *stake out* scene I missed, for I was not in the office that day to witness what took place right outside my door. It was staged to coalesce and *spring* in literally a matter of seconds in full view of the inmates, with only our Sergeant Able unaware. My clerk explained:

> [Lieutenants] White and Blue were on the other side of the hall and [Lieutenant] Green was standing over here by our door. So when [Sergeant] Able got relieved, he came over here to the bathroom. The only one he

> probably saw was [Lieutenant] Green. He didn't pay him any mind: he just
> went in there just reading and tearing up mail. Then the other two
> lieutenants across the hall moved up closer where they could see ... behind
> him. I guess when they saw him in the position they wanted him they gave
> [Lieutenant] Green the *sign* and he moved in on him.

That was it. With a lieutenant *nailing* him in the act and two others as
witnesses, plus a *trail* establishing a pattern of deliberate mail delays, Sergeant
Able had no defense. My clerk concluded:

> So they took him up to [Captains] Johnson and Rory's office ... when he
> come out of there he was sniveling and crying and begging. They had
> [Lieutenant] Enders walk him out. He cried to him too.

I do not know what transpired at that final scene. But I imagine there were
furious captains and lieutenants, eyewitnesses, documentary proof—and a confession awaiting his signature. Perhaps our sergeant was allowed to resign (and
keep his pension), perhaps not. But within minutes, with a detour to his locker to
change to his civilian clothing, he was out on State Highway 66A, unemployed.

I believe that every month and every year this kind of detective work went
on, with numbers of cases being worked on simultaneously. Captains and
lieutenants under the direction of the assistant wardens picked up suspicious cues,
put out *feelers* to their *society stool pigeons*, set up surveillance, laid paper *trails*,
and waited—months, if necessary. Sometimes they succeeded, sometimes not.
One inmate told me they would watch a guard for a year if necessary. No effort
was too great to catch a miscreant guard. The result of this was guards who did
not bring in drugs or U.S. currency, did not smuggle anything out, had no contact
with ex-convicts or inmate families, and did as Warden Ragen ordered.

The Big Stick: Days Off Without Pay

Warden Ragen could suspend a guard without pay for any period from one
hour to 29 days, and his nominal superiors in the state capitol rarely (if ever) did
anything but rubber stamp their approval. If he was generous, he would permit
a guard to work extra days without pay, but since the guard already worked a six-
day week, just one or two days of extra work meant 13 or 20 consecutive work
days. When we realize how poor and limited were these guards, we see the
financial pain which underlay the public embarrassment of these suspensions.

Each month, the Warden publicly posted a bulletin on the officers' bulletin
board giving each suspended guard's name, the amount of time lost, and the
reason for it. Each guard who was suspended also got an individual notification.
The punishments listed on these bulletins excluded guards who escaped suspension or were permitted to resign in lieu of being discharged or suspended.
Consequently, a discussion of these suspensions catalogs only the routine day-to-
day punishments, not draconian punishments such as discharge.

Table 5.1 tabulates the distribution of the 166 suspensions announced during
five months of 1958 for all branches of Joliet-Stateville. Details of this summary
Table will be explained in Tables 6.1, 7.1, and 7.2. These were routine months

with no major disturbances among inmates or officers. (For example, stealing, or trafficking with inmates by bringing uncensored letters out of the prison.)

Table 5.1

Distribution of Guard Punishments Arranged According to Importance in Preventing Escape and in Relation to the Maximum Security Yard

	Number	Suspension Without Pay
A. Crucial In Preventing Escape (For Example, Watchtowers)	25	2 Hours To 29 Days
B. Inside The Yard (For Example, Dining Room)	89	2 Hours To 15 Days
C. Outside The Yard (For Example, The Hospital)	12	2 Hours To 29 Days
D. Outside The Security Perimeter (For Example, The Farm)	40	1 Hour To 5 Days
Total	166	

Hence, while we do not include every type of offense, we do have a catalog of the routine. It shows that guards received severe punishments even if their assignments were incidental or irrelevant to preventing escapes. We will first look in more detail at punishments applied to guards on assignments which were crucial in preventing escapes.

A Note on Guard Suspensions

Although this is a limited sample, it provides some quantitative measure of the intensity of control. The 166 suspensions averaged 33 per month. Depending upon our assumptions, the minimum rate of suspension was 4.5 per 100 per month (all employees); the maximum, 9.5 per 100 per month (guards only). You may wish to consider not all suspensions, but only officers', because some guards received more than one suspension during this period. One hundred and eleven officers received one, 22 received two, two received three, and one officer received five punishments; thus these 166 punishments were meted out to 136 people. Consequently, the average number of monthly punishments is 33.2 if one considers offenses (166 divided by five months), and 27.2 if one considers offenders (136 divided by five months).

Moreover, the number of people who were available to be punished could vary, depending upon our definitions. This would change the denominator of our rate. In the abstract, the persons who could be punished included 600 employees of all ranks: regular guards, sergeants, lieutenants, captains, and the non-uniformed staff; 350 of these were guards (who really bore the brunt of it all). By whatever definition we choose, the fact is that each month approximately five to ten percent of the guards received punishment which typically cost a day's wages; of the 166 suspensions, only 51 were for less than one day; 82 were for exactly one day; the remaining 33 were for more than one day. This count of punishments is a crucial part of our argument that the Warden was no paper tiger.

There is a slight chance that these 166 suspensions cover not five, but six months. If this were so, then the monthly average would drop to 27.7 for the 166 reports, or 22.7 for the 136 custodial officers; this would cause the minimum and maximum rates to drop to 3.8 and 7.9. Such possible, though unlikely, errors might creep in because of the nature of gathering this evidence. The reports were posted on several of the guards' bulletin boards in the prison for all to see. I couldn't stand in a public corridor to copy these reports or memorize them. One of my clerks managed to tear off several months of these old bulletins after they were covered by newer ones, and just before they would have been discarded in the normal course of events.

But he had to do it one month at a time, and it was a nervous business. He had to go back time and again. He had to judge when a memo was obsolete, and reconnoiter until the corridor was clear. Then he had to peel under the newer memos to find the ones he wanted, tear them off and stuff them under his shirt. It would have been a difficult time for the two of us if he had been caught.

Endnotes

1. Most of the rules and regulations are reprinted in the compendium, Ragen and Finston (1962). That book not only contains most of Warden Ragen's more standardized rules and bulletins, but also facsimiles of more than 350 forms and record blanks used in the prison.

2. Gladys Erickson (1957, p. 107) reports as follows: Guards received $290 per month ($1,600 in 1995 dollars), meals on duty, uniforms and bus transportation; rentals in a prison supported trailer park; sergeants received $316 per month ($1,700 in 1995 dollars); lieutenants received $350 per month ($1,900 in 1995 dollars); captains received $414 per month ($2,200 in 1995 dollars) plus a home and food; the three assistant wardens received $500 per month ($2,700 in 1995 dollars) plus a home and full maintenance; the Chicago *Tribune* series of 1955 reported that Warden Ragen received $800 per month ($4,400 in 1995 dollars) plus a home and full maintenance.

3. Numerical estimates by my clerks.

6

Control of the Guards: Assignments and Events Critical for Security

Introduction

GUARDS were punished at three assignments which were crucial in preventing escapes: the 15 watchtowers built into the walls, the 3 gates which barred the entry pierced through the walls, and the armory which maintained and controlled the firearms and keys of the prison. I will discuss these punishments in detail, because some rationale exists for Warden Ragen's fierce punitiveness at these barriers. Table 6.1 explains the 25 guard punishments summarized on line A of Table 5.1. Such details will

TABLE 6.1
Punishment of Guards On Assignments Crucial In Preventing Escapes

	Number	Suspension Without Pay
Watchtowers	13	2 Hours to 29 Days
Gates 1, 2, 3	10	3 Hours to 5 Days
Armory	2	2 Hours
Total	25	

demonstrate the mind–boggling boredom and attention to minutiae which Warden Ragen's system entailed. It also suggests the calm of his prison, for violence and excitement was not the norm.

The Watchtowers

Stateville's fifteen wall watchtowers, along with the one in the dining room and the one at the prison gate house, were the only places where guards were armed, usually with two .30 caliber rifles, a revolver, tear gas grenades, and flares. The wall towers themselves were the ultimate (and most formidable) points of security of the prison, with clear sight lines over nearly all its open ground. Virtually no open space was more than 1,000 unobstructed feet from one or more tower riflemen. Thus, even an airplane or helicopter could not easily break the Warden's security because he had forbidden hostages (himself included) to be allowed as bargaining points for escape. The guards were instructed to shoot anyone approaching such a grounded aircraft.

For this classification, we list the suspensions and, in parentheses, the number of hours suspended without pay. Wording is amended to omit the guard's name, and to preserve anonymity. The ten suspensions are as follows:

"Failure to securely lock door of tower number 13. (2 hrs.)"

"For inability to promptly locate tower keys while relieving in a tower. (3 hrs.)"

"Failing to make 5:00 pm. tower call to switchboard operator. (5 hrs.)"

"The following Joliet Branch officers were suspended one (1) day each for permitting an officer and five inmates to pass their tower assignments with a 12' ladder without challenging them." (4 officers' names listed)

"Permitting a scaffold to be removed from the dining room without proper authority or notifying a supervisory officer. Also for calling another tower man and making unnecessary derogatory remarks about the incident. (2 days)"

"Failing to notice a lieutenant in vicinity of his tower, and failing to make 5:00 am call to switchboard operator. (10 days)"

"Failing to notice a lieutenant in vicinity of base of his tower without challenging and failing to make 12:30 am. phone call to switchboard. (10 days)"

"Failing to be alert in wall tower assignment. (2 days)"

"Failing to be alert in wall tower assignment. (2 days)"

"Failing to be alert in wall tower assignment. (29 days)"

The official reasons do not explain all. For example, "Failing to be alert" led to a suspension of two days, while in the last entry of the list the same reason is shown for 29 days. To know the circumstances of each incident would require a detailed investigation of all 166 suspensions, but there is sufficient detail given to outline the salient facts of control.

Note that punishments were meted out to guards who were not "prompt" with keys, failed to make a tower call, or failed to notice a lieutenant. Tower men had to call the prison switchboard every 30 minutes during their eight hours of continuous duty — no lunch hour, no coffee breaks — and they had to challenge anyone who walked near the wall by their tower. It was a job in which a guard had to remain alert, even though he was immobile and alone. As one guard told me, "After you've been up there for four to six hours—you report in every half hour— you wish you had something, anything, to break the monotony." Especially at night when the prison was still, the occasional activity one saw consisted of:

> You watch them go behind a building: when they go behind you put the spot on them, and then you wait at the other end; you put the spot on them when they walk past, after they come out the other end. A new officer, he don't know nothing, he'll be calling, but after a while you get to know. You see them coming out of assignments, you know a man'll be coming out of the dining hall; you get to know, and you can tell by watching. If they're going to the dining room, you know they're okay. If there's anything suspicious, you watch for it.

Once, I found a guard who liked this duty. He interpreted the Warden's rules very rigidly:

> I was in the cellhouse, but they transferred me [chuckling]. I was writing too many tickets... You ever see the officer's rule book? Well, I was enforcing every one of those rules. I was writing all hole tickets, but they don't like it... After I was here a while I got called in. Captain Able and Warden Baker and Warden Charles was there... Warden Charles he told me I was nervous, and after a while I'd calm down... I was going to quit, but they asked me not to: they said I'd make a good officer... They asked me, why not take a tower for a while, and maybe later you'll want to come back on the ground.

When I asked him for an example of the tickets he wrote, he said:

> Sure, I'll give you an example... I was walking the gallery in the cell house and seen these men playing cards. They was using matches—you know they got to buy their matches—they always used matches.... I stood there and watched them: they was using them for markers; they'd count them out... I was just watching them...I figured they wasn't doing anything so bad, but they was gambling, and I knowed if the Warden seen them and seen me and I didn't write a ticket I'd get it... I went downstairs I told Lieutenant Smith and asked him what to do. He said he'd take a look. .... He come back in a little while and said, "Why don't you write them up?"

In this instance, the lieutenant in question may have helped persuade the Warden that this guard was causing unrest. Few lieutenants wished to cope with a torrent of trivia from subordinates who might report even them to the Warden.

But most men found the tower a difficult assignment, particularly at night when little activity occurred in the prison. I was told by one guard who:

Spent a couple of years in the towers, up there eight hours straight. You got no radio; you can't read. Sometimes in winter you got a coal stove there: you get it red hot. I'd stand there. Couldn't sit down, I'd fall asleep. You never know when a lieutenant will come up, or even the Warden, and if you don't answer the high sign, that's it. I knew a guy fell asleep: they got a man from inside to drive over, he went up, and the other man came down, they woke up an officer in here to take the inside place, they come up, and packed this man's clothes, and it weren't no more than a half–hour, he was out on the highway, four o'clock in the morning.

Duty during the day also required alertness, as we see by the four tower men who were each suspended one day over the same incident. They each failed to challenge a guard with a work crew carrying a ladder and walking along the ground near the wall. Carrying a ladder of any length near the wall was always considered a danger sign: even though the inmates were accompanied, a man in a guard's uniform could be a convict in disguise. In effect the tower guard could not assume everything was all right because the work crew passed the tower before his. Similar reasons attached to the two day suspension for the scaffold, except here, an extra day was probably added for the guard's remarks. Supervision was ever present. If a tower man missed a call, a lieutenant was dispatched to check on him. If a tower man was being tested — or harassed if a lieutenant was angry with him — he would be continuously checked.

This did not end the unpleasant aspects of tower duty: the tower man did not leave his post for his entire eight hour tour, so he had to carry with him a bottle of water and a cold lunch. According to inmates, hot coffee was sent up by pulley by inmate *runners* until the 1940's. On a crucial occasion the innocent inmate *runner* who filched a cup of this coffee collapsed and inadvertently gave the Warden warning that the coffee had been drugged, and a large–scale breakout was planned for that very day.[1] In the towers which lacked steam heat or toilets, the tower man had to stoke a coal stove, as well as urinate and defecate in a chamber pot (which was lowered to the ground and exchanged for a clean one, once a day). Finally, the prison's walls stretched one–third of a mile, so the tower man might have to walk as many as 20 minutes to get to his assignment — no pleasant experience in rain, or the winter. One convict, a clerk to a captain, commented:

There's a lot of screws prefer the towers. Sure it's a lousy job; some of them like it though. No, they can't take it easy: they got to call in; they got 11 lieutenants prowling around, checking up on them, but what are the alternatives? A lot of them like it better than being inside the walls. You're on an assignment, a lieutenant sees anything, like two guys over a list of ball games: that's gambling, and the screw gets a ticket too. I know. I've seen a lot of them, and then the screw gets some time off — "improper supervision of assignments" covers a lot of things.

One might say this regime of the Warden was justified, though harsh, for the watchtowers were crucial points of security where his insistence on detail had some merit.

Errors At Gates 1, 2, 3

Guard punishments at the prison gates involved not only control of mistakes but also an understanding of the prison's architecture, and the regulation of illegal physical material as inmates moved through the prison by the *shakedown*. You may understand the prison by considering its architecture in relation to the medieval castle. The castle had an immense wall which was broken only by a single opening, barred by triple defenses: a moat and drawbridge, then wide swinging wooden gates, and finally the heavy iron bars of the *portcullis*, the sliding barred gate which dropped behind the wooden gates. The Stateville prison was much the same, if we leave out of consideration its specially constructed underground electrical and plumbing pipes and conduits, (which could be analogous to the castle's water well).

One exception to this comparison is that the prison also had two other holes pierced in its walls: the side sally port, through which bulky merchandise entered and left, and the coal chute for the powerhouse. Since no guard errors occurred at these other two breaches in the wall, we need only describe them briefly. The sally port was protected by special doors and fences, as well as barricades to prevent a truck from crashing through. (This was an example of how Warden Ragen did not make the same mistake twice: in Chapter 2 I recounted how Basil Banghart and his confederates in 1935 crashed out of the Menard prison in a delivery truck.)

The sally port was protected by special rules: for example, delivery trucks stopped outside the walls, were unloaded, package by package, by convict trustees who carried each box inside the walls through the Sally Port to a prison truck which then delivered the merchandise to the general store warehouse. All this occurred under the watchful eyes of the guards.

This was a massive logistical operation. All food and bulky supplies for 3,500 prisoners, a half–dozen factories, and for maintenance entered this way. Bulky garbage and factory products left this way. I remember the sally port opened and closed only on orders of a captain after the Warden had been notified. The sally port in other prisons is a route for smuggling in drugs, weapons, and contraband. But under Warden Ragen the only dereliction was minor pilferage. Occasionally the inmates could break into a shipping carton.

Likewise, coal for the powerhouse was dumped outside the walls, where convicts on the outside coal pile detail shoveled it into a chute laced with bars— spaced to pass small coal, but too small to pass a revolver—to fall inside the walls where other convicts shoveled it into wheelbarrows and then to the powerhouse coal pile. All this, too, occurred under the eyes of guards.

Let's return to the *front gate*, with its castle analogy. That gate was a single breach in the wall, protected by three major defenses which were called in the prison, Gates 1, 2, and 3. Through these three front gates passed all persons, and smaller items such as mail, office supplies, or medicine. All three of these front gates were located in the area marked as the "administration building" and the "hospital" in our outline figure of the prison. (See Figure 3.2). There was also a minor barrier at the gatehouse; here visitors (even government officials) were *shook down*, and left behind their personal possessions. A high open fence enclosed the open lawn between the gatehouse and front building of the prison itself. Once within the front building the visitor passed through a building containing business offices, and came to Gate 1. This was a series of vertical, thick round bars made of specially hardened steel which were imbedded into the concrete and stone of ceiling and floor. The bars were spaced several inches apart so as not to impede one's line of sight to Gates 2 and 3. Flat bars ran horizontally, intersecting the vertical ones.

Fitted into this was a door, manned by a sergeant assigned to the *turnkey* duty of opening and closing it for authorized persons. The only persons for whom the *turnkey* would automatically open this gate (after he first glanced up the hall to Gate 2, for Gates 1 and 2 might never be simultaneously open) were the civilians, officials and inmates with trusty status who had official duties which took them back and forth. These persons carried identification, and until every guard who manned these gates had memorized their faces, their photographs were mounted beside the gate.

The movement of visitors and all other employees was restricted: an assistant warden went to Gate 1 to give permission for the gate to open; the visitor walked through the gate, after which it closed behind him. After the *turnkey* closed the gate, he glanced at the assistant warden still standing on the other side for a second nod of approval. No visitor or convict might move through this gate together with the assistant warden or the official who okayed him, to preclude any possibility of coercion.

Once past Gate 1, the visitor was in a long hallway (with offices on either side) which continued to Gate 2. At this gate there was a structural difference, for next to this gate's *turnkey* station and in back of the prison's central telephone switchboard, the side wall (with bulletproof windows) bulged into the hallway. This bulge, the observation area of the prison armory, formed a steel plated curve spotted with ports through which rifles or machine guns might command the areas between Gates 1 and 2 in one direction, and Gates 2 and 3 in the other.

Once past Gate 2, the visitor had physically gone through the walls themselves, and was within the maximum security area of the prison. Between Gates 2 and 3 were located, in addition to various offices, the visiting room and the prison hospital, two places used by all inmates. The hallway ended soon after Gate 2, broken by an intersecting corridor. In this corridor, in direct sight line with Gates 1 and 2, was Gate 3. Gate 3 was the entrance to the prison compound itself: the *yard* or *back end*. This gate, unlike the others, carried a heavy and constant movement: mail, supplies, numbers of inmates going through to their work assignments in the hospital, inmates on sick call, or those who had a visit from family or friends. While only dozens of trustee inmates moved back and forth through Gates 1 and 2 every day, hundreds of prisoners, including the most dangerous, moved through Gate 3.

These 3 gates were crucial for security. We begin with Gate 3, where the heaviest traffic passed and where we find three of the ten guard suspensions. Two officers were suspended, each for 2 days (though each was separate from the other) for "Improper searching of inmate which resulted in inmate passing through Gate 3 with contraband on his person;" a third officer was suspended for five days for "Improper searching of inmate which resulted in an inmate passing through Gate 3 with a knife in his possession."

All three of these suspensions hinged about an inadequate shakedown where the guard searched the inmate's body and clothing. This was a chronic problem for the Warden, for the shakedown was not so much akin to a fine screen as it was to a coarse net whose strands were constantly being broken by human error.

Most shakedowns were a farce lasting four to seven seconds. But they served Warden Ragen's purpose: they limited the size of contraband that could be smuggled, and occasionally caught careless inmates. And because it was a procedure already in place, it could be tightened up instantaneously throughout the prison. It was also useful to keep guards alert. If contraband was discovered anywhere, a lieutenant retraced the inmate's steps backward to the last point of shakedown; that guard would be punished. If the contraband did not originate at that point, the retracing would continue and guards punished until the Warden was satisfied he had found its origin. Then the guard at the point of origin would be punished.

The fourth suspension on Gate 3 was for one day, for "Carelessness in permitting an unescorted inmate to pass through Gate 3, and for failure to ascertain whether or not the officer he saw was escorting the inmate to the hospital." Note that the burden of proof rested upon the *turnkey* to ascertain that the inmate was in fact, being properly escorted. There is a good chance this was one of the multitude of rule violations which constantly occurred in the prison because neither the guard nor the inmate involved knew of the rule. (There were so many that no one remembered them all.) But it could have just as likely been deliberate; not an escape attempt, but an attempt to manipulate the rules. For example, consider an inmate who had a legitimate call ticket which allowed him to leave one place to go to another. Let him go by way of a third. Just so long as he got to his proper destination or returned before the next count check—and could circumvent the in-and-out timing on his call slip by forgery, or the inattentiveness of a guard—no one would be the wiser. The volume of paper work and forms was so great that in the ordinary routine the scribbled signatures and writings on many forms received only a cursory glance. But oversight or manipulation, it mattered not: a guard was punished.

Two other suspensions were worded nearly identically: "Permitting an inmate to pass through the Gate number 2 without proper authorization (1 day)," and "Permitting an inmate and officer to pass through Gate number 1 without proper authorization (three days)." Again, the *turnkey* was responsible for all mistakes on these gates. The three day suspension for Gate 1 has the additional interest that nowhere on the same month's suspension bulletins was there a punishment for the unauthorized officer who accompanied that inmate. Again, while this could have been a minor error of detail, it is also possible that — just as with the watchtower guards — the *turnkey* was being tested by a lieutenant.

The final four suspensions were each for one day for the same incident: "Not personally checking each person who passed through the gate on August 1, and taking the word of someone else." Probably an outside baseball team came to play a game of baseball with the inmate team, and there may have been a rule violation discovered later. Perhaps the *turnkeys*, knowing who the visitors were, and seeing that they were accompanied by an officer, had simply waved the entire group in instead of counting heads and inspecting each entrance pass individually. In reality of course, such detailed inspection was the exception rather than a rule. But the outcome of this all too human failing is that somewhere or sometime an error occurred, and when discovered, ignorance was no excuse. Punishment had to follow all mistakes, no matter how trivial. Most of these mistakes at the gates, in and of themselves, could not endanger security as could a small mistake in a watchtower. But all were punished.

Of Human Frailty: The Shakedown

The shakedown exemplifies the fact that nothing in the prison, no matter how trivial, was simple. It was the human element of its details that made it difficult to carry out thoroughly. Some errors were mechanical, for searches were not made of a man's genitals or anus, nor were his shoes and socks taken off. Consequently, the routine shakedown only limited the size of contraband items. Small items were immune to search, and even so large an item as a knife with a blade long enough to kill could be concealed at the crotch with a bit of adhesive tape.

A second limit to the effectiveness of the shakedown were pressures of time. In reality, shakedowns processed a half–dozen to a dozen men a minute. A thorough shakedown could not be made of more than three or four men per minute, but this would delay the already tight prison schedule. Moreover, since a guard shaking down 50 prisoners could only watch the man he was currently shaking down, a thorough search would allow each of the other 49 prisoners to be unwatched. Having several guards shake down a line of prisoners could mitigate (but not eliminate) this problem, but this would require sufficient guards to just watch while others shook down, which by itself would require a considerable increase in the size of the guard force.

But even if the guard force were increased, shakedowns would still be routinized: some guards would have regular assignments, so that in time most prisoners would know which guard would search him. Since method leads to habit, prisoners would soon learn which guards hit (or miss) which spots on the body. In the end, convicts could still predict to some extent what sizes of contraband could be hidden on the body.

The final and perhaps the most important factor in this catalog of human frailty is the physical demand made upon the guard. To understand this, first consider it as a search. The prisoner turns to face away from the guard, empties the contents of his pockets into his hands, places his feet apart and holds his arms straight out from his shoulder, palms up, in a "spread eagle" stance. The guard stands behind him, and inspects what he holds in his hands. The guard then places his fingers (held together) inside the back of the prisoner's collar while his thumb pinches the collar from the outside. He feels the length of the collar, then runs his hands outside, out along the prisoner's shoulders and arms to the wrist, back along the underside of the arms to the armpits; then spreading his fingers, the guard runs his hands from the collarbones down over the chest and stomach, back up along the side of the convict's body, then down the rear of the man's sides to also cover the shoulder blades to the waist, around the man's belt (using his fingers and thumb as he did for the neckband of the shirt) then in two open handed sweeps, down the front, sides, and back of the legs to the ankle, and up the insides of the man's legs to his crotch; finally, the guard runs one hand down the small of the man's back to the base of the spine. At this final step, the convict steps forward back into line and another convict steps forward to begin the process anew. In Ragen's Stateville, an inmate could be *shook down* 10 to 20 times a day.

But the guard soon learned that the shakedown was a form of calisthenics. Consider it thus. The guard stands erect, his hands held close together and shoulder high. Then in succession (using finger pressure): extend arms, retract arms, bend back slightly, and run arms up and down; bend knees to a partial squat, and circle arms around and up and down; bend knees fully to a deep knee–bend, then move arms up and down; finally, stand erect. Few guards wished to do this four times per minute in one to ten minute stretches for 30 to 60 minutes per day, six days a week. Moreover, the shakedown was distasteful physical contact not usually seen in American society, for men do not ordinarily go around feeling other men's bodies. Under conditions of excitement, fear, or physical exertion, guards or inmates could become excited, afraid, or tired. Enduring a guard's hands feeling him over his body could cause a sexually repressed convict to explode.

Should violent reactions arise, the custodial staff was prevented from injuring prisoners by limiting its weapons—in Stateville guards carried none at all, not even a whistle with which to summon aid—and by Warden Ragen's discipline. But the custodial staff consisted of men who grew old, and a 50 year old guard was no match for a 25 year old inmate. Yet the guard worked in an institution where the aura of physical violence and verbal abuse hung heavy. Statistically, of course, there was probably little more chance that he would be physically attacked in Ragen's prison than a professor would be fired from a university. But guards thought no more statistically about this than professors did about renouncing tenure.

If we return again to the shakedown, for whatever physical or psychic reasons, they were quite superficial: when no lieutenant was present the typical shakedown resembled a parody of a security measure. However, as I mentioned earlier it did contribute to a system of control because it placed an upper limit on the size of contraband which could be easily carried, it caught careless inmates, and it provided an operating administrative procedure in which heightened standards could be instantaneously enforced. Moreover the shakedown provided a standard vehicle for searching when an officer was suspicious. A prisoner might be seen taking the contraband item out of its place of concealment on his body, a "pass" might be made from one prisoner to another, or an informer might report that a specific prisoner was carrying contraband. The shakedown was also extended, primarily in mild weather, to the *stick-em-up*, where a lieutenant stopped an entire line of inmates and ordered all to completely disrobe. Anything found by chance in the clothing of these nude prisoners, was of course, a *good pinch* on the lieutenant's record, and protected any informers by obscuring just who was *being fingered*.

The *stick-em-up* was rarely used, and I never saw or had notes about one. But I remember it was bitterly resented, for it was a personal insult and a vivid reminder of the inmates' lack of control. My guess is that it helped demean inmate leaders because of the ignominy of being so helpless.

Naturally, it was possible to catch some contraband without continuous shakedowns, for we can always create alternative means to ends. But the shakedown should be seen not as an isolated procedure, but as part of an endless series of routine checks (many of them trivial) which enveloped the individual guard in a fear of making mistakes. This helped to create a guard force which was infinitely obedient and alert. It is easy to be misled by the obvious fact that the average shakedown was a slovenly charade. It is less obvious, but more important, that when the inevitable mistake occurred, the system automatically tightened.

For example, how did the Warden know a shakedown was unsatisfactory? Obviously the erring guard did not know it, nor did the prisoner tell him. But another guard might find it out by a later shakedown, or the contraband may have been seen while it was being passed between prisoners. Once the contraband was found, the Warden moved swiftly and mercilessly to determine which guard made the earlier mistake. This became a problem of establishing the origin of the contraband, and the paths it followed. Depending on the type of contraband or its origin, a more or less thorough study was made. For example, the prisoner might be questioned; if he told and the Warden believed him, then a whole chain reaction of investigations and punishments might follow. In our very first example, the prisoner who carried the "knife" would be investigated to find out where it was made. Since "knife" on a suspension report could vary from a butter knife (which could be sharpened) to a lethal weapon made in an industrial shop, the investigation could go far afield. It focussed not so much on the contraband but on the leaks in the system of control: where did it come from? How did it get to where it was discovered? In the end, one result was always the same: some guard was punished for making a mistake.

The Armory

The officers in the armory were busy during the day with various housekeeping chores—reloading target practice ammunition, making new keys, checking hundreds of keys in–and–out—in addition to their responsibility for seeing that the hundreds of firearms, specialized kinds of tear gas grenades and launchers, and flares were loaded and ready for emergencies. Our two suspensions were each for two hours, one for "Failing to report to your supervisor that you knew nothing about firearms," the second for "Issuing a duplicate key that was not supposed to leave the Armory except in cases of emergency."

Here one officer was punished for causing an inconvenience, and another for issuing a duplicate key. These keys are another example of the multiplicity of detail in the prison's daily round of life, for each of the thousands of keys and locks in the prison were identified with code numbers.

Punishment for mistakes at these three places—the watchtowers, the gates, and the Armory—had a basis in immediate security, for they could not be compromised. But that was not so for the remainder of assignments in our table. These highlight the rigid nature of Warden Ragen's discipline.

Endnotes

1. Gladys Erickson, p. 112, recounts a variant of this story which probably is closer to fact than the inmate legend.

7

Control of the Guards: All Other Assignments

Introduction

WE HAVE now reached the point where mistakes by guards could not directly lead to an escape. Under Warden Ragen that did not matter, for everything, no matter how innocent, could somehow lead to something that ultimately spelled disaster. Only in some specious abstract was he right, but as a practical matter his draconian regime created an ever alert, ever diligent guard force.

I thought it repulsive, but it worked. I hope some future warden may achieve the same results in a fairer way, but for now I wish to explain how it was. We continue now with our elaboration of summary Table 5.1 of Chapter 5. Chapter 6 (and its Table 6.1) has just expanded on guard assignments crucial in preventing escapes, the 25 punishments in line A of the summary Table 5.1. Now, in the present chapter, Table 7.1 expands on the 89 guard punishments of line B of Table 5.1; these were assignments important for security, but less-than-crucial. I will deal with "disobedience" in some detail, while the remaining punishments will be summarized to minimize repeating the same dreary details.

Disobedience

You might think that punishment for "disobedience" would be severe. Not necessarily. Three suspensions, each for one day, read: "Insubordination, not carrying out Lieutenant's orders, and improper attitude toward superior officers." The final phrase, "improper attitude toward superior officers," probably explains something of the real nature of events — perhaps the guards in question poorly

TABLE 7.1
Punishment of Guards on Assignments within The Yard (Gate 3) or Mistakes which could be related to Escapes

	Number	Suspension Without Pay
A. Without Regard To Location		
Disobedience/Insolence to Superiors	8	2 Hours to 15 Days
Fire Hazard	2	1 Day
Miscount	14	2 Hours to 2 Days-
Cellhouse	6	1 Hour to 1 Day
B. Location Within Gate 3 (The Yard)		
Food (General Kitchen, Dining Room, etc)	12	2 Hours to 6 Days
Fire Station	1	2 Days
Inmate Services (Laundry, etc)	8	1 Hour to 1 Day
Maintenance (Machine Shop, etc)	14	1 Hour to 3 Days
Factories, Schools	11	1 Hour to 1 Day
Unspecified Locations	13	2 Hours to 5 Days
Total	**89**	

supervised inmates; perhaps they were not properly respectful of the lieutenants.

Some indication of this emerges from three other suspensions of a more specific nature, each for one day:

> "Failure to watch and supervise a new officer, and for not carrying out order of Lieutenant"; "Lack of ability to handle his assignment, and failure to cooperate with his supervisors"; "Failure to get required work out of inmates on his assignment"; and "Failure to cooperate with superior officers."

The case of one of these three officers illustrates the complexity of prison life. He had already received a suspension in a previous month for a "dirty assignment;" perhaps the floors were not neatly swept and mopped. His assignment was important: the repair of equipment vital to maintenance of the institution. The guard in question, who was white, was in the unenviable position of trying to be fair to black inmates. (Black inmates were generally relegated to lowly jobs such as mopping floors, while the whites learned more skilled crafts.) His attempts brought him into conflict with the white convicts on his assignment. By chance, I interviewed a white inmate on his assignment just at this time, who explained the dynamics from his point of view. First, the guard had been punished in a previous month for a dirty assignment. The inmate explained:

> He's [the guard] a misfit. He shouldn't never be here in the first place; he
> makes it hard all around. He plays the colored guys for big shots; he favors
> them. He gets them as porters over from the *Corner* [the office of the
> captain of the guards who determines inmate assignments] and when they
> come in he says, "Well, you guys can be painters," so he ain't got no
> porters to clean up the joint. Well naturally the assignment gets dirty and
> something happens, and he got wrote up, he got wrote up for having a dirty
> shop.

This guard was suspended for having a dirty assignment, and we expect there
was some irritation on his assignment over racial issues, but we must be cautious
about the reasons given by this white inmate. Racial issues were explosive. There
was little conflict over cell partners, because it was settled policy that cell
partners were segregated by race. However, on the assignments, there was
pressure by black convicts, as their proportion of the prison population grew, for
redefinitions of what should be *colored* or *white* jobs; whites usually had the
"better" jobs. When an erstwhile *white job* was challenged, it created friction.
Whatever role the guard played in the development of this friction, his solution
exacerbated the situation in the eyes of whites. The inmate I spoke with
continued:

> That was on Tuesday. Three days later—I guess it was Friday—we're all in
> the shop and he lines us all up. He holds up this pink sheet and he looks us
> over and he says, "Any you guys know what this is?" Some guys don't
> know what it is, but some guys say "No" just to give him an answer;
> nobody says they know, but they do. He says, "I got a day off, and I ain't
> never getting any more, you understand?" He says,. "From now on they
> ain't no porters in this shop: every guy cleans up his own assignment; every
> guy cleans up his own shop." So now we quit earlier because we go in at
> three: we got to knock–off at two–thirty and clean up. So there's work
> coming in all the time and the other officers complain because these jobs
> gotta be done, but we got to stop work early. They ask us why we was
> always knocking off early and we tell 'em we ain't got no porters: there's
> nobody to clean up and we gotta clean up ourselves. They say we got
> porters: why don't we have the porters clean up? We tell them no, there
> ain't no porters, and then there's a whole stink raised: he gets called in on
> the carpet.

The objective nub of this inmate's description was the growth of tension, and
the reduction of work output on this assignment. Again, consider the racial
aspects of the inmate world. In the earlier quote, for example, the lieutenant had
to inspect the shop and decide it was dirty. Why did he inspect? It may have been
a chance of routine, but more likely one of the white convicts *dropped a kite*.

This was a simple process, for each cellhouse had a large padlocked wooden
box (for all letters — to family, for assignment changes, etc.) at the front door.
Each day a runner from captain of the guards changed the box, bringing the filled
one to the captain, who opened the box and reaped the contents.

This small procedure was extremely valuable to Warden Ragen in undercutting the power of inmate leaders or errant guards. By having a single box for all notes and letters, no one could ever know if the note they saw dropped in the box was a letter home, a request to see a chaplain, or a *snitch kite*: all that was visible was a momentary flash of paper going in the box. I remember one of my clerks, to protect his reputation as a *right guy*, showed his letters home to a cellhouse clerk before they went into the box. This also points up the tremendous energy and diligence that went into Warden Ragen's system: someone had to sort through this avalanche of paper, read it, and then follow through.

Or in the last six lines of the quote above: who was the "they" that spoke with "us?" Most likely, it was white convicts on other assignments who spread the word on their assignments, and *loud talked* the issue in front of the guard on their own assignment. Prison etiquette forbade *snitching* by writing a *kite* to the Warden, but it was alright to complain about something to your friends. If enough complaining was done to enough friends, it was a sure bet that some of them would *loudtalk* it, or accidentally (on purpose) discuss it where a guard could overhear. When this happened, inmates who did it could consider themselves *right guys* who perhaps bent the rules, but still had their self respect. And finally, most guards would jump to report such information to a lieutenant: diligent guards got better assignments and had lieutenants as friends.

We can be sure that similar irritation and talk was circulating among the black convicts. Black guards and inmates benefitted from Warden Ragen's regime, because the whites had insufficient power to prevent the advancement which the Warden rewarded to all who obeyed his regime.

Finally, we progress to the suspension with which we began:

> The middle of the next week—that was after the Friday he lined us up—there's this business about the hacksaw blade. On the day shift there's a hacksaw blade disappeared. It's like losing a gun around here, and nobody could find it. Well, it was found on the next shift. He wound up getting a day off for that and course that's a big black eye for him because they disappeared on his shift, and he's supposed to be in charge of all that stuff.

We should not conclude, however, that this officer was defeated by the convicts on his assignment. Warden Ragen was wise in the ways of the prison, and after all, the "loss" and "recovery" of the hacksaw blade was perhaps too convenient. Had he wished to severely punish the officer, the usual procedure would be to suspend him for a longer period on a charge more specific than the vague one actually used, or transfer him to an undesirable assignment, like a watchtower on the night shift. Instead, the officer remained on the assignment, and a few weeks later, our inmate remembered:

> That's when all this machinery business comes up. There is only a small piece broke off from a machine in the furniture factory. It was only a small piece and it's just laying around. Somebody forgot to dispose of it. It was just a little piece that nobody would want. Well, he made a big stink about

it and we lost 30 days Yard [afternoon recreation]. That was 50 men. We all lost out for 30 days.

The officer in question, although his promotion chances were not helped by this contretemps, did not necessarily have his career destroyed by the inmates. In the prison microscopic conflict was continually in process and often erupted in the punishment reports. The Warden, (or more directly, the captain of the guards), awarded both the officer and the inmates some measure of satisfaction—the guard lost days' pay, the inmates lost recreation—but in the end, they had to live with one another.

The final two suspensions are: "Telling a supervisory officer that he was taking the word of an inmate over that of an employee (2 hours)," and "Insubordination, cursing, questioning a Lieutenant's authority, sending an inmate off of his assignment, showing preference to an inmate (15 days)." An officer might tell a lieutenant that he was taking the word of an inmate over an employee, but he had to do it in private. Probably this officer made the mistake of saying it in front of other officers, or even worse, in front of inmates. Neither guards nor inmates could openly say such things, for in public the officer was always upheld. Officers who falsely blamed convicts were punished by the Warden, but in such cases the fiction was maintained that the Warden investigated thoroughly. More likely another guard *snitched*. Among the guards, distrust was normal; they would never be openly contradicted by a colleague, but there was always the suspicion someone might inform the Warden covertly.

All Other Guard Punishments

At this point we can be less detailed because there is no chance the remaining punishments had any direct bearing on security. Instead, they kept the guards cowed and obedient, and the prison running efficiently. Paradoxically, it was this attention to and punishment for trivial detail which kept the guards ever alert and in turn kept a close control over the inmates. And that was not trivial.

Two suspensions of one day were for small fires which broke out during the night. One was waste paper which burst into flames, and was reported by the night watchman on an industrial assignment.

Fourteen suspensions were for causing miscounts. Twelve were punished by one day suspensions because they delayed the schedule of the entire prison, usually for 20 minutes.

The six suspensions for guards on cellhouse duty stemmed from routine errors of locks and keys. They reinforce the endless trivial detail of guard duty, such as the guard who was penalized one day's pay for "Giving keys to an inmate clerk to go up on the galleries in the cellhouse to open the boxes for the light switches." Light switches were covered by padlocked boxes, so turning lights on or off could become a hassle. It was easy for a guard to fall into the habit of leaving the box unlocked for his tour of duty, or assigning the job to an inmate.

Of the 12 suspensions related to food, most were in a league with the one day suspension for "Permitting fruit to be passed twice during evening meal after being instructed to pass it only once." But a few were of more serious potential such as the six day suspension for "Failing to check knives which had been issued by another officer, and for failing to immediately report that a knife was missing."

Another 47 suspensions range over a variety of mistakes, from a one hour suspension for leaving the center drawer of a desk unlocked, to a day or two for leaving equipment unlocked. A couple of these provide insight into the diligence and rectitude required of guards by Warden Ragen. First was the guard suspended for two days because he trusted an inmate too much:

> When checking the electrician's tools back into the toolroom, he was noticed checking the tools off the list with his back to an inmate as the inmate called off the tools to him. Checking in this manner made it impossible for him to see just what tools the inmate was calling, and he was taking the inmate's word for each tool checked.

How would the Warden learn of this dereliction? There are any number of possibilities, but most likely an inmate in the shop mailed a *kite* to the Warden.

Finally, another guard received a one day suspension for:

> Miscount in the furniture factory of tools on tool check, and for writing a disciplinary report on an inmate which indicates he tried to shift the blame for his mistake on the inmate.

This illustrates Warden Ragen's determination to control the guards. They were not to avoid punishment by blaming inmates, just as they were not to harass inmates.

Finally, Table 7.2 expands on guard punishments in lines C and D of the summary Table 5.1, assignments which were far removed or irrelevant to the prison's security. The 17 suspensions on assignments outside the *Yard* ranged from two hours for "Carelessness in the handling and issuing of locker keys," to a 29 day suspension for "Sleeping on duty while assigned to the Officers Kitchen." Five suspensions on the prison farm were for errors such as temporarily misplacing a knife (five hours) to letting 50 hogs heads spoil (three days). There were 23 suspensions for being absent from duty without permission, and others for such failures as not having an identification card at roll call, and a three hour suspension for "Failing to submit an award letter for the month of January 1960," probably punishment for a supervisor who failed to commend an officer for one of the Warden's $25 merit awards.

How typical are these 166 punishments? I monitored the guards' bulletin board for several years and found only two which differed. One was "Uniform coat unbuttoned" (two hours), which emphasized Warden Ragen's insistence on neatness; another was a two day suspension for "Refusing to write a report on an officer," probably a guard who refused a lieutenant's order to inform on another officer.

It is difficult to speak of "objective" knowledge about prison, but with all its

TABLE 7.2
Punishment of Guards Outside The Yard (Gate 3) or Not Crucial in
Preventing Escapes from The Yard

	Number Without Pay	Suspension
A. Location Between Gate 2 and 3 (Hospital, Officers Kitchen, etc)	7	1 Day to 29 Days
B. Location Between Gate 1 and 2 (Record Office, Business Office, etc)	0	
C. Location Before Gate 1 (Administration Building, etc)	5	2 Hours to 1 Day
D. Miscellaneous Outside The Walls (Garages, Delivery Trucks, etc)	5	3 Hours to 3 Days
E. The Farm	5	2 Hours to 1 Day
F. All Other		
Took Day Off Without Permission	22	1 Day
Repeated Absenteeism	1	5 Days
Miscellaneous	7	1 Hour to 7 Hours
Total	52	

difficulties, we think the fact that five to ten percent of the guards each month received a punishment which stung both pocketbook and ego bespeaks a system that was effective. The humiliation should not be underestimated. There were several bulletin boards where lists of these guard punishments were posted each month. Everyone — other guards, civilians, inmates — read them. We doubt there was a large volume of errors by guards which were undetected by the warden. A detailed examination of our 166 reports (and the fact that examination of several year's reports shows no difference in pattern) reflects accurately the yoke borne by the guards: no mistake or dereliction was too minor for punishment. Given this control over the guards, it should come as no surprise that, as we see in our next chapter, the guards carried out a close control over the inmates.

8

Control of Inmates: An Overview

Introduction

WARDEN Ragen's control of his custodial staff was a means to the end of controlling the convicts, our next topic. To put his system in perspective, we need to consider how, in general, inmates are controlled in American maximum security prisons.

Here we run the risk of a semantic tangle, for the term "maximum security" prison has little specific meaning. Rather it is defined within a prison system as a contrast to its opposite, the "minimum security" prison. The maximum security prison has more formidable perimeters to prevent escape, more restrictions on inmate autonomy, and more criminally experienced or dangerous inmates. All of this is only in comparison with the minimum security prison which is less formidable. Thus, the maximum security prison of one state may not be the equivalent of another's, but they are all congregate prisons in which the inmates are out of their cells eight or more hours per day, carrying out activities such as eating or working.

This relative meaning—what statisticians call an "ordinal" measurement—becomes even more imprecise when we consider a new name that has come into our vocabulary in recent years, the "super max" prison. These prisons, which are even more restrictive than maximum security prisons, have spread from the federal prison system to several of the states. They stand as a monument to the failure of existing maximum security prisons, which themselves attest to the failure of minimum security prisons, community based corrections and other more humane penal measures. We begin with a discussion of the origins and nature of the super max prison.

We may posit two reasons for the rise of the super max prison: either today's inmates are so dangerous that they can no longer be controlled by existing maximum security prisons, or our existing maximum security prisons are inadequately controlled. We discuss the first issue in the section, "Are Today's Inmates Less Controllable Than In The Past?" In the section which follows we discuss the second reason, how control is organized in today's maximum security prisons. After this, we outline just how different Warden Ragen's regime was from today's prisons.

Modern Control: The Super Max Prison

Correctional officials today have failed to control their maximum security prisons, and have turned to the super max prison instead. How did this come about? In Chapter 24 of *The Hot House*, Earley proves some insight. It began with the federal prison at Marion, Illinois, the successor to Alcatraz. Both were very small congregate prisons with segregation units for hard–core recalcitrants. When violence erupted at Marion, the federal authorities locked its inmates in their cells 23 hours a day, (with one hour outside for exercise), the working definition of the super max prison. Since prisoners could not be controlled if they were allowed out of their cells for eight or so hours a day to eat or work, they were locked in their cells continuously. This practice has spread to some states, in some cases by simply converting a prison to such a use without formally calling it a super max.

Earley recounts how the small (to house a few hundred inmates) Marion, Illinois prison was built to replace Alcatraz. In the 1980's, Marion had both a congregate prison, (where inmates were out of their cells for eight hours a day), and a special control unit in which a number of its most dangerous inmates were kept on permanent lockup, let out only to exercise and shower. Even when they were led back and forth from these destinations, it was a single inmate in handcuffs escorted by three guards.

In 1983, two guards were murdered in separate and identical attacks eight hours apart. In each of these, an inmate in the special control unit was being led out of his cell, handcuffed and under the control of three guards. In each murder, the inmate was able to have another (who was still locked up) produce a key, reach out between the bars separating them, unlock the handcuffs before the eyes of the guards who were presumably too startled to move, and then provide a knife to the now uncuffed convict. In one murder, two guards were apparently frozen with fear and did nothing to subdue the inmate who was attacking the third whom he hated. (It was a planned assassination.) In the second, which occurred only eight hours later, the inmate tried to murder all three guards; none of them attempted to subdue the inmate, but rather to escape. Two survived. At that point the prison was put on lockdown, and most inmates were confined to their cells up to 24 hours per day.

Comparing these murders with control of inmates under Warden Ragen can only be a hypothetical exercise, but it boggles my mind. I remember once seeing an inmate in brown coveralls, who had been placed under restraint (isolation, segregation, or detention), being led, shackled in chains, by a lieutenant to a special visit in an interview room across the hall from my office. This was in the busy hospital wing near the visiting room, and it is bizarre to think that with the guard watching, the inmate's shackles could be unlocked, a knife produced and handed to him. To make this approximately equivalent to those events at Marion, transfer the setting to Warden Ragen's segregation unit and then add that the guards would flee for their lives while the convict was murdering one of them. If I had proposed such scenarios to my inmate clerks I would have been laughed out of the office. Yet, Early recounts it. Even if all this could have happened in Stateville's segregation unit, it is inconceivable that three or four officers would not have clubbed the inmate to the ground in minutes.

We have confirmation of Earley's account. In 1984, the United States House of Representatives' Judiciary Committee received a report by two consultants they had hired to report on the events at the Marion prison. David Ward and Allen Breed confirmed the outline of Earley's story. Their dry prose told an even more horrific story of the breakdown of control at the Federal Bureau of Prisons institutions in the 1970's which turned Marion into a *de facto* super max in 1978. This came after assaults on inmates and guards had escalated, including gang killings at the Atlanta Penitentiary. The Bureau began to send its most recalcitrant inmates to Marion, but they were hardly controlled. Ward and Breed tabulated 14 escape attempts, ten "group disturbances," 54 "serious" inmate–on–inmate assaults (including eight homicides), and 28 "serious" inmate on staff assaults, in the 3½ years prior to June 1983. Then, until October when the guard killings took place, violence escalated. After that the prison underwent a draconian shift toward control. Not only lock–downs, but body searches of the inmates where a guard would insert his finger (presumably gloved) into an inmate's anus in search of contraband such as hacksaw blades or keys to handcuffs.

As you might expect, it is difficult to learn much about the operation of super max prisons. Published reports by those with access tend to be by supporters, such as DiIulio (1989) or Ward (1995). For example, Keve (1991) indicates Marion was calm and well run in the late 1980's. It ran with a graduation of control: some inmates were on lock–down; others had a great deal of autonomy. The Federal Bureau of Prisons now operates a second super max prison in Florence, Colorado. It was very expensive to build and even more expensive to operate. The *New York Times* of October 17, 1994 notes that its 416 inmates will be controlled by a staff of 500. Florence's 3,500 inhabitants were so anxious for these jobs that they donated 600 acres and raised $130,000 to welcome the new prison.

From those beginnings at the Marion prison in the later 1970's, the super max has spread to many states. There is no precise definition of such a prison, other than all or nearly all its inmates are locked in their cells about 23 hours per day, and they live that way for years.

The justification usually given by prison authorities for the super max prison is the breakdown of control in a state's existing maximum security prisons. This is attributed to the fierceness of today's convicts. Correctional officials never attribute it to poor management. Nor is evidence presented to justify this reasoning. For example, in the Final Report (1993) of the Illinois Task Force on Crime and Corrections, Chapter 12 took just seven pages to recommended building a super max for the state. The chapter consisted of a narrative of the breakdown of control in the state's prisons and little else. The unspoken assumption was no possibility of control existed at the state's maximum security prisons.

The claims and counterclaims about the super max prison continue to grow, and follow the usual pattern of conservative support versus liberal opposition. Unfortunately, little of it is illuminating, particularly because the shroud of secrecy is tightly drawn by state corrections departments. This veil is torn only by proceedings in the courts. Unfortunately, this happens only when failure occurs, not when a prison operates smoothly.

An example of this exposure occurred in the 1993 Federal District Court in San Francisco, where a two month trial investigated allegations of brutality at the California Department of Corrections Pelican Bay super max prison. In 1995 (the *New York Times* of January 13 and the *Wall Street Journal* of November 20) the judge held the authorities guilty, but allowed the prison to continue its regime, albeit with modifications and restrictions. The *Wall Street Journal* pointed up an unexpected reason why Pelican Bay is expensive to maintain: the *pro bono* law firm which sued the state was awarded $4.25 million in fees, after submitting a bill for $8.3 million, indicating that for lawyers, *pro bono* work is sometimes very profitable.

The super max is now a fixture of the prison landscape. It is very expensive to build and operate, and from the Pelican Bay example, to defend in its lawsuits. Most importantly, it is based upon an assumption that failed management is not a major reason control has broken down in a state's maximum security prisons, an assumption no one questions. What then do we know about the uncontrollability of today's convicts?

Are Today's' Convicts Less Controllable than those of the Past?

From time to time I have emphasized how violent society was in America at the turn of the 20th century and into Warden Ragen's day. For example, in Chapter 2, I described how the Chicago police shot and killed ten union workers on strike in 1937, while in comparison there were no deaths a generation later when the Chicago police rioted during the Democratic National Convention of 1968. In Chapter 9 I relate how one of my clerks, a product of Chicago in the 1930's, planned to murder another inmate in the event the offending convict did not stop his harassment. Today's violence may be different, but hardly unique.

I have provided such anecdotes to dispute the claim that today's convicts are so much more violent and uncontrollable than those of previous generations. This is the standard nostrum of prison administrators when violence breaks out. One such example in the *New York Times* of February 9, 1995 had the warden of the U.S. Penitentiary in Atlanta claiming this to a reporter after one of his guards was killed, the first such killing in a Federal prison since 1987. Violence is so common that the numerous assaults on guards in America's prisons which do not result in death are minor news.

Certainly there is evidence that by the 1970's, American prisons became more violent. This is graphically portrayed by the sociologist John Irwin (1980). He attributed it to a new phenomenon, a great increase in the number and percentage of convict "lowriders," who were violent, hostile, and uncontrollable young hoodlums. However, in an aside, Irwin commented (p.189): "When there were no successful countermoves against them [the "lowriders"], they took over the convict world." Irwin did not discuss these "countermoves," but I surmise there were times when the "lowriders" were contained.

The idea that today's convicts are so much worse goes beyond the United States. Thomas (1972) reports that it was widespread among British correctional officials decades ago. For example (p.176), he cites the annual report of the prison commissioners: "There has been in recent years a change in the character of the prison population, which adds materially to the difficulty of control." Then Thomas makes clear his own skepticism of this claim (p.177): "Whether or not prisoners were more difficult during this period than previously is not only questionable but irrelevant. Prison staff suffers from the common tendency to detect 'change and decay' all around"

His history of British prisons is striking in its parallel to the United States, where prisons went through a wave of riots around 1950. Thomas discusses the breakdown of control after World War II when gang leaders took over British prisons and "violence between prisoners became usual, when the strong terrorized the weak" (p. 191).

A growing number of American investigators have developed a skepticism that today's inmates are inherently more violent. This was expressed by Colvin (1992) in his study of the 1990 New Mexico prison riot. Colvin accepted the idea that a new type of disruptive inmate was emerging, but he asked if inmates were entering prison that way, or whether they got that way in prison.

Colvin drew on his experience as an employee in New Mexico corrections years before his transition to an academic, and on similar thoughts by others.[1] He concluded that there had been two developments: in New Mexico prisons, inmates who demanded their rights and questioned staff authority emerged in the late 1960's and continued into the 1970's; then after 1976 there was, "A more violent inmate who no longer 'did his own time,' but 'messed with' other inmates before they could 'mess with' him" (p.201).

But Colvin suggests this violent inmate was actually produced by the prison environment. Thus, if the more violent prisoner is a reality, his origin may be as much or more in the failure of control in prison than in a change in society. This idea implies that if prison control changes, so would prison violence.

Thus, even if today's inmates are somehow more violent than those of yesteryear, a controlled maximum security prison could change the situation. My suggested model in Chapter 12 is based on Warden Ragen's regime. Other approaches could be developed. But before we turn to Warden Ragen's system, we should consider control in the maximum security prisons of today.

The Maximum Security Prison Today: A Metaphor Based Upon Stateville Penitentiary

In January 1991 and August 1995 the wardens of the Stateville penitentiary kindly allowed me to be escorted on brief tours (a few hours each) of the prison. I was guided by young civilian counselors: in 1991 a black woman; in 1995 a white man. My observations about some cellhouses I saw, (in conjunction with the frame of reference I developed in Chapters 3 and 4, on the need to control time and space in the prison), lead me to make some educated guesses about maximum security prisons today.[2]

One striking difference between the Stateville of 1991 and 1995, compared with my 1957 to 1963 tenure, was the presence of women correctional officers. There were none in my time. I do not know their percentage of the present staff, but I saw them at the front end of the prison and also in the *yard*, the maximum security enclosure. On both tours my guides directed me to the newer cellhouses, replete with electronic controls. There were two of these electronic cellhouses, built on the sites where three of the old round cellhouses of my day had been torn down. (One round cellhouse remains.) Their electronic control panels were impressive. I saw women guards there, a few of them clustered and socializing with others, male and female. Also, the inmates I saw in those electronic cellhouses were a higher percentage of white inmates than was generally so in the older cellhouses. (In 1993 Stateville was 11 percent Hispanic, with a remainder of non–Hispanic whites 14 percent, and blacks 75 percent.)

But when I asked my guides if I might see the cellhouses of my day, my view of Stateville changed. In 1991, my young woman guide seemed uncomfortable, but took to me to the old rectangular cellhouse B shown in Figure 4.2. She refused to take me afterwards to the one remaining round cellhouse. All the cellhouses now were ringed by wire fences topped with razor–edged barbed wire.

At the front door of the old rectangular cellhouse B, I realized we were entering a different world from Warden Ragen's era. The cellhouse had been split lengthwise down the center into two separate facilities called B–East and B–West. If you look at Figure 4.2 of the old cellhouse B, in the "bird's eye view" there is a label "alley: walk in rear of cells." This alley ran between the backs of the banks of the cells. Imagine a wall built filling this alley and extending to the outer walls of the old cellhouse (labeled "cellhouse wall" in Figure 4.2). The new cellhouses are like a sandwich in which B–East is one slice of bread and B–West is the other, while the wall filling the old alley resembles the filling of the sandwich.

My young woman guide in 1991 would let me see only the cellblock to the left. (I think it was B–East.) She indicated that B–West was a "problem," suggesting inmates who were too hostile. Since I wanted to be an agreeable guest, I did not probe her reasons. We entered B–East. We were now in a world of almost all black inmates, and all male guards. It was a world of grunge, and looking into a few cells on the ground floor flag by the entrance door, sometimes close to a pigsty.

I sensed a diffuse tension, as if I were in an alien and ominous world. The cellhouse guards and my guide chatted by the entrance door and never budged. When I walked out perhaps 100 feet on the flag along the line of cells, no one stopped me, no one came with me, and no one offered any commentary.

I was startled by the decor. Concertina razor wire flanked the end of the building by the entrance. The walkway in front of the cells, labeled "gallery: walk around front of cells" in the "birdseye view" of Figure 4.2, was a concrete floor. The upper tiers, (2-4, shown in the side view of Figure 4.2), had been a simple railing when I worked at Stateville. But now the entire length of the railing of these upper tiers had fastened to it a steel mesh designed to keep guards and inmates from being hurled over the railing to the concrete flag below. A fall from tier 4, the height of a four or five story building, would probably mean death.

An even more amazing addition faced the cells from the outer wall of the cellhouse itself, shown on the "birdseye view" of Figure 4.2 as "cellhouse wall." High above my head, bolted to the concrete wall and running the length of the cellhouse, was a steel catwalk. It was protected against objects thrown from the cells facing it by a wire fencing. Patrolling this catwalk were guards armed with shotguns.

During my tenure at Stateville the only firearms inside the walls were the rifles in the dining room tower, carried there via an underground tunnel from the armory three times a day for mealtime surveillance. Now the inmates faced shotguns across from their cells all day. The change of weapons is significant. A rifle is a weapon designed to allow a marksman to drop a specific target, even at a distance. A shotgun, however, is designed for undifferentiated shorter–range killing in its cone of fire; it is deadly against a group of men. If it is crucial to drop an individual, bystanders may be hit.

Later, on my 1994 tour, I saw the same B–East cellblock. My guide again demurred at showing me B–West. B–East was the same, but dirtier. It may have been so because on the day of my scheduled visit the prison was just coming off a lock-down—inmates locked in their cells 24 hours a day—of several days because, as my guide explained, "A couple of guards got hurt." When I asked what happened, I was told tersely, "I don't know," in a tone which indicated it was none of my business. None of the Chicago papers picked up this lock-down, presumably because it wasn't news. During my tenure at Stateville there had never been a time when "a couple of guards got hurt," and the only time lock-down occured was for the duration of heavy fog rolling over the prison.

On this second visit, I watched as the guards on the flag stayed close to the cellhouse entrance, while the shotgun guards fanned out across the catwalk. I saw inmates raise and lower buckets from the upper tiers to the flag, a transportation system unhindered by the guards.

On this second tour, my young man guide was less nervous than the young woman guide I had in 1991. Although he too refused to show me the other, B–West side of the old cellhouse, he did take me to the remaining round cellhouse. Inside, there were only male guards. My guide and the guards stayed by the entrance, with one exception: there was a guard in the tower shown in Figure 4.1, with a shotgun at the ready; in Warden Ragen's regime no cellhouse guards were ever armed. Again, there was the same grunginess, the same milling about of inmates, my same feeling of tension. I felt I was intruding into the inmates' turf. I saw one young inmate bypass the stairs to climb from the ground floor flag over the railings to an upper tier, as if he were rock–climbing. The basement had been renovated, and I walked over to look down to see a large room in which the convicts came and went, showering and washing clothes.

What do these impressions mean? Some things are evident. Modern cell-houses with their electronic surveillance and remote control of doors create barriers to distance guards from inmates; in these cellhouses there were women guards and a higher than average percentage of white prisoners. The older cellhouses, which appear to house a majority of the inmates, were grungy, sullen places where male guards watch overwhelmingly black inmates. There were no barriers between the guards and inmates. My other conclusions are more abstract and require a perspective. Who better to provide it than the Warden?

Warden Godinez (1995) in an essay for the *Keepers Voice*, recently revealed for the first time details of a riot which occurred in the old round cellhouse F on July 13, 1991. This was six months after my guide had refused to take me to that cellhouse on my first tour in January 1991. We have only the Warden's brief essay, so I must infer some details. That round cellhouse, which under Warden Ragen had been run by a sergeant and four guards supervising 500 to 700 inmates, had devolved by 1991 to a captain and ten guards supervising 240 inmates.

At 7:20 pm. of July 13th, an inmate gang member under orders to murder the captain attacked, but the would–be assassin was killed by a shotgun blast from the guard in the cellhouse tower. (You can see the essential spatial layout in Figure 4.1.) That blast probably wounded the captain and other guards. Perhaps inmates wounded guards; the Warden's account is not clear. The captain managed to lead his guards out of the cellhouse, taking their wounded with them. I imagine they escaped because, as I saw on my 1991 and 1994 tours, guards stayed close to the entrance doors. Then the captain led the prison's riot squad to storm and retake the cellhouse.

The Warden's account is not clear about how many inmates and guards were involved or wounded, if inmates had weapons, what role was played by the shotgun guard in the cellhouse tower, whether the cellhouse was retaken by hand–

to–hand combat or if the inmates surrendered, and what was the aftermath. Indeed, he does not recount the events which led to the assassination attempt. Nor do we have an account of these events by the inmates or guards involved.

Stateville has been no stranger to dramatic events. During the five years leading to this 1991 riot, it was listed many times in the Chicago *Tribune* Index. In 1987, one inmate was killed and three stabbed, one inmate escaped, and a guard was arrested for smuggling cocaine. In 1988, a guard was murdered, an inmate was caught with a firearm, $14,000 was extorted from an inmate's family to protect him from death, an inmate gang fight injured six, another inmate was stabbed, three employees (guards and civilians) were caught smuggling drugs, and one acted as a pimp. In 1989, a prisoner held four people hostage for over four hours before he surrendered. In 1990, an inmate was killed.

After the July 13, 1991 riot, the July Chicago *Tribune* (July 16) reported a gang uprising at Stateville because the inmate who had been killed by the guard in the riot on July 13 had been a member of their gang. Then on July 18, an inmate in the Menard prison stabbed a guard in retaliation for the July 13 killing of his fellow gang member in Stateville. Finally, on December 9, a former Stateville superintendent went on trial for selling drugs.

The Chicago *Tribune* Index had no listings for Stateville in 1992 or 1993. However, New York *Newsday* and the *New York Times* reported on May 14 and May 16, 1996, that Richard Speck, a notorious mass murderer, and two other Stateville inmates had used the prison's video equipment, apparently in 1988, to produce and act in a pornographic film. They then smuggled the film out of the prison.

During all this time Stateville was officially recognized as a model maximum security prison. The American Correctional Association (ACA) initially accredited Stateville on January 16, 1985, and reaccredited it January 12, 1988 and January 14, 1991 (Illinois Department of Corrections: 1). The ACA is the premier American organization of wardens and high level correctional officials, and accreditation is an elaborate process of inspection and review of a prison to certify that it is well run. This review must be repeated every three years for a prison to retain its approved status. We will discuss the meaning of the ACA accreditation in Chapter 12, but for now it suffices to indicate that modern Stateville meets the highest official standards for a maximum security prison.

What kind of perspective can I provide for this account? Reflecting on my impressions from my 1991 and 1994 tours and the recent events recorded about Stateville requires some sort of unifying metaphor, a theory of how the prison is controlled. I suggest an analogy to a military society. There have been many countries in which a military dictatorship contained a guerilla insurgency, but could neither win the allegiance of the populace nor conquer them. Often the result in such cases is that the military holds the major city and a few strongholds such as the airport and main highways, while the guerrillas, who are not necessarily unified among themselves, hold all else. There are varying conditions of uneasy mutual accommodation, low level conflict, or escalating violence.

This metaphor is actually suggested by Stateville's warden in an essay on the July 13, 1991 riot (Godinez: 7):

> *Imagine yourself in war–like conditions with the smell of gunfire in the air and all hell breaking loose in front of you. Now picture one of your soldiers laying near death while an adversary is laying next to him lifeless but with a weapon still clutched in his hand. You have no time to think because time has deserted you and you are on your own with your army of 10 against 240 of the state's toughest, roughest, and most notorious inmates.* (Italics in original.)

My own point of departure is framed in Chapters 3 and 4, that a warden must control the time and space of his prison. However, the Stateville warden's military analogy may be useful in combination with my discussion of the control of time and space in understanding today's maximum security prisons.

The control at Stateville, and perhaps at other maximum security prisons, may accord with this script. For example, the concept of "unit management" in which each cellhouse is a kind of mini–prison expresses this. If the warden loses control of one cellhouse, he still controls the others. Or for feeding the inmates, Warden Ragen's Stateville, with a single mealtime in a dining hall holding 1,500 prisoners, has changed to a couple of small rooms large enough to hold perhaps 200 inmates, so that clusters of them come and go continuously all day long. As I watched, inmates were hardly controlled by today's guards. They did not walk in any kind of formation, nor did they have their prison register numbers stenciled on the wide variety of clothing they wore. (If a guard saw any misbehavior, he had no way to identify the inmate.) Warden Ragen's kitchen and bakery of perhaps a half–dozen staff supervisors and 100 to 200 inmate workers to feed 3,500 prisoners has been replaced by today's 40 civilian staff and 160 inmates to feed 2,400 inmates.

Similarly, Stateville has no mass showering today; each cellhouse has its own facility. Some cellhouses, such as the modern electronically operated ones, seem quiet and safe, while the old rectangular and round cellhouses are ceded to the inmates, and may be dangerous. Perhaps my tour impressions are not exact, but it did seem that women correctional officers were stationed at the modern cellhouses, rather than at the older ones.

Certainly, one major aim of all this is to prevent inmates from killing guards. It seems to work. Two guards were killed in the 1970's and two in the 1980's, but thus far, none in the 1990's. From Warden Godinez' account above, at least one attempt was made in the old round cellhouse in 1991, six months after my tour. Judging from Stateville's coverage in the Chicago *Tribune's* Index since the mid 1980's, only the murder of guard would seriously embarrass a governor before a jaded public.

Perhaps the Warden's implied military metaphor in conjunction with my emphasis of the need to control time and space provides a frame of reference. Analogous to containing a guerilla operation, the warden cedes the inmates some of their own areas of control. Some cellhouses and assignments belong to the inmates, some to the warden. Essential functions such as food and medical service are largely taken over by an expanded staff. As long as there is no bloodshed or media outcry, inmate goods and services, U.S. currency, and co-optation and bribery of guards is largely dominated by the inmates. Now, with Stateville in mind, we can turn to academic ideas of how maximum security prisons are controlled.

Academics Look At Maximum Security Prisons

Observers have described American workhouses and correctional facilities since the 18th century, and where we focus in this long history must be arbitrary. We begin with Donald Clemmer's *The Prison Community*, published in 1940. Before Clemmer, descriptions of prisons were memoirs, inspections, and other stories written from various philosophical and intellectual points of view.

Clemmer's book was an intellectual watershed: for the first time he looked at the prison as urban sociologists had started looking at communities in the free world. He asked questions such as how do inmates learn to fit into this world, what are the various niches into which they fit, and how does this world run? It may have an old–fashioned ring to it now, but it was a great intellectual accomplishment, born of Clemmer's years working as a sociologist with the Division of the Criminologist of the Illinois Department of Public Safety. It synthesized his observations of the Menard prison in southern Illinois and the Joliet prison in the north during the 1930's. As I have already mentioned in Chapter 2, it even included a discussion of Warden Ragen as the young reform warden at the Menard prison in 1934.

After World War II, Clemmer's work led to academic interest in prisons, for many reasons. Among them, the numbers of prisoners rose in the years after the war ended, and I suspect the horrors of the German concentration camps heightened our awareness of prisons. Another reason was the educational benefits which the U.S. Congress voted for the millions of returning veterans—the G.I. Bill—which produced more academic Ph.D.s, who in turn looked for subjects of study. Violence is the engine which drives society's interest in prison studies, and provides a platform from which academics have investigated many facets of prison life. The violence is to be expected.

If a society concentrates its most violent, rebellious, and predatory young men in the iron cages of prisons, periodically there will be outbreaks of violence. Around 1950 riots began, and from time to time since, they have continued. All this time journalists, media types and governmental commissions have rushed in afterwards to explain everything to the public. We now have academics developing this into a field of study, (for example, Martin and Zimmerman 1990), for an audience of other academics.

To the credit of academics, a body of research has evolved without the prod of riots. Many disciplines from anthropology to psychology to sociology have developed an interest in corrections. But little has been done with the concern of this book: how are prisons controlled. Clemmer's book itself, except for tangential remarks, (see pages 61–64), does not discuss the organization of control. The post–World War II research can be divided into two periods: from the riot–born studies of the 1950's well into the 1980's ideologically liberal sociologists denigrated the idea of control; since the late 1980's, ideological conservatives have injected the idea that how administrators control their prisons is important.

The material of the first, liberal, period varied from outright hostility toward controlling the prison to simply assuming control was impossible. An example of hostility was Cressey's (1965) pejorative description of the "ideal–type" of "punitive–custodial" prison. This essay is one of Cressey's more moderate attacks on prisons, perhaps because it was an authoritative statement of the academic establishment in a compendium of received wisdom about social organization.

Empirical research of this period is best represented by one of the influential books of the period, Gresham Sykes' 1958 study of the Trenton, New Jersey prison after it rioted in 1952. This is one of the period's reports closest to a study of control, but it is basically an interpretive essay rather than an empirical report. Sykes analyzed the prison from a "functionalist" viewpoint, that is, he formed a plausible conjecture of how and why guards and inmates complemented one another to keep the prison operating. For us, the most interesting conclusion was that it was not possible for the warden and the guards to control a prison. His third chapter pointed out that because of the complexity of the prison and the lack of any sense of duty among the inmates—their lack of belief in the "authority" of the custodians—the warden must fail to obtain any semblance of complete authoritarian control. For one thing, the warden had few rewards, and punishments were irrelevant when compared with liberty already lost. Guards had no chance to control for diverse reasons: they were forced into too great a face–to–face intimacy with their charges; they needed the inmates' help to keep assignments running smoothly; they feared the inmates because they were outnumbered and because the inmates might sometimes be able to blackmail them for past derelictions.

Sykes organized these points well, and made a plausible case that it was impossible to control the Trenton prison of 1,200 prisoners. It is unfortunate that he and the academic establishment (for example, Cloward, et. al. 1960) were unable to learn from Warden Ragen's feat of imposing the impossible on the 3,500 inmates of Stateville.

In the 1980's, perhaps as a result of growing political and financial support to ideological conservatives, the issue of management and control surfaced again. Academics who extolled management and control published studies which had major impact, as for example, DiIulio (1987) and Useem and Kimball (1989). They are beginning to be published in the literature of prison administrators. (See Useem, 1990.) Just as we considered in some detail Sykes' study as a representative of the ideological liberals, DiIulio (1987) stands as a representative of the conservative view.

DiIulio postulates three basic qualities of good prison management (or in his words, "the quality of prison life"): "order," or the absence of assault, rape or riots, and the presence of personal safety; "amenity," or good food, cleanliness, recreation, and television; and "service," or education and vocational training.

All these are sensible and empirical. That is, an outside observer can, with some degree of certainty, learn if inmates have been killed; if the food is adequate and the premises clean; if schools are in operation. In the end, DiIulio's ideas devolve empirically to the same things homemakers know about supermarkets: those with clean floors, neat shelves, crisp fruits and vegetables, and neat and helpful employees are better than those without. And he is right. But DiIulio's supermarket methodology does not let us know who controls, who is in charge.

For example, I remember the Menard prison in southern Illinois which I visited once a year: clean guard halls and cellblocks, whitewashed stone curbs, bright red caps on the inmate runners, some in ironed uniforms. It looked the clean, orderly place, easily on a par with Ragen's Stateville. I remember it was a given that the warden ran it in collaboration with inmate leaders. I remember my clerks talking about Menard and its inmate toughs who provided the warden's *muscle* to keep order. It was better than the anarchy of gang warfare, but I expect the average inmate was subject to the will of those stronger, and woe to the weakling.

DiIulio examines sociological analyses of prisons, prison riots, and various ideas such as inmate participation in prison governance. In the end, he concludes that none of these approaches are relevant to the questions of improving the quality of prison life. Instead, he concludes that his touchstones of order, amenity, and service are the consequences of good management by the custodial staff.

He also evaluates ten factors believed to be causes of order and disorder in prisons: the racial characteristics of the inmates, governmental expenditures, overcrowding, inmate–staff ratios, staff training, architecture, the inmate social system, educational programs, race relations, and repressive measures. He evaluates these factors by examining them in relation to three prison systems: Texas, California, and Michigan, asserting that Texas has the highest degree of order, amenity, and service, and Michigan the lowest. He makes a convincing case that none of the ten factors explain differences in the quality of life in these prisons. He suggests that management is the key. These various factors are themselves part of an academic industry. For example, overcrowding strains all kinds of prison services from food preparation to medical care. In addition, it requires more inmates per cell.

A useful stream of research, while it leads to no definitive conclusion, provides an ongoing commentary on the issue. For example, in 1985 Gaes and McGuire concluded that overcrowding did contribute to prison violence; a decade later, Gaes (1994) concluded that the latest reading of research indicated that it did not.

All of this literature, however, suffers the disability that it is based on no information, or worse, erroneous information. Sykes (1958) and the liberals of the immediate post–World War II period were busy stating it was impossible to do what Warden Ragen was already doing. Later conservatives such as DiIulio (1987), (as we have seen in Chapter 3), base much of what they write on material which is certainly in error—their understanding of Warden Ragen's regime—or probably in error—their understanding of Director Beto's regime. Perhaps we can turn now to how close control existed once in real time and space under Warden Ragen at Stateville prison.

Warden Ragen's Control of Stateville Inmates

Warden Ragen's control of the guards was the means to control the inmates, who got away with little things continuously, but important things only on occasion. The Warden's system was not a battleship cruising the seas, impervious to all but the most massive of assaults; think of it instead as a clumsy raft careening through white water rapids. Only by the minute direction of its Warden, and the frantic and disciplined endeavors of its guards—and a bit of plain luck––did it withstand chaotic challenges from the inmates. Our business now is to outline the structure of this control, something which follows the same pattern we saw with the guards: few rewards but many punishments. This system welded the guards into an unified force, while the inmates became fragmented and powerless.

The Carrot: Rewards for Conforming

Because Stateville's convicts had so little, all rewards were important. Few pertained to the world outside, most to life inside. The world outside impinged primarily because of the larger society's requirements. The right to petition the federal courts for writs of *habeas corpus* was obtained in the face of Warden Ragen's opposition. Other rights, like receiving personal visits from family at regular intervals, were only moderately limited, even in the case of the most extreme recalcitrance against the prison's rules, and were never revoked.

But most things which involved the Warden's discretion and the outside world were limited: for example, occasional permission to write more than one letter in a given week to family, friends, or prospective employers, or an assignment which accorded some extra remission of sentence if an inmate had already seen the Parole Board and had his case continued for rehearing at a future date. In such cases Warden Ragen could shorten the length of this "continuance" by up to a few months by assigning the inmate to a front end job.

In contrast, he had many rewards to make an inmate's enforced stay more tolerable. Some benefits were automatic: without exception, inmates lived in cells with running water, flush toilets, electric light bulbs, heat in winter, fresh air ventilation all year and sunlight during the day. Some involved the American standard of living combined with the Warden's control. Thus, an efficient extermination program kept the insect and rodent population at very low levels for so old and densely populated an institution. Food, clothing, and medical service were above the level available to many Americans who lived in poverty. The diet might have been monotonous, but it was ample and nutritious; clothing might be uniform, but it was warm in winter; medical and dental services were bureaucratized, but efficient. Even inmates who were punished by placement in segregation enjoyed these. Finally, although Stateville was at base a world which required inmates to be ever alert, none needed to fear guard brutality or convict gangs. These were no small accomplishments. Inmates under Ragen needed no connections to be treated fairly, for there were no inmate gatekeepers. It was also difficult for guards to harass inmates they disliked over a long period of time.

In the day–to–day life of the inmates, money, comfort, and autonomy were the important things. Which inmate needed what to make his stay more tolerable varied according to his temperament, resources and sentence. The *short–timer* with a one or two year sentence and a family that sent him money needed very little. On the other hand, an *old dog* who had lost all contact with the outside world, and whose sentence precluded release for another decade needed much. Between these extremes of objective situation, there were also the factors of behavior in the prison. Recalcitrant inmates might become more amenable to control if they were offered a pay job. An *executive*, one of the small number of inmates who were important to the Warden in conveying to him the "tone" or "tension" in various assignments of the prison, also were rewarded. The Warden's barber, for example, slept in a cellhouse by night like everyone else, but after shaving him in the morning, went to a comfortable assignment by day.

The triple benefits of money, comfort and autonomy were often intertwined. Pay jobs, which provided the inmate with money to buy some physical comfort, sometimes permitted greater autonomy in daily life. Comfort was the ability to eat better food, keep clean more easily, or have a cell in a quieter cellhouse. Closely allied to these was greater autonomy: freedom from the multitude of petty rules; an opportunity to cell alone; to have a job that kept one on duty and out of the cell longer periods of time; to have a radio or television set on assignment; to shave oneself; to learn a skilled trade; or to have more relaxed visits from one's family (which was possible on the prison farm). Also valued were jobs which involved "clean," "easier," or "more interesting" work.

The Warden restricted money payment to assignments which earned money for his budget, so only one fifth of the inmates had pay jobs in the prison factories. A few jobs such as those at the inmate's commissary received pay. Warden Ragen padded these payrolls. For example, the commissary paid inmate clerks assigned to the Veteran's Affairs office, and a captain. Another inducement was the opportunity to eat better food than what was served on the main line, a benefit accorded mostly to the cooks or waiters in the main kitchen. A select group were authorized to eat—although in a separate dining room—the same food as the guards, and informally, inmates on nearby assignments (including my clerks) could sometimes score for this food. A large proportion of the inmates assigned to the front end were authorized to use a small shower room installed near the hospital, and thus avoid mass showering. And a very few, such as those assigned as nurses in the psychiatric ward of the hospital wing (the Detention Hospital), were provided with facilities for brewing their own coffee and preparing some of their own meals.

The unanticipated consequences of routine decisions also created reward and punishment, and the cumulative effect tended to turn B cellhouse into a "punishment" house. Trivial rules, such as talking in line, having your hands in pockets while in line, or having a button of your shirt unbuttoned were enforced more stringently in cellhouse B than elsewhere, because the newly employed guards were usually assigned there. These *fish screws* took their training literally, and as a consequence, were more likely than an experienced guard to *shoot down* an inmate for a minor violation. Other benefits were the ability to cell by oneself; here, cellhouse B offered some attraction, for it was the only cellhouse which was less than full, and usually had but one man to a cell. Some inmates who wished to concentrate on legal appeals of their cases preferred to shovel coal on the B house coal gang in the morning, be finished by lunch, and stay in their cells alone the rest of the day. For other men, the ability to be out of their cell as much as possible was an inducement; many clerical jobs, especially in the front end of the institution had evening details which permitted an inmate to stay on assignment as late as 10:00 pm (with less rigid custodial supervision). Also, some assignments had radio and television available, and on the farm inmates were allowed to shave themselves.

Paradoxically, it was the rigidity and effectiveness of Warden Ragen's control which provided the greatest freedoms for average convicts. They were almost entirely free from the threat of physical violence by guards, for the Warden closely regulated coercion so that the limited physical violence invoked against inmates came exclusively from lieutenants, or the few guards who were in the riot squad or assigned to segregation or detention duty, and only occurred when a convict swung at a guard. Moreover, weaker inmates were also, by and large, free from physical violence or sexual assault by other inmates.

Beyond these broad categories were rewards for a conglomerate of the Warden's needs: he needed trustworthy, intelligent inmates to carry out certain assignments; he needed to pacify certain kinds of recalcitrants and he needed to reward useful inmates.

The need for trustworthy intelligent inmates occurred because the Warden's budget had no provision for clerical or skilled positions. For example, only Warden Ragen had a civilian secretary. Few of these positions were officially *pay jobs*, although the supervisors (especially civilian ones) often brought in cigarettes for their clerks, as I did. This use of inmates even extended to positions effecting security: for example, the switchboard operator was always a woman civilian during the day, but when she went to the toilet, for a coffee break, or to lunch, her relief was a trusted inmate.

A small number of inmates, like the Warden's barber, were considered in the *Executive Club*, useful in helping the warden to keep his finger on the emotional tone of the institution. Unquantifiable, perhaps, but a crucial part of Ragen's system of control, and one of the reasons why every weekday at noon he met for a conference with his assistant wardens and captains. Similarly, each assistant warden, captain, and lieutenant had his own *Executive Club*, contacts with shrewd inmates he trusted. This was not part of a *stool pigeon* system of specific rewards for specific items of information which we judge was more prevalent among the lower ranks. The Warden's main fears were riots and escapes, for these were the major breaches of his control that would directly affect his public standing. He needed inmates who could be depended upon, not so much to divulge discrete wrongdoing—he got large numbers of these in unsolicited *kites*—but to let him know if and where there was a slackness or tension in the institution, so his lieutenants could focus efficiently. Among such dependable inmates a great deal of autonomy was allowed, sometimes in relation to the kinds of assignments they received, other times by their being given such latitude as the informal "right" to obtain illicit coffee.

Other kinds of inmates given informal latitude were those with exceedingly long sentences who could not hope for parole consideration for ten or twenty years. If such an inmate was recalcitrant, as many were during their first few years, punishment was swift. But after a few years these men tended to quiet down, and many of them moved into *pay jobs*, and the rules were bent. Experienced guards knew this, and left them alone if they quietly and discretely gambled or developed homosexual liaisons.

But absent from Warden Ragen's system were inmates who kept others in line by violence. The only inmates in Ragen's system allowed to use coercion were the few assigned as nurses in the small group of cells for psychological observation in the hospital wing. These nurses were authorized to subdue *bugs*, inmates under observation for mental illness. But Warden Ragen's rewards were insufficient to persuade his unwilling charges to bend to his yoke.

The Big Stick: Punishment

The basis of Warden Ragen's control was punishment. It began when a custodial officer wrote a report of a rule violation. This ticket was forwarded to a captain of the guards who evaluated it, and, except in rare instances when a report was disregarded, called in the inmate to ask him his version of the offense, before deciding on the punishment. Recent Supreme Court decisions make such decisions more cumbersome, but hardly cripple it. Basically, the autocratic power of Warden Ragen's captain has been now circumscribed in the name of due process, so punishment must bear some relationship to the offense, inmates have a limited right to challenge the charges, and hearing officers must be used to decide and review appeals.

The quality of guards' reports varied, for new officers tended to write more and trivial reports. I remember hearing two young guards discussing their ticket–writing competition to see which one could *shoot down* the most inmates, a species of innocent arrogance not unknown among the newer officers. These *fish screws* often came out of their training with compulsive worries about catching rule violations, and no experience in sorting the trivial from the important.

Which officer wrote the ticket, and the disciplinary record of the inmate involved affected the punishment meted out by a captain. Jacobs (1974: 43), presumably based on his access to records, reported 25 to 30 per day.

To dispose of this volume required a number of short–cuts, and probably many reports by newer guards received only cursory attention. The disciplinarian captain disposed of approximately 25 to 30 punishments during every working day's three hours allocated to tickets. This averaged perhaps ten minutes per report: reading it, quizzing the inmate, then deciding whether to give a "reprimand and excused"—a *pass*—or whether to punish. From this workload a routine emerged, so that the trivial reports were quickly disposed of: a talking while in line ticket might be disposed of in seconds, rather than in minutes. In prisons today, the effect of United States Supreme Court decisions has been to make the selfsame process more cumbersome and bureaucratic, but no less effective. This is because inmates in the modern prison have only limited rights to due process if they are to be punished. They may contest the guard's accusation and appeal the initial decision of punishment, but all of this is carried out by prison staff; inmates have no right to outside lawyers, and they have no chance to clog the appeals process and bring the punishment system to a halt.

The overwhelming majority of punishments in Warden Ragen's Stateville were minor: loss of privilege to spend one summer's Saturday afternoon in the prison ballpark watching the prison team play outside civilians; loss of permission to go to a weekly movie in the chapel in the winter; loss of the one hour of recreation yard each day for a month; loss of one's radio earphones for a week or month. I don't mean they caused no pain, but they were the milder punishments. Once beyond these minor punishments, the next step was an isolation cell for one to fifteen days.

Isolation

A small building of 20 cells was kept specially for this purpose, although the name "isolation" is a misnomer, since the average daily population was 33 prisoners, or more than one per cell. Periodically it went higher, as for example, when some prisoners "booed" an officer in the dining room, and part of an entire bank of tables was marched to isolation for five days per man; then, the population of the isolation cells rose to 79 prisoners, or nearly eight men per cell. I recall no widespread stories of fights or sexual assaults in Isolation, although I expect some consensual homosexual activity took place on occasion.

Inmates were not allowed cigarettes or playing cards in Isolation, so they were thoroughly searched. The isolation wing was a long corridor with high ceilings lined with solid steel cell doors that had small shuttered openings for observation set into the green walls. I once observed an inmate being *laid down*:

> The guard sergeant, a little man, stood on one side of the corridor, the convict facing him from the other, an inmate porter watching aside. The convict removed his trousers, emptied the pockets, shook them out, and laid the trousers on the floor in front of him. Then he took off his undershorts, shook them, and handed them to the guard who shook them, and then dropped them on the trousers. The convict unbuttoned and took off his shirt, and dropped it on the pile.

Then the naked inmate was inspected:

> The guard gave low orders, and simultaneously the convict acted. Extended his arms and open hands to show nothing was in them, while tilting his head back, opening his mouth and sticking out his tongue, the guard watching from six or seven feet away. Then turning around, lifting up one and then the other foot to show his soles to the guards, then bending slightly forward, and spreading the cheeks of his buttocks.

Finally, the inspection over, the inmate went to his cell:

> Then, the convict moved as the guard gestured, picked up his undershorts from his pile, then to another pile where he picked up his isolation coveralls and carried them down the corridor in front of the guard to where the inmate porter had an isolation door open. Then as the convict filed in and the guard locked the door, the inmate porter began picking up the convict's clothing, shaking out the shoes for inspection.

During his stay in Isolation, an inmate slept on blankets on the floor and received one afternoon meal per day in these monotonous, but not uncomfortable surroundings (lighted and heated, with flush toilet and running cold water). He saw guards when his meal was served and the physician on his daily round. During the time he was in isolation he could receive no visits, write no letters, and if he was to see the parole board, his case was continued to the next month.

Segregation

To ratchet up the punishment, the next step was segregation in the same building. This was a small unit of 32 one man cells—usually at least half full—with its own small recreation yard. These were standard–sized cells, with bunk and mattress, running cold water, a flush toilet, and three regular meals each day. These men were restricted to their cell all 24 hours, except for one hour of recreation each day (weather permitting) in their special recreation yard, and one visit each month (with a guard present) at the front end of the prison, instead of the regular two each month. Moreover, they lost all such ordinary privileges as permission to purchase cigarettes, although they did retain magazine and library privileges. They did not see the parole board during their stay in segregation. Prisoners might be kept here any length of time, and some few were for months or years; in practice, however, stays were short, and the Warden tried to keep some cells vacant to maintain segregation as a credible threat. Consequently, he constantly pressured its residents for a pledge of good behavior so he could put them back in the general population. If they refused he could summon up his strongest punishment, a Merit Staff referral.

The Merit Staff

The Merit Staff was an amorphous group I could never precisely define. It probably consisted of assistant wardens, captains, and favored non–custodial personnel, such as one of the chaplains. They did not interview the prisoner, but read the official files and made recommendations (invariably approved by the Director of Prisons) for loss of statutory "good time," or reduction in "grade." "Good time" was the name given to the administrative process whereby a prisoner might be discharged earlier than his legal maximum if he did not cause difficulties to the Warden. For example, a prisoner doing five years could be released in less than four years, or a prisoner doing a ten year sentence could be discharged in slightly more than six years. Reduction in "grade" was part of a complicated "progressive merit system," officially designed, "for the purpose of encouraging and rewarding good conduct and industry," but which in fact was no more than an adjunct to the efficient operation of the prison. This was a system of five levels ("grades") through which inmates progressed, and only if an inmate was in the highest level would the parole board consider him for parole. Hence, the Warden could prevent a prisoner from seeing the parole board by reducing him in grade. In addition, if a prisoner was seen by the parole board and continued to a later date for reconsideration, not only did the prisoner need to be in the top grade to see the board again, but he shortened the interval if he remained in the highest grade.

In effect, a prisoner who received a one to ten year sentence from the courts had nine calendar years of his life controlled by the Warden because the parole board cooperated with him. By coopting the board and controlling *good time*, the Warden could make him *do* all ten calendar years of the sentence. In addition, placement in the lower grades barred the prisoner from minor privileges such as purchasing sundries in the commissary, listening to radio earphones, and going to movies or baseball games. The Merit Staff could reduce an inmate to the lowest, "E" grade, revoke his good time, or do both. Which was more painful depended upon the sentence; a newly arrived *lifer* was not affected at all by good time, while a man with a one to ten year sentence was affected by both the parole board and good time. Loss of good time was the average inmate's greatest fear.

Thus the Merit Staff was the apex of the punishment pyramid.[3] Guards did not see all rule violations, or write tickets on all that they did see, nor did the disciplinarian captain punish inmates for every ticket. For those inmates who were punished, the numbers diminished as we progress from the suspension of privileges (for example, use of radio earphones), to placement in isolation (for one to fifteen days), to segregation, to referral to the Merit Staff.

Each year, the Merit Staff rescinded its punishment for a few inmates, thereby introducing some mercy to its proceedings, and holding out an induce-

TABLE 8.1
Merit Staff Decisions During a Twelve Month Period
October 1959 - September 1960

A. INMATES IN CONFLICT WITH AUTHORITY OR
POWER OF THE OFFICIALS
   1. Inmate Challenges to Official Authority
     a. Physical Violence, Hitting an Officer 1
     b. Other Than Physical Violence
       1.Insolence, coupled with gestures or threats of bodily harm .. 29
       2.Insolence 23
       3.Accusing an Officer falsely.. 2
       4.Refusing to accept work, or an assignment placement 24
       5.Misbehaviour in Isolation or Segregation 24
       6."Agitating" other inmates 3
       7.Criticism of prison officials in letters 2

   2. Inmate Subversion of Official Resources
     a.Improper contact with persons outside the prison 6
     b.Falsifying prison records 4
     c.Stealing from officials.. 3
     d.Possessing contraband.. 8
     e.Not being at proper assignment at proper time 5

   3. Miscellaneous Nuisances
     a.Continuous minor punishment reports 47
     b.Uncouth speech in the presence of visitors to the prison 2
     c.Damaging property 1
     d.Injuring one's self 1

B. OFFICIALS IN CONFLICT WITH EXCHANGE OR
POWER AMONG INMATES

   1. The Possibility of Exerting Control Among Inmates
     a.Fighting with other inmates 45
     b.Possession of a weapon 3
     c.Extortion or confidence game against inmates 3
     d.Stealing from inmates 2

   2. Services Rendered Among Inmates
     a.Homosexuality 19
     b.Gambling 3
     c.Legal practice 2

     TOTAL 262

ment to cooperate to men who had been already punished.[4]

Punishment was balanced by the need to fit the inmate, the infraction, and the operation of the prison. A prisoner who had been recalcitrant in the past might be considered a *troublemaker* and be in several layers of trouble. He might be punished heavily for a rule infraction that might have been punished lightly for other prisoners. Hence the decisions of the Merit Staff constitute an outline of what the Warden considered the major problems of controlling inmates.

Table 8.1 classifies the 262 Merit Staff decisions during a routine year by our primary concern, control. Inmates were severely punished for two kinds of behavior: first, when they challenged the Warden's web of control; and second, when they tried to control other inmates, or provide services such as sex or gambling to others. In the first, where they challenged the Warden, they could try either direct challenges or subversion. In the first, "Inmate Challenges to Official Authority," inmates directly challenged guards. A common example of this was verbal hostility, as for example, the inmate who was reported for insolence:

> This inmate refused to work. I asked him to clean dust off pipe on his assignment. He told me: "If you fuck with me, I'll kill you. I mean it, so help me God."

Some verbal and body language was less violent than this, some more so. But it almost never got beyond the verbal; in Warden Ragen's Stateville, physical attacks on guards were rare. Next is "Inmate Subversion of Official Resources," such as stealing prison supplies or falsifying records. Another grouping contains "Miscellaneous Nuisances," a catchall which illustrates that the Warden hunted mice with an elephant gun — no misbehavior was so trivial that the Merit Staff could not be called in.

Entirely different in this table is "Officials in Conflict With Exchange or Power among Inmates." These were inmates who were punished for attempting to "control" other inmates by force or stealth, or who provided services such as sex, gambling or legal advice.

Can You Believe the Guards?

But first, we should consider the limits of these reports, for they are only the guards' side of the story. Complete fabrication of events were rare, for these were routine reports used for internal administration, and false information was dysfunctional. The guards were controlled too closely for falsehood, which leads to the self–serving aspect of these reports, for they were biased. Consider one report by a guard against one of my clerks: The guard's report was:

> Insolence and having a line strung up in his cell. At about 6:35 am this date, I went up to cell number 999 to get a line. When I asked this inmate if those were his clothes on the line he said "Yes." I told him to take the clothes off and give me the line. He said, "That fucking line has been up for a month, now you make up your mind that you want the line."

My clerk had not been trouble to the officials, for he had received only three punishment reports (all trivial) during his nearly three years in the prison. However, he had been one of the principals in a riot at another prison a few years previously, which might be relevant to the severity of punishment, for Warden Ragen punished by who you were as well as what you did. "Insolence" to a guard was a standard cause for Merit Staff referral. My clerk's version was that:

> It was just a little piece of string that long [holding up his hands, a few feet apart]. It'd been up there I don't know how long, and you go in just about any cell, you'll find one [used to dry handkerchiefs and socks after washing]. They're in my cell every day, shaking down, rapping bars, nobody ever said a word about it, but this one screw, I guess he was feeling rotten or something, he woke me up—I was sleeping—he woke me up and told me to take it down. I just blew my cork.

Obviously, the divergence between guard and inmate accounts was over the circumstances, motivation, and justice. Objectively, they both agreed that the guard wanted a piece of string, the inmate spoke angrily, and this was sufficient for the Merit Staff to demote my clerk to the lowest of conduct grades.

It is important that you are convinced that these reports were biased but accurate accounts of what occurred. They were the guards' punishment reports which informed their superiors of what happened, and major lies or omissions were dysfunctional for Warden Ragen, something he would not tolerate. This is critical to evaluate the next chapter on violence inflicted on inmates, for ultimate power in the maximum security prison resides with whomever controls physical violence. If the warden does not, then it automatically devolves to fiefdoms of custodial officers and inmates.

Endnotes

1. Bennett 1976:151; DiIulio 1987:69–71; Ellis *et al* 1974:38; Garson 1972:551; Jacobs 1977:160.
2. While my observations were in 1991 and 1994, I assume the correctional regimes I saw were organized many years previously by the Corrections Department in Springfield, the state capital. I do not mean to imply that the wardens in 1991 and 1994 created those regimes.
3. The rate of punishment varied. Consider just Merit Staff referrals during three consecutive years. We find the following monthly averages of punishment per 1,000 inmates: 2.5, 3.4, 4.3.

Percent Distribution by Punishment

	Total	Reduction in Grade Only	Loss of Statutory Time Only	Both
Year 1	100	71	27	2
Year 2	100	52	30	19
Year 3	100	51	31	18

4. During three consecutive years, there were 7, 5, and 1 remissions granted (usually for Merit Staff referrals of previous years) for each 100 Merit Staff punishments actually imposed that year.

9

Control of Inmates: Beatings And Violence

An Overview

THE issue of violence against inmates, whether by guards or by other inmates, requires special discussion. Violence was the ultimate power in Warden Ragen's Stateville, as it is in today's maximum security prisons. How it is controlled defines whether the prison is a moral universe. (See Newman, 1979: 258.) In a maximum security prison, it is axiomatic that if the warden does not dominate, then power will devolve to fiefdoms of his staff and inmates. In the end, that power is based on who controls face-to-face physical violence.

If the guards and inmates in today's prison view the violence used as "reasonable" or "fair," then they are more likely to bend their necks to the warden's yoke. Otherwise, either guards or inmates will see their lot as unwilling subjects of an "unfair" system. Fair or not, inmates will never be enthusiastic about their prison, but a system judged fair will have a smaller proportion of prisoners seething and looking to riot.

More practically, the courts may grow less tolerant of the inability of prison authorities to control violence. Supreme Court decisions have consistently ruled against purposeful brutality inflicted by guards on inmates (Mushlin 1993:53), something I discuss later in this chapter. But practical enforcement of these strictures is difficult. It requires lawyers for inmates ready to do battle in court. If the courts enforce these Supreme Court decisions, state corrections departments will be forced to create disciplined corrections staffs. Unfortunately, under the adversarial tradition of American courts, lawyers for each side operate on the intellectual level of Hollywood movies. Lawyers for the inmates argue that their clients are pure as driven snow, while the lawyers for the state do the same for the guards who have been accused. If the lawyers cannot broker some kind of agreement, then the judiciary must sort equity out of the half truths of a courtroom battle. But at least the Supreme Court has ruled that it is impermissible for guards to brutalize inmates.

Even more crucial to the issue of control is the right of an inmate to be protected against purposeful brutality by other inmates. (For a discussion of its myriad forms, see Bowker 1980.) Most brutality originates with inmate predators who wardens cannot control, but some is purposeful: wardens and custodial staffs may use inmate toughs and aggressive homosexuals as their enforcers to keep order, or even to terrorize obstreperous inmates by beatings and rapes. At present, custodial staffs can act with impunity through their surrogates. Recently, the courts have begun to consider these issues (Vaughn and Del Carmen 1995; Vaughn 1996). Perhaps, over time, court decisions will lead to further control.

I think the courts will gradually rule against failures of control, as American prison populations expand and fester. At present, wardens are most concerned about protecting guards from being killed and wounded. Some control is afforded by such labor intensive procedures as "unit management" or capital intensive investments in electronically sophisticated low density cellhouses. But prison costs will soon exceed the willingness of the taxpayers to fund many of these alternatives, and the search will be on for cheaper prisons. As larger inmate populations outstrip the increase in correctional staff and expensive gadgetry, control will become more difficult. One result will be increasing violence. Wardens and correctional staff may tolerate violence by staff against inmates, or by inmates against other inmates, but that of inmates against staff frightens them.

At present ideological liberals and conservatives are committed to their own visions of large expenditures. The liberals move for social services and the conservatives for capital investment. As funds grow scarce while misery and violence increase, the courts will be faced with these issues. And whether the courts are conservative or liberal, they may—they certainly should—rule against wardens who are unable to control violence, whether by guards or inmates.

Paradoxically, there was relatively little violence in Warden Ragen's prison because his own use of violence was so effective. But it loomed large as an ultimate sanction then, as it will loom large in any modern prison. This is because violence exists on the razor's edge between the necessary use of force to subdue an inmate, and unnecessary brutality by guards against a helpless inmate. Only a small minority of guards will ever become brutal, just as only a small minority will become corrupt or gratuitously harass inmates. But unless these rogue officers are ruthlessly suppressed and fired, they will rot the moral justification of the prison for both inmates and guards. Because the guard who is the model of probity one year may become corrupt the next, the warden's vigilance must be perpetual.

I have tried to place the use of violence within the context of Warden Ragen's system of control. I think it fair to say that neither guards nor inmates considered it "brutality," although my guess is that the black inmates resented the fact that it was always white lieutenants who beat up black inmates. My memory is that by the time I resigned, Warden Pate had promoted the first black lieutenant. (My memory may be wrong: Jacobs [1977:184] states this happened after Pate resigned.) The challenge in a modern prison will be to create a system in which the custodial staff uses physical violence on inmates in such a way that neither the inmates nor the courts consider it brutality.

I can only speculate, but I think the modern warden will ultimately develop his own version of Warden Ragen's system. Ragen's first rule was that neither ordinary guards nor any inmate *goons* were allowed to use violence. Violence was the province of only a few selected and trained officers. With Warden Ragen these were primarily his lieutenants. He had a riot squad, but I don't remember any occasion where they actually used violence against inmates, although I assume they were ready to do so. Beatings may have been administered by guards on duty within the isolation-segregation building, but I believe this was the exception. Inmates assigned there were not involved in beatings, for they were porters and clerks. However, they could be compromised. For example, if they were present when an officer was getting the worst of it, they would be expected to come to the assistance of the guard.

Warden Ragen's second rule was that in the *yard* only minimum force was allowed to subdue a violent inmate. Of course, Stateville was a world of working class—lower class, if you prefer—men. Some were guards and some were inmates. This might not be your world; I expect if there was a fight in the *yard*, "minimum force" could include a fist in the face or a knee in the stomach. But Stateville's guards and inmates would not think of this as a "beating."

Third, inmates were not beaten unless they hit or fought with a guard. Not that the guard in question was allowed to beat up the errant inmate. If he tried to, he'd be in trouble with Warden Ragen. Beatings were the province of lieutenants, and they took place in the isolation-segregation building. These statements beg definitions, but I doubt that cursing a guard was the pretext for a beating, although it could have, on occasion, resulted in a sock in the jaw—by a lieutenant, in the isolation building.

Control of violence will be difficult for the modern warden, because it is no easy thing to control the aggression of some guards who will *ride* inmates they take a dislike to until the inmate explodes. Especially when some hostile inmates bring it on themselves. Warden Ragen's basic tool was the fear of punishment by both guards and inmates. And something else: a psychological edge. His guards had a subliminal self-confidence because they intuited that they were in charge. And the inmates carried a not so subliminal resentment for the same reason.

The beatings at Stateville probably exerted control on two levels. First, the inmate himself was rarely willing to repeat the process: the physical and psychological shock was too much. Since other inmates got the message, inmate leaders found it difficult to recruit followers who would risk such retribution.

I believe beatings were brief, with personnel and weapons carefully controlled. Ordinary guards and sergeants carried no weapons, not even a whistle with which to summon aid. The only things they had in their pockets were a pencil and a pad of blank punishment tickets, supplemented by a handkerchief and a pack of cigarettes. Lieutenants had a special pocket sewn in place of the back pocket of their trousers, the *sap pocket*, to hold a blackjack. This was the only weapon they carried routinely and had available for a spontaneous fight. In the isolation and segregation building, or when lieutenants or guards assigned to the riot squad were called out, the officers had clubs, shields, and dogs. Ragen's lieutenants, in my judgment, were confident that three or four of them using clubs could do all the damage necessary in short order. As I remember, none of Ragen's lieutenants were magnificent muscular specimens. While they looked fit enough, they were mainly the kind of men who were not afraid of hand-to-hand combat, albeit with one-sided odds. And they were skilled: I never heard of their doing any permanent damage. I have no doubt that after a fight with lieutenants, an inmate would be beaten all over again if he provided the slightest provocation. I have no reliable measure of how often guard-inmate violence occurred in Warden Ragen's prison, but I think the evidence of Table 8.1 makes it apparent that it was relatively rare. Only one report of violence appears for 262 Merit Staff reports in a year.

The rarity of inmates hitting officers is just as consistently revealed in Merit Staff reports for other years. Given how closely Warden Ragen controlled his guards and how they wrote punishment reports to put themselves in the best light, I think it certain that if guards hit inmates it would have been written up as the response to inmate attacks, and there would have been many more reports. The only other claim could be gratuitous widespread violence upon inmates which was not written up. Given how closely Warden Ragen controlled his staff, such omission is unlikely. I certainly do not remember hearing this from believable inmates.

Finally, I remember the time one of my clerks managed to "borrow" the hospital admission ledger for an hour or two one evening. If inmates were often beaten, there should have been mistakes. In the heat of hand-to-hand combat, a club aimed at the ribs might crack a vertebra. Such consequences would have shown up in the hospital as fractured skulls, spines, arms or other broken bones; or as torn shoulder or joint cartilage; or as crippling ligament or tendon tears; or as kidneys smashed. I recall nothing but a boring catalog of infirmities.

Inmates in Conflict with Official Power:
When Staff Beat Inmates. Interpreting the Official Versions

Direct challenges meld into one another, for there are no clear lines between striking a blow and cocking a fist; nor between insolence with a threatening posture, and insolence only; nor between insolence alone and making a false accusation. We can illustrate some of these situations by selecting representative reports from Table 8.1. The one official report for hitting an officer summarizes the behavior simply as:

> Fighting, striking a lieutenant, running from a lieutenant, threatening a lieutenant with bodily harm after being discharged from this institution, and calling a lieutenant every profane name and word he could think of.

The inmate was injured, so three lieutenants took him to the hospital for a medical examination and an x-ray. The inmate cursed them the entire way, and spat in the face of the guard who opened the hospital gate for them. X-raying prisoners and guards in situations like this had as one consequence more control for the Warden. He knew how severely each was injured.

This inmate was a young white man (transferred from the Pontiac Prison for younger offenders) whose warden was unable to prevent him from dominating other youngsters. In Stateville he was placed on the coal gang, an outdoor assignment of heavy and dirty physical labor which was often used for recalcitrants. There he continued to accumulate punishment reports and isolation placements. Since this did not make him more amenable, the next step was to warn him that in addition to isolation, subsequent punishment reports would accrue toward the revocation of his good time. Then, in the three months preceding his fight with the lieutenants, the inmate accumulated a series of the following minor punishment reports, and for each he was docked a few days good time. The offenses were:

> "Going to the [recreation] yard in violation of privilege denial order;" "Talking in the Dining Room after the bell had rung;" "Talking in line;" "Going to the Dining Room with the wrong line;" "Being out of cell formation in line;" "Talking and humming in line;" "Being off his work assignment;" "Loitering and talking on the gallery;" "Whistling in cellhouse, seemingly in answer to the whistles of inmate Jones, which has been going on for weeks."

Then the day of the fight itself, a guard told our convict:

> [T]o move to the back of the church line. He did not move. He asked why he had to move. I told him because I wanted him to, at which time he said I didn't have the right to move him.

At this point the officer called for a lieutenant to take the inmate to isolation; when the lieutenant arrived, the fight started.

I was not able to track this inmate to determine if he was beaten afterwards, but I expect he was beaten after he was taken to the isolation building. After his x-ray the inmate was removed to isolation, and his cell was searched with great care by the guards in his cellhouse. They entered as contraband, two pairs of extra gloves, two scrub brushes, and an "excess amount" of string. However, in addition to this trivia, and because of the care with which trivia was sifted, they also found, "one love letter, found in a magazine on the shelf over the cell door." This letter bears testimony to the thoroughness with which guards looked for items easily concealed. They checked every single page of the inmate's books, magazines, folded up letters, and the underside of flat surfaces. This evidence of homosexual activity was now part of the inmate's prison dossier.

He was demoted to the lowest of conduct grades. Also, he had one year of his statutory good time revoked, which meant that if the Parole Board decided to have him do the maximum of his sentence, he would have lost 12 months remission on this maximum. However, should he "calm down" the Warden could recommend (and Warden Ragen's recommendations were always followed) that the inmate's demotion in grades or revoking of statutory good time be themselves revoked, and his record cleared. For this prisoner none of this mattered, for his sentence had a minimum of one year and a maximum of two; so small a *spread* would not influence such a prisoner to calm down. Wide *spreads* in sentence such as 1 to 10 years were helpful—perhaps essential—to Warden Ragen for controlling the inmates. With a 1 to 10 year sentence, Warden Ragen directly or indirectly held 9 years of the inmate's life in his hands. The only step missing in the above inmate's case is probable placement in Segregation.

Placement in Segregation would complete the full cycle of control of recalcitrants. First, the inmate experienced close supervision by guards on an undesirable assignment like the Coal Pile. This could lead to the unremitting use of punishment reports and Isolation placements. Next, the situation might culminate in Merit Staff referral and if necessary, Segregation placement. Many prisoners traversed this cycle, but few repeatedly. The strain on their nerves wore down most recalcitrants, and long-term prisoners rarely took more than a few years of this cycle before they found themselves more amenable to the Warden's control. At this point, such an inmate might be offered the carrot— perhaps a *pay job* in a prison factory. Then the inmate could enjoy some money to spend in the commissary. Again, because of Warden Ragen's control of the guards, they would not carry out any retribution against the inmate for past offenses.

Only on rare occasions did convicts plan attacks against guards. The only one I recall happened shortly before my employment when three powerful prisoners were being walked to Isolation by two lieutenants. When they were between some buildings (cutting off sight lines to the watchtowers) the inmates turned on the lieutenants, beating them to the ground. Perhaps race played a part: the lieutenants were White, the inmates Black. Another lieutenant who came to the rescue was held off, and I believe all were mauled. I never learned the aftermath, but I assume the inmates were finally subdued and then taken to the Isolation building where they were beaten. Some years later, another case occurred when an inmate went berserk and held a lieutenant hostage with a straight razor (abruptly seized at the Barber Shop) to his throat until a chaplain could talk him into surrendering. This happened during my employment, and I tried to follow the consequences. There appear to have been none; the inmate was defined as a *bug*, so he wasn't beaten.

Finally, captains, lieutenants, and guards in isolation-segregation had to be capable of hand-to-hand fighting, albeit with one-sided odds. An example appears in another year from our table and describes an inmate who was reported "for listening to his cellmate's earphones in violation of phone denial order." When he was called up to the isolation building on these charges, the inmate denied them and began arguing with the captains. At that point, another captain, and a guard:

> [E]ntered the office and ordered inmate Jones to calm down in an orderly manner, but instead, he became more belligerent and argumentative. When subject refused to obey repeated orders to keep quiet, he was ordered to proceed to the Isolation confinement quarters, to which he refused.

Then, the two captains and the two guards, in their words:

> [P]roceeded to escort subject out of the office. Inmate Jones simultaneously began to struggle, swinging and kicking violently at every one around him, making it necessary to forcibly remove him into Isolation confinement quarters.

In short, four officers forcibly put one inmate in an isolation cell. In the process, the inmate:

> [B]it Captain Jones on the right wrist, kicked, bit Officer Smith on the right biceps and tore his shirt. Officer Doe sustained a fractured index finger, while Captain Johnson was hit several times but sustained no injury.

The officers were bandaged by the prison physician, but when the physician went to isolation to see the inmate, "he refused to be examined."

When Staff Beat Inmates: What the Inmates Said

Beyond these official reports, I had to rely upon accounts by inmates. After discussing the matter with convicts I believed, a picture emerged in which violence was strictly controlled. In a case recounted by one of my clerks, an inmate in the Dining Room:

> [S]creamed he was tired of eating that garbage. He threw his plate. He saw he was all alone. He saw a bunch of screws was converging on him. He grabbed a big pot of coffee. He held them all back, threatening to throw it on them. Finally, there was 8 or 10 of them around him, and a couple of them dived on him: they just went fighting then.

Fist fights and scuffles such as these were part of the guards' workaday world. Since a guard had only limited opportunities for getting away unobserved once such an outbreak occurred, he had to be the kind of man who could face such possibilities. This was not a pleasant prospect for a 50-year-old guard faced by a 25-year-old inmate. I think the situation was ameliorated for such an older guard by several factors. First, of course, he had been working in the prison for years and it was part of his world. More importantly, it was usually one-sided, with several younger officers pitching in. Warden Ragen's guards were no more physically fit than any group of men their age.

After violence came control. A few blows and the inmate's arms and legs were pinned. This inmate was not beaten in the dining room. However, he was "subdued" in isolation, before he was taken to detention (the psychiatric observation cells of the hospital). As I remember, this was a common occurrence. After a beating an inmate might be tended for a short time by inmate nurses in detention, and then placed in segregation. An inmate seriously injured with say, broken bones, would have been placed in the prison hospital; it was the only facility Warden Ragen had to treat a serious injury. When I asked my clerk how he knew his friend had been beaten, he replied:

> I know what happened at the time it happened [in the Dining Room]; he didn't get hurt there. And then from the guys in detention, I know what kind of shape he was in when they brought him up there. I knew him pretty well, for a couple of years — he told me the same thing.

What my clerk had been told was:

> When they got him over to the hole afterwards, well, he knew they'd be coming back after him, from past experience. So later they come over there with their clubs and shields, went in the cell, crowded him into a corner or something, just beat him up, that's about it. They beat him up pretty bad for the average guy, but he's pretty big, pretty rough. They brought him up to detention later on.

This violence was governed by expectations accepted by both convict and guard. Differently, I think. I believe guards considered it justice, while inmates considered it retribution. But within that prison world, I think these expectations were the basis for considering Warden Ragen's regime a moral society. This judgement came out in an interview I had with an inmate who had fought with the guards. He was quite matter-of-fact in discussing it with me. He had been placed in segregation after the Warden had exhausted other means of control. While he was there, he told me, "When I was out of my cell, I busted a window, I put a hole in it—with my fist." This started a fight. He continued:

> There was an officer with me, and the other officer was at the end of the corridor. He had a club. He come in, swung on me. I grabbed at the club and pushed him away. I told him, "I don't want to fight a guard, and don't hit me." He swung again and I hit on him. I knocked both of them out; they come to and run out. Then a bunch of lieutenants, the Warden come. I busted out a screen. They threw in tear gas, but it was winter and the window was out; it's windy, and the stuff blew out. They hollered at me: the Warden he say, "Come on out," and I say, "I'll come out, but I don't want you to beat me." They say ain't nobody gonna. I come out and they grabbed me; one guard swung at me, I broke out and ran back in, they come in and grabbed me, pulled me out. They didn't hit me much. Then we got to the steps: then the lights went out. I woke up in isolation on the concrete. The guard say, "Take off your clothes." I had on a segregation outfit, and I put on a isolation outfit. They started to walk me to the cell, the guard he hit me. I turned to hit him back; they grabbed me and beat me down.

Moreover, after the inmate struck back, (or claims to—the guards would claim the inmate hit first), the guards did not go beyond the point of what may be a "fair" whipping. When I asked this inmate how badly he had been *worked over*, he said:

> No, they didn't do no damage, permanent like, but I wouldn't want to take any more beatings like that again. I had it coming, just like outside: you hit a policeman, you know you're gonna get it.

While this inmate himself would have admired any *heavy screws* capable of taking him on man-to-man in a fight without weapons, he knew he would be put down by superior numbers. But the inmates also expected the justice in Warden Ragen's Stateville which they would not receive on the street. In the Chicago from which most of these inmates came, the savagery of policemen was legendary. If the police wanted information they would beat a suspect for hours. Even that brutality was mild compared with the permanent injuries or death imposed by other thieves. The justice the inmates received in Ragen's prison was three-fold: beatings were "reasonable" (compared with policemen or other thieves), occurred only for a "reasonable" cause, and were never administered by inmate goons. Furthermore, after the event the Warden was not vindictive, and his system of control protected them from any private vengeance by the guards. This same inmate said:

> No, nobody ride me since. They keep their eye on me. The captain told me that, but 'cept I can't get some jobs in here. I tried for the barber shop, but they turned me down. They don't want me with a razor in my hand: I hit a guard. But they ain't like that; they got too many men in here. You stay clean, they don't bother you.

All of these factors together are why I have characterized Warden Ragen's use of violence as part of a "moral universe" for the inmates and the guards. Unless they were part of a trained riot squad or on duty in the isolation-segregation building, guards below the rank of lieutenant were not allowed to use more than the minimal force necessary to immobilize an inmate. Breaches of this rule were the exception. Even lieutenants did not beat inmates except in the isolation-segregation building. In the heat of a fight none of this was clear-cut, but generally an inmate would be beaten only if he hit or swung on a guard. Of course, this leaves a gray area. For example, if a guard broke up a fight between two inmates and caught a punch in the process, the consequences could go either way.

The question for today's prisons is how much and what kind of violence could withstand the scrutiny of the courts? The parameters are outlined by Mushlin (1993:53) in relation to a 1992 decision of the United States Supreme Court:

> In *Hudson v. McMillan* the court held that the use of force by prison guards violates the Eighth Amendment when it is not applied "in a good-faith effort to maintain or restore discipline," but rather is administered

"maliciously and sadistically to cause harm." To determine whether the use of force is unconstitutional, a court must consider such factors as "the need for application of force, the relationship between that need and the amount of force used, the threat "reasonably perceived by the responsible officials" and any efforts made to temper the severity of a forceful response. In addition, factored into this equation is the extent of the injury to the inmate from the use of force by the prison guards.

Thus, suppose a case before the courts was like the one I described in Chapter 5, where an inmate of the Auburn, N.Y. prison accused eight guards and a sergeant of a gratuitous beating which broke his leg (among other injuries). Hypothetically, if the same charge were made against three or four lieutenants, minus the broken leg, I think the warden would have a better chance to prevail. There never will be a clear and simple line dividing necessary force from brutality. But a warden who delegates a monopoly of violence to a select cadre such as Ragen's lieutenants should be in a defensible position. Staff who are skilled in the use of violence without leaving crippling injuries, in clearly defined circumstances, would have credibility before the courts that is lacking in the Auburn cases.

Perhaps this sounds cold-blooded. But violence is the touchstone of the world of the maximum security prison. Violence permeates Earley's (1992) and Fleisher's (1989) books on two federal maximum security prisons, Leavenworth and Lompoc. It is instructive that in both prisons, one seen by a journalist and the other by an academic, a guard's status and respect came from his fists. The true test of correctional officers was fearlessness in hand-to-hand combat with inmates, including inmates with weapons. Prisons are perhaps the only remaining arenas of criminal justice in which hand-to-hand combat is the norm. In other venues, such as police work, the emphasis is on firearms. This may be one of the reasons why it is easier to incorporate women into police forces than in maximum security prisons. The ultimate police weapon is the gun, which equalizes physical strength. Earley and Fleisher illustrate how fearlessness in hand-to-hand combat defines the admired—and promoted—correctional officer.

A final note. You may be put off by the one-sidedness of the odds, because Warden Ragen's lieutenants ganged up on individual inmates. You have to realize that this is part of the matter-of-fact world of violence, no matter where it occurs. For example, professional killers such as military fighter pilots and organized crime assassins (*hit men*) use the same standard operating procedure: take the enemy by surprise, and with overwhelming firepower. Images of one-on-one battles with the protagonists face-to-face exist only in the minds of adolescent boys and in old John Wayne movies, not in the real world.

Inmates Who were Authorized to Use Force on Other Inmates

Another aspect of violence against inmates in Warden Ragen's Stateville was the absence of inmates who had the informal authority to beat others. In some prisons, that practice has apparently been a way to use violence on inmates without the correctional staff being held liable. I have heard credible statements that there have been prisons where the correctional staff placed recalcitrant inmates in situations where they could be raped. This was absent in Warden Ragen's Stateville. However, there was one situation where inmates did have authority to use coercion and force on other inmates. This came from the need to control inmate *bugs*, those mentally ill or acting out psychological stress.

For such cases, Stateville had the Detention Hospital, a 32 cell psychiatric prison holding area on the second floor of the hospital wing. Inmates were housed there for observation if they were emotionally upset, under observation for mental illness, or were diagnosed as mentally ill and awaiting transfer to the Menard Psychiatric Prison. These patients were watched by several inmate "nurses" who, as far as I remember, were self-trained. I imagine new nurses were apprenticed to experienced ones to learn their trade. I also remember that some inmates who had been beaten by lieutenants in the isolation-segregation building were temporarily placed in the Detention Hospital for observation and care by the inmate nurses. These nurses had self-contained living quarters in the Detention Hospital with hot plates and coffee pots for preparing meals.

Inmates put in the Detention Hospital were the only ones subject to physical coercion by other inmates, but that coercion carried a stringent etiquette. A *bug* might be subdued, but not beaten. As one inmate nurse explained to me, a medical doctor (often a psychiatrist who came to the prison on regular rounds) had general responsibility:

> When they come up, they talk to the doctor first. He's gotta prescribe the medication; he'll tell the guy, "I'm gonna prescribe something," so he knows about it beforehand. When we go to give it, the guy usually knows. I'll explain it, if in case he's forgot, it's slipped his mind...Almost all guys just take off their jackets and take it.

If simple explanation did not work, persuasion was tried:

> If he objects, I'll try to talk to him, explain the doctor prescribed it...It's maybe easier for me, I'm a con. I can talk to them, ask them what they're gonna get out of it. They can't beat these people, like if I acted up, it'd be the same thing.

If persuasion fails, the next step is physical force: "If he still won't, then we use restraint, we have to restrain him." However, these inmate nurses were supervised:

> There's three of us and the officer is standing there. The cells are small so he can't move around. Like say I'm the first guy in, the first thing I go for is his legs so he can't kick nobody in the nuts, and the other guys follow me in and grab his arms, until we give the injection....Most guys will calm down after that.

Such force was usually sufficient, but not always. As the inmate nurse continued, "After that if he don't, then we put him a strip cell," a cell with no furniture, so sleeping, defecation and urination, and eating are carried out with minimal equipment. Then, for the very few who remain recalcitrant, there is the final step, again under supervision:

> The officer will call a lieutenant and the lieutenant will call the Warden, and we'll put him in restraint....It's a table with a little mattress not much bigger than your desk [motioning to my office desk] and he's tied down. We only take off the straps for one arm when he eats. After a week his joints are so stiff, you know, from not using them...And if that don't work, then he's mentally ill.

On occasion the force used by the inmate nurses escalated. Another nurse recounted such an occasion:

> I grabbed his feet so he couldn't kick; another guy grabbed his arm. Next thing we know, he's in the other corner. He didn't have his arm; I didn't have his feet. I tried an arm lock, then when I saw [I] wasn't getting no place [we] used a towel. We finally got a towel on and that did it.

This "choke hold" with a towel is the only example of inmate use of force which was potentially dangerous. I have no notes, but I suspect the custodial staff looked the other way, or possibly no one realized the dangers. (I never heard of any permanent damage.) The inmate nurse explained:

> You take a wet towel. No, not a bath towel, a regular hand towel and you get it on, you get it around their neck till he goes out. The harder he struggles the faster he goes....You choke him off for a few seconds, it takes maybe as much as three minutes for him to come back, for his mind to begin working. By that time you have him strapped down.

Their use of a towel to administer a choke hold was the height of physical force used by the inmate nurses. It can be dangerous because it cuts off oxygen and blood to the lungs and the brain. There are two issues about choke holds to be considered: what are the alternatives, and how can it be controlled. The problem is to subdue a berserk inmate as humanely as possible in a confined space such as a cell where only two or three nurses can attack him.

Charles Duke, a police sergeant who instructed the Los Angeles police in the use of force, wrote an interesting essay in New York *Newsday* (April 1, 1994). He made the point that the Los Angeles police department eliminated the use of choke holds in subduing violent suspects. But the police were not provided with alternative methods with which to subdue suspects—other than to beat them with their clubs (called batons) or to shoot them. Sergeant Duke claimed that this was the direct cause of an exponential growth in injuries to suspects and police officers, including the infamous 1991 Rodney King episode in which several Los Angeles policemen beat a suspect unmercifully with their clubs. I doubt that certainty is attainable, but a prison must develop some means of subduing inmates who are having psychologically-caused seizures of violence.

The closest example I could find in Warden Ragen's Stateville comparable to the *goon* squad of other prisons was the use of these Detention Hospital nurses to subdue inmates in a cell of the isolation-segregation building. Their purpose was to bring the inmate to the Detention Hospital itself. As best I can judge, if the authorities in isolation-segregation decided an inmate was a *bug*, they would not beat him, but would call for a nurse. Even making allowance for inmate nurse bravado, I think the lieutenants did defer to the nurses when it came to subduing a *bug*:

> I went over there [segregation] last Sunday. A guy had a towel with soap in it; [he] made a blackjack, three or four new state soaps in a towel or in a sock. I walked in, and when I saw his eyes widen, I put my foot in his stomach and grabbed him so we went over on the bed with him on top and the other nurse was able to grab him.

Parenthetically, this interview was the only one where I have notes on gratuitous violence by the custodial staff. The nurse continued:

> One of the lieutenants, he grabs the guy [making a twisting motion with his hand by his groin] and twists. He went out fast. That guy's [the lieutenant] a real sadist. None of them other guys [other lieutenants] will do that. I learned never grab a man by the balls. He does it. He likes to. Sometimes I think I'd like to get him on the outside. I'd see how tough he was....No, I can't say who he is, you gotta have some discretion.

In my judgment, the lieutenant referred to above was an exception, and inmate *bugs* were subdued with minimal force. The use of the towel to *choke off* a *bug* was inherently dangerous, a practice which the warden in today's prison would need to restrict, or supervise more closely than Warden Ragen did.

The overriding question is not whether there will be violence in a prison, but who will control it. There will be physical violence between staff and inmates, and physical coercion will have to be imposed on psychologically upset inmates. If the warden does this through a disciplined staff which does not harass or *ride* inmates until they explode, then violence can be minimal. Such minimal violence will be accepted as "fair" by both inmates and staff—the prison equivalent of a moral society. If the warden does not control violence, then it will automatically devolve to fiefdoms of guards and inmates, and their control is sure to be nasty and brutish.

Exerting Control Among Inmates: Fights Between Inmates

When inmates are unconstrained in the use of violence against other inmates, it is a form of Gresham's Law of Economics, which asserts that bad money drives out good. Except in prison, the more violent and reckless convicts degrade and dominate those less so. In such a system, the weak must submit or buy whatever accommodation or defense they can. In Warden Ragen's prison, these fundamental forces still existed, but they operated in a pale version. Fights were one-on-one with fists, not gangs or weapons, and they were brief. Consequently, inmate leaders were without the ultimate power of violence, which limited their ability to develop gangs.

We see this in the Merit Staff reports which involved inmates exerting control by force or guile over other inmates—fighting, possessing weapons, extortion, confidence game, or stealing.

The first factor to be considered about fights were their locations, which were determined by the system of control. Naturally, we have here only that fraction of all fights which occurred, were reported, and which came to the attention of the Merit Staff. However, we doubt that their reasons differ significantly from the undetected ones. Table 9.1 shows the location of these 30 fights in which 45 inmates were punished. Since these were all two-man fights, of the 60 inmates involved in the 30 fights, 15 inmates were judged blameless, and 45 at fault.

Whether one or both inmates were punished was the consequence of what the guard saw: if an officer believed he saw the entire fight and the behavior of both inmates during the entire fracas, there is a good chance that the inmate whom he called the aggressor would be the only one referred to the Merit Staff. (There were no fights during this year that had more than two participants.) Where an officer did not see the entire fight, the chances are that both participants were referred to the Merit Staff.

The largest single place of occurrence was the cellhouse, outside the cell itself; 22 inmates were punished for being involved in 13 fights. However, these fights should be seen in conjunction with the seven inmates who were punished for being involved in five fights in the dining room. Most cellhouse fights occurred in conjunction with the men going to or returning from the dining room. The reason for such locations are simple: they were among the few places where inmates who had grudges to settle could get at one another. The closeness of Warden Ragen's control prevented men who were enemies being either cell partners or near one another on the same assignment. In fact, if enmity was strong, men would not even be in the same cellhouse. This left limited possibilities for contact: in the dining room, church, movies, recreation yard and ball games. Only when nearly all the inmates of a cellhouse were out of their cells and moving in masses could enemies get at one another, a phenomenon which occurred most often as lines moved to and from the dining room.

This element shows up in the five inmates punished for three fights while they were "elsewhere on line." Other places where men could get at one another were recreation yard or work assignment. There were few fights in the recreation yard because of the ease of observation, both for the inmates and the guards. Unless one could muster a group of inmates to trap someone, it was difficult for a single inmate to trap another when both were free to move about. Inmates were not able to form groups to trap individual inmates in the open space of the recreation yard for several reasons. The main reason was Warden Ragen's attentive custodial staff, as well as the certainty and severity of punishment. Officers were walking about on the ground, and those in the watchtowers on the walls had nearly unobstructed views of the inmates.

The limited locations of fights was one of the end products of the general

Table 9.1
**Location of Fights Punished By Merit Staff During the 12 Month Period
October 1959-September 1960
(No Weapons Involved Unless Cited Below)**

Location	NUMBER OF FIGHTS			NUMBER OF INMATES PUNISHED		
	Number Of Fights Where Of Two Inmates Fighting Punishment Given To			With Two Inmates Fighting, Punishment Given To		
	Total	Only One	Both	Total	Only One	Both
While Eating In the Dining Room	5	3(a)	2	7	3(a)	4
In Cellhouse						
Outside Cell	13	4	9	22	4	18
In Cell	2	2(c)	0	2	2(c)	0
Elsewhere						
Recreation Yard	2	1	1(e)	3	1	2(e)
On Line	3	1	2	5	1	4
On Assignment	1	1(b)	0	1	1(b)	0
Not Stated	4	3(d)	1	5	3(d)	2
TOTAL	30	15	15	45	15	30

(a)One case where an iron pipe was used
(b)Officers' Kitchen-butcher knife used
(c)One case where leg of a stool was broken off and used as a club
(d)One case where a fountain pen was used to stab
(e)Both inmates used ball bats
Note: There were no fights involving more than two inmates

system of control. Bitter enemies could be separated into different cellhouses, and even if they were assigned to the same cellhouse, no inmate's ability to control others allowed him to create concerted action. In fact, probably the only place where our present tabulation seriously undercounts the number of fights which did take place are for those on assignment. The various factories and buildings where the inmates worked were the only places where it was possible to readily avoid detection. There were few guards for the large numbers of inmates, and more importantly, each physical structure had so many floors, rooms, cabinets, and corners, that a fight which was over quickly (as most were) could take place out of sight or hearing of a guard.

Another factor to consider in the seriousness of fights is the absence of weapons: of 30 fights, weapons or implements were involved in only five. One was for, "Trying to stab inmate Jones with a fountain pen," not a dangerous weapon except in the eye or eardrum. Serious injury was possible in the remaining four fights. In one, two inmates went at one another in recreation yard, each with a ball bat; here, both inmates were punished. Of the remaining three fights in which only one inmate was punished, one involved, "Hitting inmate Smith in the back of his head with a piece of pipe," during the supper meal. Of the two remaining, one took place in the cell, the other on assignment. The one in the cell took place after the evening meal, while the cellhouse was on deadlock. A cellhouse officer heard the commotion, ran to the cell and:

> [R]ushed down there and found inmate Jones standing with the leg of what had been a stool in his hand, threatening inmate Smith who was laying on the floor under the lower bunk. He was bleeding at the mouth. I ordered inmate Jones to throw down the club which he held, and he refused to do so. I repeated the order five times and he still refused to do so. I then ordered inmate Smith to lay down the piece of stool that he had in his hand. He did so, while begging me not to let inmate Jones hit him again. I then ordered inmate Jones to lay down the leg of the stool and he did so, but reached for it again when inmate Smith started to get up from the floor.

In this case, inmate Smith was badly beaten, with skull abrasions, lacerations of the lip, and a fracture of a leg bone.

The remaining case took place in the kitchen of the officer's dining room. Two inmates assigned there got into an argument and one, "grabbed a knife from the cook and started after inmate Able who ran into the officer's dining room. Inmate Able fell." One startled officer reported that he:

> [H]eard a loud racket. Upon turning around I saw this inmate standing over inmate Able who had fallen down. Inmate Baker had a large knife with about a ten inch blade raised and seemed about ready to strike inmate Able. Three to four officers and myself immediately jumped this inmate at which time I managed to take the knife from him.

This last incident illustrates the fact that guards could not be squeamish about violence. They had to be prepared to grapple occasionally with violent inmates, and on rare occasions, violent inmates with weapons.

None of the other 30 fights mentioned involved any weapons, and in most cases were little more than a short flurry of punches before they were stopped. A typical fight occurred in the dining room where an officer:

> [S]aw inmate Charles jump up from his seat on the inside and dive over an inmate who was sitting between him and inmate Fox. He was swinging and was on top of Fox all the time. I never saw Fox swing at all.

No fight lasted long in the dining room—in this case, the officer quickly stopped it. Why was inmate Charles enraged? Inmate Fox accused him of sticking his thumb in inmates Fox's bowl, while passing it back from being refilled by a waiter.

Of the entire 25 fights which did not involve a weapon, probably only about three seemed to be more serious than this. In one case it took the officer a minute to get to the scene, and he reported:

> [M]y next view of the fight showed inmate Jones laying on the floor with
> inmate Smith pounding him about the head and face. Inmate Jones was
> bleeding about the face.

In another case, two cell partners were fighting after the cellhouse had been
put on deadlock. When the officer at the cellhouse ordered them to stop, one man
refused, and kept swinging while the other pleaded with him to stop. A lieutenant
was called from the night patrol with his trained police dog, and found:

> [I]nmate Jones was clinched with inmate Smith and he was trying to ram
> Smith's head against the bed. I told him to stop or I would bring the dog in.
> He said to me: "Bring the god-damned dog in." I then had officer Johnson
> open the cell door and entered. Inmate Jones still wanted to fight.

In the final case, two inmates were fighting on the cellhouse gallery, and
even though they were pulled apart by officers they kept swinging, breaking
away from the officers, and going back at one another:

> I grabbed inmate Jones with Officer Johnson, and Officer Enright got
> inmate Smith over to the side of the cellhouse. While Officer Johnson and I
> were trying to hold inmate Smith and keep him from breaking loose, he
> gave Officer Johnson and I quite a battle. Lieutenant George came in and
> got Smith. Then Lieutenant Fox and I took inmate Jones over to Isolation.
> During the time of the fight, I either got hit in the ribs or when I got
> knocked into the wall I got my ribs bruised because, about two hours later, I
> could not move without hurting in my ribs. I told Officer Johnson, and he
> told me to go to the hospital, which I did. I went to the hospital and the
> doctor had an x-ray taken of my chest. He said there were no broken ribs,
> just bruised and I would be sore for a few days.

And when inmate Jones was taken to isolation, he was by no means
subdued, for he:

> [B]ecame belligerent and demanded that he be told how many days he was
> to serve in Isolation. Inmate was told to go back to Isolation and that he
> would be called out as soon as we received the reports. He refused and had
> to be forcibly removed from the Captain's office by Lieutenants Able,
> Baker, and Officers Doe and Roe. While he was changing clothes into
> Isolation uniform he was boisterous, making sarcastic remarks.

In a case such as this, when the inmate was a young adult with his adrenaline
and fists moving, how much force was the minimum required? We do not know.
But my guess is that sometime during this inmate's sojourn in isolation, the staff
found some provocation to beat him.

The reason for these fights were undoubtedly varied, and may have ranged
from the trivia of momentary irritation, to the desire to force payment of
gambling debts, or the violent emotions of homosexual attraction or demands.
But they were all attempts to control other inmates.

Defense is implied in the three reports which involved "Possessing a
weapon." Only one of these three was something which might be called an

offensive weapon, where the officer reported:

> I caught this inmate in the bath-room putting a cloth handle on a piece of
> steel. When he spotted me, he threw it in a corner. As I picked it up, he told
> me he would throw it away for me. I called Lieutenant Jones and he took
> the inmate and the dagger to Isolation.

While the officer did not specifically mention the size of the weapon, it is
likely that it was large enough to kill. Moreover, the bathroom, where an
intended victim would be naked and without weapons, was an ideal place for an
attack. Note that this is our only knife, a far cry from their prevalence in other
prisons.

The remaining two reports indicate implements that I doubt were lethal
weapons. In one case, an officer found an inmate had:

> [C]ontraband hidden in his shoe when he was searched this p.m., in the
> Clothing Factory preparatory to going to the cellhouse. He had hidden in his
> shoe a small pocket knife in a Bull Durham sack.

In the other case, the inmate was found, "Carrying and having a home-made
knife in his front pants pocket while eating the noon meal in the farm
dormitory."

Of course, even the stubbiest knife or razor can cause death by severing a
jugular vein, and one may consider any implement as dangerous. But if we
define a dangerous weapon as one in which a single blow reasonably well given
will cause death, then a knife with a blade of at least three or four inches is
necessary. In our three cases, we can guess that a least one of the "knives" could
not have been this long. It is possible, of course, that the inmate was carrying
the knife for other reasons—perhaps to use as a nail file, or an eating utensil—
but considering the penalties for being caught with a knife we doubt this. All in
all, I guess that a least one of these men wanted a small knife as an *equalizer*,
to defend himself from a stronger enemy.

Homicide

Don't underestimate the role of luck in Warden Ragen's ability to suppress
violence. As I will recount below, there was only one homicide which occurred
during my six years at Stateville. Most of this is to Warden Ragen's credit, for
his system eliminated weapons from the prison. But I'm sure he had the luck to
escape near-misses on many occasions.

One such occasion impinged on my office, but I learned of it only after the
fact, something I was grateful for. I did not know beforehand that one of my
clerks was planning an attack in which he might kill another inmate. A rule in
our office was that if anything *heavy* were coming off, I would not be told. It was
for my protection. If my clerks were caught, I would not be suspected of
snitching.

My clerk was a short middle aged thief who had engaged in violence before
prison, and after. He had almost killed a guard during an escape attempt from

Menard many years ago, and had been dangerous when younger. But he had been locked up well over a decade, and a few years previously had a severe heart attack; his vigorous days were over. What created the crisis was a young inmate on a nearby assignment who had taken to harassing, or *riding* him. Why? Some of it may have been racial, for my clerk was white, the other inmate was black. I never learned who this other inmate was, so I can only speculate that it was the arrogance of the young, something which happened frequently in the prison. Young men sometimes took pleasure in taunting older inmates who had been incarcerated for many years.

My clerk, call him Able, felt humiliated, and believed if he did not take some action quickly, he would be demeaned as the butt of derision. He had many friends, and in fact his closest friend was also a clerk in my office, a young man who would gladly have taken on the offending inmate in a fight. But Able felt he had to fight his own fights, even though his heart attack made it impossible for him to fight with his fists.

The solution came from a chink in Warden Ragen's control that had escaped notice. The prison had a radio system piped into earphones in individual cells, which necessitated a disk jockey who played records and controlled the radio. This required the disk jockey to have some tools for routine maintenance of his equipment. This office was near my own in the front end. Able borrowed a long sharp-slotted screwdriver from the disk jockey (who may or may not have known anything was afoot). In effect, Able now had the equivalent of an ice-pick.

He planned it out. Also in the front end was a shower room, a perk for inmates who worked there. They had the autonomy to avoid the mass showering of the Yard by taking time from their assignment at the front end. Able kept watch, which probably required enlisting some of his friends to *stake out* the tormentor, and learn when he took showers. Crucially, the offending inmate did not have a friend keep guard.

Then Able sprung. He waited until his victim was in the shower room; the shower had started and the windows were fogged. Able then sneaked in. He grabbed the startled and naked inmate by an arm and slammed him against the wall as he pressed the tip of the screwdriver just under the solar plexus hard enough to "freeze" the inmate. Able demanded of the other did he "want it" now, or was he going to *back off.* The answer was obviously "Yes," and Able quickly left. The entire incident probably took a minute. The sequel was that Able was never again spoken to by that other inmate.

Able told me about it afterwards. I asked him if he really would have killed the other. He said yes. I believed him. Remember this the next time you read how today's convicts are so much more violent than they were in that golden age of the past.

Rape

Rape in prison is a horror that haunts the popular imagination. It is a staple of Hollywood movies about prisons, and in recent years Ann Landers, the syndicated newspaper columnist, has printed several heartrending columns about it. (For example: *Gannett Suburban Newspapers*, October 29, 1995; Hollywood, Florida *Sun Sentinal*, January 31, 1996.)

Moreover, there is evidence of its destructiveness. The feminist movement has documented that rape often scars women psychologically for life. It seems plausible that if a man is raped the psychological damage may be even worse, especially if we consider that when it happens in prison, it may be repeated for months or years. I can only speculate, but perhaps degradation as a victim may be a cause of violence perpetuated by ex-convicts after release.

This visceral revulsion over prison rape is a powerful force which may eventually lead the courts to penalize correctional administrators who do not control inmate-against-inmate violence. For that reason, it is worth discussing popular outrage in its own right. Afterwards, I will turn to sexual assaults in Stateville, and finally, a discussion of the growing academic literature on the subject.

The pathos underlying the lack of control of prison rape has been expressed nowhere as poignantly as in the indictment a generation ago by David Rothenberg in *The New York Times*, January 29, 1977. Rothenberg was then the executive director of the Fortune Society, a liberal self-help group for ex-convicts:

> Sexual assault in jails and prisons remain an issue shadowed in fear and embarrassment.
> It is a grim reality that causes uncomfortable silence among prison administrators and politicians. The subject, too intimidating, is refused the honest airing it desperately needs.
> Rape exists in most jails, reformatories and prisons. It has devastating effects on the participants. Often it is the unspoken cause of jail suicides, and it is closely linked to much "inexplicable" violence nurtured in our "correctional" facilities. Some prison administrators admitted at recent conference workshops that their greatest single difficulty is the violence that emerges from sexual assaults. Yet of the several hundred workshops not one concerned the sexual aspects of caged human beings.

Sometimes the print media provides contributions to knowledge about sexual assaults. Such was the May 1, 2, and 3, 1994 series by Charles Sennot in the *Boston Globe* on rape in prison, primarily in Massachusetts. Although the series follows the usual genre of personal human drama, it is an excellent empirical report on rape in prison. Equally compelling is its claim that rape in Massachusetts' prisons is widespread.

This chamber of horrors can be contrasted with the six years I was employed at Stateville. The atmosphere hung heavy with repressed sexuality. Voluntary homosexual activity was pervasive (though by no means rampant). I heard of cases in which fearful inmates were intimidated by verbal assaults into submission to sodomy. But I only heard of one case of gang rape, and it is possible that it took place before my employment. However even this, I was told, was ruthlessly prosecuted by Warden Ragen, complete with polygraph, medical tests for sperm, and forwarding the evidence to the Will County States Attorney to see if it warranted criminal indictment. All this was in addition to the physical protection of the victim, and segregation and Merit Staff referral for the rapists. Undoubtedly there may have been rapes I never heard of, but when you contrast my Stateville recollections of six years with Rothenberg's account, it is evident that sexual assault was not a severe problem in Warden Ragen's Stateville. Even those who had been intimidated into submission were probably few in number, and sad to say, had no idea how effectively they were physically safe from their tormentors.

Jacobs' history of Stateville prison (1977) is an example of the all too common lofty view of academics who ignore the issue. In his discussion of Warden Ragen's regime, he never mentions that the inmates were safe from sexual assault. Then in Chapter 6, which discusses how the inmate gangs took Stateville over during the liberal ascendancy, he notes in passing that, "Whites within vulnerable cliques were exposed to physical assault, rape, extortion, and constant harassment" (p.159).

In contrast, Grant Pick, writing in a weekly Chicago newspaper *The Reader* (February 16, 1996) carries the profile of an inmate named Hudson who had been imprisoned at Stateville in the 1950's (during Warden Ragen's regime) and then again in the 1970's (in the period of anarchy which followed):

> The Stateville that Hudson returned to in 1970 had deteriorated from the prison he remembered from the 50's and 60's. Joe Ragen, a tough warden Hudson credits for keeping order, had moved on to become state director of public safety and then had retired. "Now the gangs ran the place," says Hudson. "It was a madhouse. Although I never had any trouble myself because I used to box, still the situation bothered me. I'd go to the officials to get them to exert control, and they'd say, 'We know what's going on, but there's nothing we can do.' "
>
> In 1972 Hudson made his own attempt at control. "A young white kid I had befriended, the son of a mayor downstate, was raped by several gang members," he says, "and I took it upon myself to do something about it. I called this one gangster by the name Bo Diddley down off the stairs, and I hit him in the chest with a shank [a makeshift knife]."

I have no doubt that after the fall of Warden Ragen's regime rape became as pervasive as all the other forms of violence and degradation at Stateville. But to generalize about prisons in general is no easy matter. For one thing, its prevalence may vary greatly between prisons, and for another, inmates may not wish to admit they have been raped.

Academic researchers on the subject may be following a path similar to the one I noted in Chapter 8, when I pointed out that there was a growing academic literature on the relationship between overcrowding and control in prisons. It may not lead to a definitive conclusion, but it constitutes ongoing reports which keep us aware of the issue. And as with the research on overcrowding that I noted in Chapter 8, major reasons for this growing literature stem from the larger number of academics interested in prisons, and the ascendancy of ideological conservatives who are concerned with prison control.

Until the last few decades, there really was little concern with the issue of sexual assault in prisons. For example, such major works of the liberal period as Sykes (1958) ignored it. From time to time it was discussed, and the original *Kinsey Report* included some material. Then empirical research about prison rape increased in the 1970's.

It is likely that the prevalence of rape in prison varies enormously. For example, Fleisher (1989) suggests (p.167) that rape at the U.S. maximum security prison at Lompoc, California was rare. Given the quality and detail of this ethnographic study (although its focus is prison guards), this is a believable conclusion. A number of other studies (e.g., Saum, *et. al.* [1995], or Lockwood [1980]) also come to the same conclusion. On the other hand, Carrol (1974) estimated 40 to 50 men were raped each year in an eastern prison of about 300 inmates, while Wooden and Parker (1982) estimated 14 percent of the inmates of a California prison were raped. Research has increased so that the 1989 *Prison Journal* published three articles on the subject by Chonco, Jones and Schmid, and Tewksbury. The value of this research remains to be seen, but at least an attempt is being made to understand the subject.

Race, Sex, and Sudden Death

An example of an event which encapsulated the elements of sex, violence, and racial hostility was illustrated by the only homicide which occurred during my six years at Stateville, the murder of a black by a white inmate. A young white inmate, while temporarily alone in an industrial shop with a black inmate, killed him by beating in his skull with an iron bar. There were no witnesses. The white inmate testified in a closed hearing of inquest by a Will county grand jury in the nearby city of Joliet. The grand jury decided there were no grounds for any indictment that a crime had occurred. This decision of "no bill" by the grand jury and a radio report that the inmates had fought over possession of a package of cigarettes concluded the incident. To the public, it was an irrational flare-up. The incident may have been reported in the Joliet newspapers and was quickly forgotten. I have no newspaper clippings, so it probably was not picked up by the Chicago papers.

But the white inmate's story contradicted the story in the public media, and he, after all, was the source of all information of what actually transpired. He told the same story to me, some inmates, and a psychiatrist and a sociologist with the state criminologist:

> I was alone in the shop when he came in. He tried to get friendly with me before. The white guys I don't have any trouble with. I just tell them, "I don't wanna hear any of that shit, get away from me," and they leave me alone. But these colored guys, some of these baboons just gotta be shown. He come up and he started to talk to me. He told me I was good looking; he said, "I heard about you." He asked me for some pussy. Well one thing led to another, and we started scuffling, and I grabbed this pipe, and laid into him. I cracked in his head in front and the side.

When I asked him why this story contradicted the official story about his testimony, he told me:

> I testified downtown at the inquest, but I didn't go in before the jury. I know the newspaper said it was over a pack of cigarettes but that's not what I told them. I guess they don't want the publicity. They don't want the sexual angle to come out. I guess if I went to trial, it would come out. I don't think they really believe me, but they had to take my word. There weren't any witnesses when the murder—I mean accident— happened.

After the event was over, everyone was willing to let it fade into the past. The Warden treated it as past history, and the inmate had no desire to see reporters. He told me:

> I haven't got any notification from these officials. I got the newspaper clipping. I heard it on the radio first. They just said "no bill." I guess that's only if they decide its justifiable homicide or something.

No one wanted a recurrence. The inmate was a young man, *state raised*, who knew that he could not afford it:

> I'm 21. I've got ten years in. I know I don't look it, but I've been in several places before. I've been in the federal joint. I can take care of myself. I'm not afraid of any personal harm. I can protect myself. Ninety percent of these guys would be afraid to come up to your face, and I don't let nobody come up behind my back. I'm just afraid it'll happen again, and I don't care what the consequences are: if I feel I'm justified, I'll defend myself, and I don't want to spend the rest of my life in this place cause of some silly con, and I won't beat it the next time. They'll say: "See, we thought so."

To protect him, at least till the *heat died down*, the Warden severely restricted his assignment:

> They transferred me here and they put me in the cellhouse help. I'm restricted to an area about the size of these three rooms, the concrete floor of the flag. They won't put me where there's any knives or wrenches or weapons. I couldn't get into the vocational school or the furniture shop.

Moreover, the inmate himself was quite alert to his own danger, and to the psychological stresses he faced, especially from black inmates:

> I stopped going to Yard till the grand jury was over. Now it's over I'll go again. It seems to be getting worse, especially the colored guys. They stare at me. I went out on Yard, I saw them looking at me. A couple of guys

come up to me, one guy says, "You Abel?" and I say, "Yeah." He said, "You the guy that cobbled the guy in the factory? He was a friend of mine." Right away I get my back up—how can I take it? The only way I can take it is he's telling me look out. I won't worry about him: I can take care of myself, and if one of them comes at me, I'll take care of myself again. Some nigger'll get hurt.

Bordering On Violence

This was the only killing of an inmate I remember happening during my time at Stateville. Guards were rarely assaulted, and no one could remember when one had been killed. Jacobs (1977: 243) tabulates inmate assaults which resulted in injuries to guards, beginning in 1966. I expect he tabulated none earlier because there were none, except the minor injuries I have already noted. There probably were undetected attacks by inmates with weapons on other inmates, but I doubt there were many. Surveillance was so thorough that any wounded inmate would have been hard put to go undetected, although I'm sure undetected fist fights happened regularly on assignments where rooms, nooks and crannies were available.

The only time that Warden Ragen's control was really seriously breached during my employment occurred when several convicts subverted the hydraulic locking system of their cells in one cellhouse. Theirs was an ingenious and daring accomplishment. It was probably only days away from allowing these inmates to get out of their cells at night, and seize control of the cellhouse. I doubt they would have escaped because I learned of no plan to scale the walls. I never learned how the Warden was tipped off, but the media and newspapers, as usual, simply printed what Warden Ragen told them. They printed stories which grossly underestimated reality and saved Warden Ragen from ridicule.

Although rape, especially inter-racial rape was a recurring theme, (at least among whites—I could never get black inmates to discuss it), in the tensions of the prison actual sexual behavior ran along a more even path. Inmates constantly fantasized about sex. However, only when the system of custodial control slipped up and a willing partner was available did some furtive and rapid sexual intercourse take place.

We now shade off from the foregoing reports on actual fights and possession of weapons to consider the remaining methods of control among the inmates: threats, guile, and stealth. We have two Merit Staff reports for the use of threatening letters, such as the one in which one inmate wrote:

> Say Baby: You know who this is from, so get upset. You understand, I need something and also something to smoke. From this day on it will be me and you. OK Look, I don't want any bull-shit like you pulled in the Textile. You and me from now on. You can give me the smokes tomorrow when you see me. I know you have until you get your pay from Textile, then you can turn me on. I don't want any of your bull-shit.

Another method was the guile of swindling other inmates, although the actual report we have only verges on this. It concerns an inmate who worked on the outside detail, and during a shakedown of his cell, an officer found, "what we believed to be marijuana and marijuana cigarettes." When he was questioned, the inmate:

> [A]dmitted carrying the weed in and that he was going to try to see if mixing it with tobacco would get him high. Also, admitted he was going to give inmate Jones some of the weed. After tests were made on this weed it was found that it was not marijuana.

Since the marijuana plant was widespread and grew wild, it would have been possible for the inmates to find some, and even cultivate it on a place like the farm. However, it appeared to be a minor racket with some inmates to *fast talk* others into believing that they had marijuana, when in actuality they were selling some miscellaneous weeds from the prison yard.

The final way of getting what they wanted from other inmates was theft. In two cases, one inmate was found, "having and wearing the enclosed commissary shoes belonging to inmate Jones," and the other inmate for:

> [T]aking a T-shirt from the laundry bag of inmate Smith. We have had various complaints of inmates' personal property being broken into, and I know this inmate is one that is doing part of it.

The Good Old Days

It may be a useful perspective to consider alternative means of control. We can consider the opposite extreme of little custodial control because, a generation earlier, custodial organization consisted of little more than a perimeter control which guarded the walls. Stateville was almost completely run by the inmates. The stories I heard corroborate those published by Erickson and Jacobs. As one inmate who was there remembered:

> It was a playhouse. Everybody was stealing food, they were eating good, they had stoves, they had night life, they had gangs, they had killings. I'd say there was an average of about once a week, there was an actual killing...I've seen them laying in the yard. They'd be walking in the yard, see, and all of a sudden you'd see men shuffle and all of a sudden a man would be laying on the ground with a knife in him.

The figure of once a week killings is an exaggeration; this inmate himself later reduced this figure to perhaps a half-dozen or so each year, with several men wounded by knife for every man killed. This higher level of violence was not necessarily due to any more dramatic conflicts than contemporary ones, but rather to the system of control:

> Knives were prevalent and shakedowns were not like they are now. There were gangsters, I mean guys who thought they were gunmen with their shivs. They even had holsters for them. Then there were young gangs and it could grow out of any little thing. I've seen a guy get killed down there for

taking a cigarette out of a guy's pocket.

Out of this different prison grew an earlier inmate subculture, in which suspicion of being an informer could bring death or serious injury. Inmates did not glance into someone's cell unless they knew him and were invited to. When an inmate heard a scuffle in the cellhouse or dining room, he continued to look straight ahead. When the common level of violence available among inmates included knives instead of flurries of fists, the inmate subculture was far different. Warden Ragen's system did not eliminate this subculture, but rather changed it to a pale version of its former self. Violence, homosexuality, and gambling still existed, as did all other aspects of former days. But their level of activity was reduced, and new inmates learned to adapt to an institution in which their main fears were of guards looking for violations of trivial rules.

10

Control of Inmates: Other than Violence

Introduction

ONCE past actual physical violence and coercion, the objective need for punishment as severe as Merit Staff referral diminished. And informally, it did. There *were* minor punishments for trivial offenses. But sometimes, Warden Ragen's system hunted mice with an elephant gun, and inmates were referred to the Merit Staff for punishments out of proportion to their offenses. Because the Merit Staff was such an autocratic, shadowy creation of Warden Ragen, it was basically unfair, and the inmates felt it. I believe that this was a great source of tension, and a major reason inmates hated his system. Paradoxically, I think Warden Ragen's use of physical force was considered just because it was congruent with the street justice inmates accepted. One of the benefits of judicial intervention in corrections can be that a greater sense of fairness is required when a warden imposes punishments. Because there is so much repetition in the explanations of many of the following punishments, I will be selective in providing examples and summaries.

A. Challenges to the Authority of Guards

Mouthing Off

Moving away from actual violence, we first enter the grey area where it hangs heavy. In Table 8.1, the 29 Merit Staff decisions called "Insolence, coupled with gestures or threats of bodily harm" concern behavior where the situation stopped short of actual physical violence. In one of these cases, an inmate standing to one side observed an officer write a punishment report on two other inmates in the dining room. Another guard, watching the inmate who was standing to one side, reported:

> As the officer turned away, this inmate turned, his eyes flashing at the officer's back, and I heard him say, "The dirty son–of–a bitch."

Our inmate was demoted to "E" grade and had one month of his good time revoked. In another seven reports of this category, the officers felt the hostility of barely controlled anger. In one case, the officer reported:

> This inmate came complaining about his back to sick–call this morning to see the Doctor. The Doctor ordered him an X–ray. After he came out of the X–ray room he wanted to see the Doctor again. I told him that one trip was enough. He started to argue with me and said that he was going to see the Doctor anyway. I told him that he wasn't and for him to stand against the wall. This he refused to do. He just stood there with his fists doubled. I told him too that if he kept messing around, he would probably lose his good time. Then he said, "You are probably right."

This inmate had already been up for disciplinary action many times, including one refusal to accept an assignment transfer, and another for "discourtesy to an officer," so the Merit Staff decision routinely followed his most recent conflict.

The remaining 21 reports of this category included instances which conveyed less hostility than gestures of contempt. But an inmate did not have to indicate hostility by gesture or language to be referred to Merit Staff. The 23 Merit Staff reports for "Insolence" contain reports on inmates who either argued with, or were overheard cursing officers. For example, the officer who reported an inmate for:

> Calling me a son–of–a–bitch. I told this inmate to go over to the south fence and cut the grass away from the cement. He went inside and told the inmate barber on the first floor that he was going to ask for a transfer. He said, "I am not going to work for that son–of–a–bitch any longer." I was standing by the door and heard him.

After these 23 Merit Staff referrals for "Insolence" we begin to move away from direct personal hostility and move to assorted challenges.

ACCUSATIONS

Two instances cited inmates for trying to intimidate officers by threatening them with false accusations. The first case involved an inmate assigned as an *officers flunky*, one of the porters in the guards' dormitory in the administration building. During a shakedown, contraband was found and the officer accused the inmate of:

> [T]hreatening an officer. When I was searching inmate Jones, I found a nudist book in his shirt. He asked me not to write him up. After I got off work, Jones came up to my room. He said if I wrote him up, he would say that he found the nudist book in my room.

REFUSING TO WORK

This applied to inmates who contested their work assignments, a paradox. The prison was overcrowded, and there were many more inmates than work, so it was easy for an inmate to *slide into* a spot that required little of him. A little patience with an onerous assignment could soon lead to a transfer to something easier. The 24 men who received Merit Staff referrals, however, violated the rule that no inmate might openly refuse to work. Seven of these cases were variations on:

> Refusing to accept an assignment transfer, and refusing to work. Inmate Jones stated, "I'm not going to work out in the population. Take my good time."

Eight of these refusals, the largest number on a single assignment, involved the coal pile, which was used as a punishment assignment for it included dirty, manual labor outdoors for half a day. According to one report:

> Inmate Jones was going back and forth wheeling coal with a wheelbarrow, from the hole in the wall to the pit at the powerhouse in the coal yard, with from one to two shovels of coal this a.m. I asked him to let the shovel man put on more coal. He ran the wheelbarrow at me, said get the hell out of the way, went on down to pit, emptied his shovel of coal, made a circle down there with the empty wheelbarrow, and then returned. I walked over and had the shovel–man fill up the wheelbarrow. He dumped it and started to take off. I told him to walk out to one side. He shoved me and said the hell with you. I shoved him away from me and called a lieutenant.

The remaining cases were scattered through other assignments. The closest common denominator among them was a desire to avoid physical labor.

THE RECALCITRANT IN SEGREGATION

The 24 reports for inmates who misbehaved after they had been placed in isolation or segregation encompass a variety of recalcitrant behavior: cursing the guards or the prison doctor on his visits; throwing food at the guards; throwing spoons into their toilets; urinating out of their cells; screaming and banging metal cups; engaging in screaming matches with other inmates; more determined souls stopped up their toilets. I can only speculate, but I believe that these inmates were not subject to beatings unless they, say, threw feces at a guard. Even then it was not a situation where a guard lost his temper and beat up the inmate, but of lieutenants coolly deciding to do something about the behavior. One of my clerks referred to this sardonically as the "parties" the lieutenants sometimes attended in segregation.

Rather than creating a litany, the report on one inmate in segregation will serve as an illustration. For three days in a row, the officer in segregation reported this inmate almost identically:

> Refusing to clean his cell. This inmate had been issued soap, floor rags and scouring power to use in cleaning his cell, but he refused to clean it. His floor and clothes are dirty and his cell causes a stink on the gallery, as it is filthy.

Then two weeks later, in one day there came three reports. At two o'clock in the afternoon, one officer reported:

> Creating a disturbance, throwing food and water into the next cell, where inmate Jones is confined. Around 2:00 p.m. this date, inmate Smith was throwing food and water, and creating a disturbance. When I asked Smith what the trouble was he told me that inmate Jones had started calling him names like he was a no good son of bitch; he was "just a punk;" he would sure like to get into his old ladies pants, then she would leave him for good.

Then, two hours later, another officer reported:

> Throwing water and soap at 4:00 p.m. I caught this inmate engaged in a water fight with inmate Jones in the next cell. I told them to stop it and when they started again about ten minutes later, I reported it to the Lieutenant, and he came over and talked to them. Smith then settled down to calling loudly "nigger" for the rest of the night.

This report came simultaneously with that of another officer who said:

> Throwing water into inmate Jones cell, and standing in his cell and yelling "Nigger," just "Nigger." This inmate has been causing disturbances and keeping the whole gallery awake for several nights.

Finally, much later that night, another officer reported:

> At 11:00 p.m. I heard this inmate kicking his bars. As I started through the tunnel door, and when I stopped at his cell, he said, "Get me a Lieutenant, and get me out of this mother fucking place. I am the only white man here, the rest are all fucking niggers." When I told him to shut up, the Lieutenant wasn't coming over again, he said, "Now you listen, I'm telling you, you cock sucker, I'm going to turn in a complaint when I get a visit, and get your job!" Then he went on cursing the "Niggers" as he called them. He raised hell all night since he had the water fight at 2:00 p.m. The rest of the men on the cell block are colored and are giving him the works to try and bug him up, with inmate Jones carrying the ball.

Recalcitrants such as this may have assisted the Warden, for few inmates in segregation enjoyed continual uproar. Consequently, during the day or two that our inmate wore himself down, some of the men in his segregation block may have become irritated, and more amenable to giving the Warden the promise to behave if he allowed them back into the general population. Inmates in segregation had sight privacy from other inmates, but none from sound and smell. I expect few enjoyed gagging on the stink of neighbors who refused to bathe or who threw their urine or feces at the guards, especially if this was combined with the bedlam of screaming which could go on all night. I suspect there was always someone in a fury to make life miserable in segregation. To secure his release an inmate had only to promise to obey the prison rules, and most did.

MISCELLANY

Next, we have three reports on two inmates for setting fire to the mattress in their cell, and purportedly "Trying to incite a riot." The third inmate was punished for what the custodial authorities more commonly consider "agitating," an attempt to disrupt the operation of an assignment, or even complaining about the prison to the State Superintendent of Prisons. Not all recalcitrance on the part of inmates is so overt as these, however. When we turn to the next section, we see cases where inmates avoided outright opposition.

SUBVERSION

The conflict over control between the custodial staff and the inmates did not end with direct confrontation. A more profitable contest was waged by those inmates who wished to subvert the Warden's system in such a way that he must first discover the attempt, and then track down unknown perpetrators. Here Warden Ragen usually discovered these actions only after he had been *beat*, and the efficiency of his system was tested by the speed with which he gained sufficient information to identify and punish whom he believed to be the culprits. Previously, we have seen inmates rise up, so to speak, against the Warden—only to be immediately cut down in an unequal contest. This may have a certain appeal of the heroic confrontation—at least to spectators—between the gladiator and the lion, in which the lion always wins.

We now deal with another kind of conflict, that of the *cool hustler* who outwitted the Warden. Because of the conspiratorial nature of this conflict, the Warden's control became analogous to a leaky container which held its contents only by virtue of constant inspection and repair. It was quite an accomplishment that inmates with no resources but their wits could so effectively probe the weak spots in Ragen's control, and an equal accomplishment that he so effectively controlled this kind of conflict with scarcely a half–dozen assistant wardens and captains seconded by a dozen lieutenants who supervised hundreds of guards and thousands of inmates.

But all assignments were vulnerable to being *beat*. I remember one of my clerks showed me the key with which they *beat* the secured file cabinet in my office. It looked like a metal scrap, but it worked perfectly, and had for years before he showed it to me. I could not object because it would have jarred the culture of our office, and my clerks could always make another.

The six reports in the category "Improper Contact with Persons Outside the Prison" might be considered challenges, rather than subversions. Most of them were so crude and simple–minded, that they could with equal justice be called the simple absence of common sense. Examples were asking a guard to make a telephone call for him, or falsifying the payroll records in one of the prison factories to increase someone's paycheck.

Four of these offenses involve the writing of unauthorized letters. The one letter each week which a convict was allowed to write to his family or friends and the unlimited number which he was allowed to receive from them (or anyone), were read by guards. But he might write only to those on his "mailing list" of people he had already specified by name, relationship, and address. Moreover, the inmate was limited in the kinds of things he could write, for he was not permitted to criticize the institution, make any complaints, or ask for money.

A couple of cases involved inmates assigned to keep the guard dormitory clean, who stole a guard's underwear. Eight inmates were punished for possessing contraband, in most cases excess commissary items; this helped keep down organized gambling or extortion, for bookies or musclemen were easily detected by growing hoards of cigarettes and other sundries. Five inmates were punished for being out of place: they were in someone else's cell during recreation, or had snuck off a work assignment. (These were usually for innocent reasons such as socializing with friends, rather than any sexual reasons.) Finally, Merit Staff referral was also used for miscellaneous nuisances, such as inmates who were caught over and over again in trivial rule violations such as "talking in line," "being rude to an officer," or "loafing on work assignment." A string of these, and a convict would be referred to the Merit Staff.

B. Officials in Conflict with Exchange among Inmates

This category involved mutually desired services and moves us toward the inmate underground economy, the subject of our next chapter. These services were ongoing and concealed, so I cannot quantify what percentage were actually detected. But success was hard to conceal if it was paid for, for a *kite* would alert the guards, and an accumulation of cigarettes or other payment was hard to hide.

SEX

Of the 19 inmates referred to the Merit Staff for homosexual behavior, the largest single group consisted of five pairs of cell–partners in bed with one another at night, as in the case where:

> Inmate Jones bunk is on top and inmate Smith's bunk is on the bottom. When I found them, I was on my 12:00 o'clock walk. I found them at 12:10. When I first found them they were in inmate Smith's bed, under the covers. As I got in front of the cell I found them kissing each other. After I got there inmate Jones jumped out of the bunk and sat down on the commode. He didn't have anything on. I then called the Lieutenant and had the two inmates escorted to Isolation.

In one case, an inmate caught in homosexuality attempted to commit suicide:

> At approximately 1 p.m. this date while making Isolation dinner relief, inmate Johnson was pounding on his cell door and when I went to see what he wanted, he was crying and said, "Get me out of this cell." I told him that I couldn't move him. He then said, "If I don't get out, I will hang it up." I went back to his cell again, very shortly thereafter, and he had his jacket sleeve tied to the top bar of the cell door. Meanwhile Lieutenant Able was in Captain Baker's office, so I immediately notified him what was about to happen. Lieutenant Able informed me to put a close supervision notice over his door. I left the Captain's office, got the sign, went straight to the cell. When I looked in he was hanging by his jacket. Time: approximately 1:08

p.m. I summoned Lieutenant Able and we went in and got him down, took all his clothes away, and moved him to another cell.

In addition to the five pairs discussed above, two other inmates were discovered in an act of sexual intercourse—but they were not cell partners. In their case one inmate had switched cells by going into the other's.

The remaining seven inmates were punished, not for intercourse, but for sending or receiving "love letters," such as, "Attempting to pass this note, in a Life magazine, from cell 444 to 666." The wording shown is exactly as the inmate wrote it:

> Hi baby! I really don't know how to begin this letter. But I ain't going round the butchies. I am going to tell you the real thing. By now your mind is working already. I have been wasting you at the yard for sometime. An believe me I have eyes for you. Your looks and your eyes are what have me going around. Your lips are the ones I like to kiss, and hold your body close to mine, make love to you all night long. Show you how much I really love you and go for you baby. They say that love at first site is the real one. So baby I like to hear from you. Say what you have to say. Don't be afraid. Say it. I have been put down before. But don't forget, that I'm one of a guy that really goes for you. Okey. If you answer me. And want you to give it to me are Billy on Four gallery. From Willie B. Throw it away when you finish it. Don't let nobody read it. So be cool babie and think about it. Am your man if you go for me.

Among four of these inmates the letters were found on the recipient, and both sender and receiver were punished by the Merit Staff; in the other three cases the letters were found in transit. The most common means of sending letters were in the magazines that were legally passed between cells, and often tripped by the guards as in the case where one guard reported:

> At 5:55 p.m. as I was checking the magazines on two gallery, I found these two magazines with two notes in them. One was going to cell 111 and the other was going to cell 333.

When this happened the cellhouse runner (paperboy) was on the spot to tell from which cells he got the magazines. Any haziness of memory would cost him a stay in isolation and a purge to a less remunerative job—cellhouse runners operated a *hustle* by charging to deliver messages and goods at night after the other inmates were locked in— and quite likely, a Merit Staff referral.

In addition to overt behavior, repressed sexuality pervaded the prison, to the point where the custodial force knew not where it lurked, and suspected it everywhere. In one case the custodial authorities carried out an intensive investigation which seemed obsessive to me. It began with a letter sent to a captain, outlining how the anonymous writer was going to kill another inmate by stabbing him on the assignment, or throwing him off the gallery in their cellhouse. The captain combined informers' tips as well as checks of the handwriting of numbers of inmates, and finally narrowed the search to someone who worked on the assignment adjoining that of the threatened inmate. Confronted with the anonymous letter, along with several specimens of his handwriting, the inmate confessed. I would have thought it was over, for a potentially dangerous situation was forestalled. But it was only the beginning.

The inmate who made these threats, (let us call him inmate Jones), when unmasked, explained to the authorities a complicated story which devolved to a con game. Inmate Jones explained that he paid $40.00 for legal material to the other inmate, Smith. How did he do this? He sent a member of his family the money from his own prison account, after telling the person during a visit to mail the money on to a girlfriend of Smith's. She in turn used this money to add regular sums to Smith's account on the prison's books, his dollar account in the front office. Jones said he had written his anonymous letter to the captain when Smith not only failed to get Jones the legal materials for his case as promised, but had also sent Jones a kite for more money, trying to extend the con game. At this point Jones wrote the letter in an attempt to get Smith transferred from his normal assignment, in the hope that this transfer would, when presented to Smith by the authorities, scare Smith into carrying out his original bargain.

It is possible that this was indeed the background of the threatening letter. But when the authorities questioned Smith they were less interested in moving him than they were in getting him to divulge the names of his enemies; from the Warden's point of view this was the most effective solution to this case. However they did their detective work, they did wind up with a guilty party who was referred to the Merit Staff.

So far, there has been nothing sexual in this matter. But in fact, as in so many other cases, the custodial authorities did not know the real motivations of the convicts. They could only speculate:

> Inmate Smith has been suspicioned of sex perversion. Therefore it is possible that inmate Jones deliberately attempted to convey the impression in his anonymous letter that he was in the same shop with Smith, and gambled that the authorities, as a precautionary measure, would move Smith from 4 C [gallery 4 of cellhouse C] Furniture Factory to the same shop Jones was in, 2 A Furniture Factory.
>
> Furthermore, inmate Jones did not explain his references to inmate Johnson. The latter inmate was just transferred to 4C Furniture Factory. In checking the cell card of inmate Smith, I find that he and Johnson celled together while assigned to 1F High School. This gives rise to the alternative possibility that subject may have suspected a relationship between Smith and Johnson, and jealousy may have prompted him to write the anonymous letter with the object of separating the two.

This last example completes this phantasmagoria of suspicion. While the custodial authorities retained a firm grip on power, their minds were pervaded by sexual suspicions.

At this point, we have exhausted our empirical knowledge. We think, however, that virtually all long-term prisoners had some sexual experience in the prison, for as one of my clerks told me:

> Every guy you know and I know, anybody you can name, all of them been involved in one way or the other either fucking or fucked.

In our opinion, short-term prisoners also had sexual intercourse, but relatively rarely. The reason for such limited behavior is the same we have seen time and time before: the system of control. At one extreme, long–term regular sexual intercourse was possible when cell partners were involved, but this was difficult. My clerk continued:

> You can't have affairs like it used to be since they tightened the joint up. Like in my cell. I share it, there's Smith and Jones, they're in there, I guess Smith is in his 30's and Jones, he's much younger. They're both big guys, all wrapped up in body beautiful. They both lift weights; nobody thinks of sex. But after I go home, suppose they get a *broad* in the cell, they'll both fuck. They'll have a ball, but when he leaves, they'll say, "Well, that was a good thing," but they won't try to get another.

They were not likely to try because there was little chance of success. Warden Ragen eliminated the power of inmates to control assignment transfers:

> You can't control it anymore, like you used to. It used to be one could follow the other. When there was money in the place before they dried it up, you could give Bill Smith [the inmate clerk for the assignment captain] a *fin*, he'd slip [Captain] Johnson a few bucks and you'd get a transfer wherever you want. No more. Now, one goes to the furniture shop, the other tries to follow, he might wind up on the coal pile.

Moreover, even men on the same assignment who were automatically assigned to contiguous cells in the same cellhouse could no longer use the cellhouse clerk to control cell placement. Once it was routine:

> In those days, the joint wasn't as tight: a clerk could put anybody in whatever cell he wanted. I remember the cellhouse B clerk, Abel, he was a good guy. He wouldn't put nobody in a cell unless it was okay. There was this nigger kid, high yeller, good looking. This other nigger told Abel, put that kid in his cell. So Abel went to the kid and asked him. "Hell no, I don't," the kid told him, so he didn't move. That nigger came back and told Abel put that kid in by tonight. So Abel didn't do it. Next day Abel was in his cell washing his hands after chow, this nigger and two friends came in and they had *shivs*, and they must of cut him maybe 80 times.

Still, during my experience, Warden Ragen's control was not absolute, and sexuality did pervade the minds of inmates. While the Warden controlled much of the sexuality which might occur in the cellhouse, he had less success with the encounters on assignment. Where an orgasm was achieved quickly, there was little chance of detection.

The reasons the Warden wanted to control sexuality were undoubtedly complex, and I imagine Freudians would have a field day analyzing him. But he did need to control it to maintain his position. Not only could sexuality bring violence, but it was a volatile subject for the general public: any embarrassment would have allowed opponents such as political liberals or the embryonic guards' trade union an opportunity to attack him through adverse publicity.

GAMBLING

As actual behavior, gambling was more common than sexuality. Warden Ragen effectively controlled it, so the *bookie*, the gambler who made a business of gambling by taking the bets of others was almost sure to be *knocked off* sooner or later. All three Merit Staff punishments for gambling referred to such *bookies*. One guard said: "While going down three gallery, I saw this inmate put something in his pocket. I stopped him and took it. It turned out to be a parley gambling slip."

We can be sure these men were *bookies*, for they were the only inmates who carried gambling records. They were but shadows of their former selves. Years ago when cash circulated in the institution, a prison *bookie* had the scope of the present day bookie on the street: bets were taken on all sports, and bankers were available to insure against heavy losses.

But under Warden Ragen *making book* was usually restricted to betting in season on football, baseball, and basketball. *Keeping a book* was a much diminished vocation, reduced by the tighter controls of the institution, greater risks of detection, the elimination of cash, and the rescheduling of radio programs and the receipt of newspapers to delay knowledge of results which dampened general interest in keeping the daily *play* going. Consequently, the pervasive gambling which did occur now consisted primarily of personal bets between individuals.

LEGAL PRACTICE

Our final two Merit Staff reports involved inmates who practiced law, a situation akin to that of gambling. The Warden was faced with a pervasive activity which he wished to keep from being organized. Of the two men punished here, one was a self–taught inmate "lawyer," and the other was one of his clerks. The lawyer himself seemed to have an extensive practice and employed a typist. The officer who shook down his cell reported that he had "in his cell legal documents belonging to other inmates." Investigation disclosed his typist who admitted:

> [T]yping approximately 60 pages of manuscript for inmate Jones, cellhouse C help, at 5 cents a page. Inmate Smith admitted to me that he had accepted $1.50 worth of commissary items from Inmate Jones, and he told me that Jones still owed him $1.50.

But profitable law practices were few in the prison, squashed by the Warden's system of control.

This ends our discussion of the Merit Staff reports. It is subjective interpretation based upon objective evidence, and it outlines the reality of control. Finally, we turn to perhaps the major result of Warden Ragen's system, his control of the inmate economy.

11

The Inmate Economy

Introduction

THUS far, I have discussed power and control in three ways. First, we considered the overriding issue of the power to control the distribution of goods and services needed to keep the inmates fed, clothed, housed, and in good health. To accomplish this, Warden Ragen had to control the ecology of the prison, the hurdles of time and space. Second, we looked at the foundation of Warden Ragen's power, which resided in his control of the guards, and third, how he then used his guards to control the inmates. Now, let's add a new dimension: who got what, the control of the prison's economy. This area entailed a contest between the Warden and the inmates over control of finances, in its simples terms; the flow of U.S. currency and cigarettes.

This was the penultimate contest of power, for unless Warden Ragen controlled the economy, the inmates did. If they did, they could bribe his guards for better food, work assignments, cell partners, or freedom from punishment and any other restrictions. Furthermore, with the ability to pay off and reward other inmates, leaders and their gangs could exert their own economic power over the inmate society. In some prisons this is just what happens. The warden exerts so little control that the inmate economy resembles the market economy of a municipality. Kalinich (1980) describes such a prison, for which he even calculated demand and supply curves. Such a prison's inmate economy would bear no resemblance to the one at Warden Ragen's Stateville. The relationships of economics and power in the contest between Warden Ragen and the inmates for control are outlined in Figure 11.1, "The Inmate Economy."

This chart considers the inmate economy in three ways, labeled Parts 1, 2, and 3. The Warden's Official Economy is discussed in Part 1; the inmates' Underground Economy and its ties to the outside world are discussed in Part 2;

Figure 11.1
The Inmate Economy

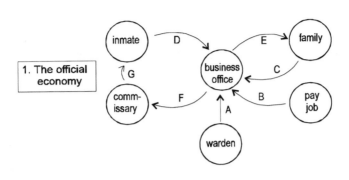

1. The official economy

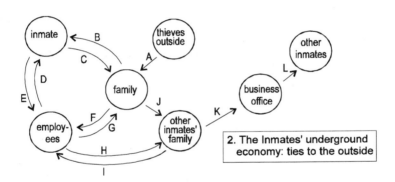

2. The Inmates' underground economy: ties to the outside

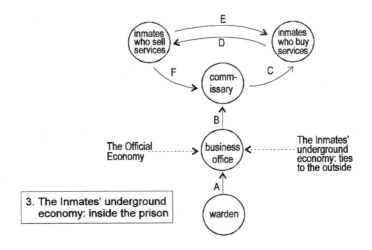

3. The Inmates' underground economy: inside the prison

and finally, the inmates' Underground Economy inside the walls as it was tied to the first two parts, is discussed in Part 3.

Each of these economies revolved about its own center, and was tied to the others. First, there was the Official Economy (Part 1) which the Warden recognized as the only legitimate one, where inmates bought supplies for themselves such as food, shaving lotion, and cigarettes. In this economy, the prison's business office was the central agency because it doled out money earned by inmates in pay jobs or deposited by their families.

The business office of the Official Economy intersected Part 2, the inmate Underground Economy on one edge where it was connected to the outside world. The central institution of this economy was the inmate's family and friends who controlled the transfer of inmate money outside the prison.

Finally, the inmates' Underground Economy as it existed inside the prison is shown in Part 3. This underground was tied to the first two (Parts 1 and 2) by the prison's business office, the conduit for money flow. The central institution of the internal economy was the inmates' commissary. Here the rewards of inmates who bought and sold services among themselves were translated into the goods of a barter economy: for example, cigarettes were smoked, but also used to pay debts. (I elaborate below.) Thus, whoever controlled the commissary dominated the Underground Economy. There was no contest in Stateville, for Warden Ragen did.

Part 1: The Official Economy

Figure 11.1 shows the businessoOffice, which was located at the prison's front end and was the focus of Part 1, the official economy. This office kept a running tally as the dollar accounts of each prisoner changed with deposits and withdrawals. The circle labelled "Warden" with its arrow to the business office (labelled "A"), represents the fact that the Warden decided what inmates could do with the money in their accounts. He decided, for example, that inmates could spend five dollars per week. Processes B and C indicate that the sources of this money were either pay jobs in the prison or money sent by family or friends. Not shown separately, but included in C, is a small money stream by which visitors could buy sundries, subscriptions, or typewriters at the officers' commissary at the prison's front end. While it is also not shown here, inmates could sell a pint of their blood to a blood bank every few months, I believe for $5.00 ($26 in 1995 dollars). My inmate sources thought that few inmates had much money sent in from *the street*, and only about one–fourth had pay jobs, from which they earned between 5 and 15 dollars a month ($26 to $77 in 1995 dollars). Probably the unequal distribution of income between inmates would have led to a inmate class structure even more extreme than Stateville actually had, if Warden Ragen had not controlled the economy.

Processes D and E, whereby an inmate could order the business office to send money from his account to his family was a minor cash flow. Because of the low wages in the prison industries, pay jobs could usually provide for only processes F and G, when inmates drew on their Business Office accounts for purchases at the commissary. Thus, the Warden's official economy provided a one-way street whereby money from the inmates' families or prison pay jobs were channeled to them as consumers. This official economy was the mainstay of the inmate economy at Stateville, because Warden Ragen had so effectively choked off the Underground Economy. As a prerequisite for his control, he eliminated U.S. currency from the prison. Today, drugs might be added to the U.S. currency of the earlier day.

Part 2. The Underground Economy

The Fatal Flaw: United States Currency

The lack of U.S. currency was a serious blow to the Underground Economy, for the norms of reciprocity, mutual support, and other social factors of the inmate subculture went only so far without cash. Currency was unparalleled as a bribe for guards, for everyone accepted it, and it was easy to hide. A perspective on the Ragen era provided by various sources, (such as the Chicago *Tribune*'s series in 1955), was buttressed by an older inmate, who remembered a previous generation when money circulated freely:

> There was quite a bit of money. They had regular poker games going; they had watchmen out there. They had chips on the table....There was quite a bit of money here. But I don't know too much. I've seen money on the table, I've heard of $12,000 [$140,000 in 1995 dollars] games, I've seen men with $100 [$1,200 in 1995 dollars] bills, I've seen guys bet horses, I've seen guys bet everything, baseball, everything, but I've never seen a large money exchange hands. I've seen as much as $1,000 [$11,700 in 1995 dollars] on cons.

The dollar amounts here may be exaggerated, for this inmate *fell* around 1933, and he is talking about a time long past. But in a world of open gambling, the cumulative winnings of successful gamblers who *took* large numbers of those less skillful, and then played off between themselves, could have given rise to these legendary card games.

Things began to change, probably around 1950 after Ragen had been re–employed as Warden for five or ten years. One inmate explained:

> At one time you used to be able to go to the commissary, lay your fucking cash on the counter and get your dollar–thirty or dollar–and–a–quarter for your dollar. Now you can't do that anymore, because nobody in the commissary will touch it. So that kills an *out* right there. All the old *screws* that used to be contacts and all that, they went by the wayside, and, ah, the *connections* of sending anything out and having it put on your books [credited to the inmate's account at the prison business office], that's pretty slim now because you just don't have the connections.

As inmates could no longer pay cash for goods in the commissary, as guards began to shy away from trafficking in it,[1] as it became too dangerous to *make a pass* to or from your wife in the visiting room, and as its possession ran the danger of referral to the Merit Staff, U.S. currency disappeared from the prison. And with it, much of the financial power disappeared among inmates. Cigarettes and other consumer items constituted the money of only a barter economy. With cash, an inmate could buy inmate services or bribe a guard; with cigarettes, he could only buy inmate services. True, he could bet on a ball game, pay for homosexual services, or trade, but in the end, the network of exchanges for any one pack of cigarettes went up in smoke. Even this could have been partially surmounted if there had been an operable system of credit, but there existed no power to enforce payment of debts, for Warden Ragen's control was too thorough. In fact, a successful entrepreneur who accumulated too many cigarettes was quite vulnerable, for a single *stool pigeon kite* to the *corner* [the captain of the guards] would immediately bring a shakedown of his cell or assignment, easy discovery (cigarettes are bulky), and a referral to the Merit Staff. When U.S. currency was available, storage was immeasurably easier. For example, inmate gardeners could *stash* large sums in tobacco cans buried in the flower beds.

This lack of currency and power meant that there was no money market, no inmate *bankers* to extend credit, and no inmate *insurance pools* to spread risks for heavy gambling. This in turn limited the marketplace, which would have provided opportunities for entrepreneurship, as well as circulation, accumulation, and redistribution of wealth. Only minor vestiges of an inmate economy that used-to-be survived in Warden Ragen's prison. The only financial power available to inmates was the limited surplus they could accumulate through purchases at the inmate commissary, supplemented by whatever they could steal from its inventory, (almost nothing, as you will see), or they could earn: perhaps a pack or so to wash another inmate's underwear, provide homosexual sex, or win bets.

TIES TO THE OUTSIDE WORLD

As Figure 11.1, Part 2, indicates, the center of the Underground Economy in its ties to the outside world was the family, or in some cases, friends. Process A, money provided by fellow *thieves* to his family, probably was a minimal cash flow, since it depended upon membership in some organized criminal activity, something beyond many of Stateville's inmates. Processes B and C, the smuggling of cash into or out of the prison via family or friends was also rare in Warden Ragen's Stateville. Before he tightened security, smuggling cash was relatively easy, for cooperative guards or contact visits did the trick. In Ragen's Stateville, a visitor—especially a woman—could still smuggle cash *stashed* in her underwear or even her vagina. I think searches of visitors were mainly capable of detecting large items such as revolvers. But to actually make the *pass* to an inmate via a handoff or a kiss was difficult because the inmate had to turn to the guard before and after the kiss, arms extended with hands and mouth open (tongue extended). Or sitting at the long visiting table—all visitors on one side, all inmates opposite on the other—with a low glass pane running the length of the room between them, and a guard watching from the end (as well as all the other inmates and their visitors present), the wife might try to throw it over the glass pane. But it was rarely done, as one inmate explained:

> Now if the guy wants to take a chance and make a pass in the visiting room and get it out that way, ah, he can still do it, but he's taking his own chance there, and, ah, if he goofed on that he might wind up with a blue shingle, lose his visiting privileges, and yeah, there's a lot of consequences that follow.

The "blue shingle" reference meant a reduction in grade, which could take as much as 27 months to overcome, and had many penalties. For example, an inmate would not have a hearing by the Parole Board.

But even if such a visiting room pass were successful, the inmate had to beat the shakedown before the visit (smuggling out) or after (smuggling in). The result was that Warden Ragen effectively choked off the flow of cash from family and friends. Smuggling did continue, of course: some passes were successful in the visiting room; inmates on the outside detail who left and re–entered the prison walls every day brought cash in from the farm where contact visits were allowed. But it was a trickle: the inmate inside the walls who went this route had to have a lot of connections he could trust (and pay off) and who themselves were willing to take a chance that had severe penalties for failure.

The modern warden has a choice between the humaneness of contact visits, where families sit together without barriers, and control of the flow of currency, not to mention drugs. But it is a delusion that today's warden can have both.

Smuggling with Civilians

Processes D and E, the smuggling between employees and inmates, was another matter, because hundreds of employees entered and left the prison every day. Warden Ragen had few volunteer civilians in Stateville; today's wardens may have numbers of them. Piercing the fog of Warden Ragen's overblown rhetoric, I have concluded his system actually worked on two levels. The first, a sort of "Don't ask, don't tell" applied to civilian employees. I have no evidence, but I am fairly certain that it existed and the Warden looked the other way. I have already illustrated it with my own office in Chapter 1, "The Accidental Observer."

I cannot be sure this practice was widespread, for I did not trust employees outside my office well enough to ask. But one inmate who was a skilled tailor and worked in the Warden's quarters told me that Mrs. Ragen, the Warden's wife, gave him cigarettes for sewing drapes. I believed him. I remember my clerks told me that one of the Protestant chaplains, a very kind and humble man, episodically smuggled letters out for his parishioners. Sometimes he was tripped up (attributed to stool pigeons' snitching) and lectured about it, but he persisted, and Warden Ragen tolerated it. Also, once a month when I gave out research questionnaires at the school to men on the current parole docket, I brought in a briefcase of candy and cigarettes for these inmates, and to pay off the inmate porters at the school. The guards on duty saw all this. Over the two years this went on, some guard or lieutenant or *snitch kite* must have informed the Warden, but I was never asked about it. In my six years employment I was never shook down, except perhaps the first day or so, nor were my co–workers, except one who was fired. His replacement was never searched.

Several things about these delinquencies are important: none of them involved *doing business*, that is bribery with U.S. currency; none of them involved stealing; and finally, none of them involved guards.

Warden Ragen effectively sealed off his Sally Port, the opening in the walls which was used to ship bulk cargo in and out of the prison. (I introduced the Sally Port in Chapter 3.) In many prisons this is a major route for smuggling bulky items. Compact contraband such as currency or heroin might be smuggled in by an individual visitor, but bulky contraband such as marijuana or a revolver might better be smuggled through the Sally Port with bulk cargo. There are many ways this could be done, but for criminals who have sufficient funds and organization, it is hard to stop. For example, at an outside wholesaler, factory sealed television sets or cartons of cereal could be unsealed, contraband inserted, resealed, and shrink wrapped as new. This may be why Warden Ragen dealt with wholesalers and suppliers he trusted.

Smuggling with Guards

If any employee, civilian or guard, were involved in stealing or *doing business*, or if a guard were involved with an inmate under any conditions, then Warden Ragen spared no effort in tracking him down. Guards smuggled for many reasons, and I expect some were psychological, such as the thrill of beating the system. But on a more ordinary level, in keeping with such paragons of virtue as businessmen, professors, or politicians, they did it because the way of the world is money, sex, and power, and guards were men like other men, a fact recognized by the thief who commented: "It takes money, but it can be done. There's an old saying, 'A hair [a woman] can move a mountain,' and a smart broad and money can do anything. Anything."

Sexual corruptions need not be straightforward lust, for the guard who humanely inquired of an inmate about his father's health might meet a sister, a situation which might lead to friendship as well as infatuation or liason. But once a guard crossed that emotional bridge, the Warden's control was breached. In the prison, knowledge of sexual corruption was an amalgam of secrecy and wishful thinking. I never really learned anything. The closest I came was when a sociologist who worked with me was fired or was pressured to resign: he told me he was disgusted with the Warden's lack of rehabilitation; one of my inmate clerks who was friendly with him thought it was involvement with a convict's wife; the Warden said nothing.

Probably the largest number of corruptions involved the manipulation of money and ego, something that required a shrewd judge of character, like one inmate who explained:

> You can't use no muscle on a guard, but Christ, they're people. If you had machines out there, I guess it wouldn't go, but you ain't. If you get a totalitarian system, I guess you can control it more. I guess Hitler had a bunch of people they done what he told them, and the Warden's got some like that too. But he ain't got them all, and that's your shot.

The guards were the main focus of subversion only because there were so many of them in close contact with inmates, but these remarks could also apply to civilian employees. And in those front offices where a few inmates worked with women civilians, romance might have played a role. (I never heard of homosexual affairs between guards and inmates.) The actual process of subverting a guard was a matter of intuition, shrewdness, and luck. My informant explained that the first step was to find a likely prospect among the guards:

> Some guys like to get a new guy, a *fish*. They figure he ain't had time to get into the system, and I seen it work sometimes. I don't like to work that way. I think it's better to wait for a guy who's been in the system a while, who can see it's all shit, who can see it's graft from top to bottom. The graft at the top takes off the cream. If you get a guy that's making $85 a week and it takes $85 a week to live, he's just existing. And if you get a guy that's a little disgruntled, maybe you can work him. If you spot a guy like that, he can't be a stoop; he's got to have some brains, even if he ain't a mental giant, and you start to butter him up.

Depending upon what the inmate wanted and who the *mark* was, seduction could take a multitude of forms: I remember I was approached to play the horses by having an inmate pick my bets, and promised a percentage of my winnings. I declined, but had I accepted, I would have been drawn into doing business with the inmate—and probably at the end, bringing in U.S. currency. At the other extreme, the inmate I am now quoting told me (and I believed him) how he had used gambling debts years before to get a guard at the Menard prison to bring in a hacksaw blade for an escape attempt. The approach to the *mark* must be a shrewd one. As my informant explained:

> Like I say, you just got to learn to figure these *rubes*. Some guys can be had for a bottle of whiskey or a few bucks, another guy may need a few hundred bucks. And the guy who takes a bottle of whiskey won't take a hundred bucks, he'll back off and run a mile: he'll get scared; he'll think you want the First National Bank. But he'll do things for a lousy couple of bucks. And if you soften a guy up, and then you put it to him, he backs off? Well, hell, that's happend, you shot craps, but what've you lost? A lousy few bucks, but that don't matter as long as you can get more.

These few examples of conniving do not exhaust the nearly infinite variations possible. Indeed, several of Warden Ragen's trusted subordinates had *the rap* for having dealt with inmates in bygone years when a substantial number of custodial officers *connived* with convicts, among them a few shrewd officers who dealt with a few trusted inmates. As Warden Ragen tightened control, some of these men were promoted to higher ranks in the custodial force, or to front office jobs, where they bore responsibility for important operations. Once the net of control began to tighten, these men progressively severed their connections with inmates to become Warden Ragen's trusted subordinates of unshakable probity.

By the time of my employment, the guard who trafficked with inmates took enormous risks, for the Warden rewarded inmates who entrapped them. Here, Warden Ragen's challenge was to sift accurate intelligence from exaggeration and lies, so it was important for his lieutenants to develop reliable informers. One inmate explained:

> Now if it gets a little loose, and it's hard for it not to become loose, and suppose it gets to some con who's administration; whoever's got him, it don't have to be the Warden. It can be a lieutenant, and this is a big thing for a lieutenant. And he'll [the con who's administration] buzz him [the lieutenant] and say '[Officer] so–and–so's doing business with [inmate] Smith,' and the lieutenant says, 'Do you think he'll [officer so–and–so] do business with you?'

Once the Warden decided to trap a guard, everything depended upon the ability of some inmate to gain that guard's confidence. Once this occured, the guard was ready to be *set up*. One common way was to persuade the guard that cash was a safe way of bribery. Then, since:

> Every guard can't wear his uniform off duty: he's got to change it in the basement. Consequently, they'll let this guy change his clothes and make all the transfers. He'll have a bill, usually a five dollar bill [$26 in 1995 dollars] and a letter—suppose he's a letter *route*, he'll have a marked bill and the letter. Now, the *screws* will be there. These lieutenants will be watching. You gotta realize that a shift comes off together and there's a lot of guys down there changing clothes, and it's not unusual for a few lieutenants to be down there. So they'll be watching him and when they see he's made the transfer, they'll go up to him and *put the arm on*: they'll ask him 'What've you got there?' and they'll take him up to the Warden's office and shake him down. Well, that's it.

Once the guard who was the *route* was *pinched* however, it was not possible to completely protect the identity of the inmate who did him in because the prison was a small world. My informant explained: "Well, supposing you and I are *doing business* [bribing] a guard and he gets it. Well, I know it's not me, so it's got to be you."

Or it might be that an inmate and a guard are *doing business* and that guard sought business advice from that inmate. My informant continued:

> Or maybe somebody [another inmate] might have propositioned you [the guard], and you asked me about him. [Gesture that "me" warned the guard not to.] But suppose you don't take my word, and you're money hungry or something. Well, when you get it, I put two and two together.

Even more difficult to prevent was knowledge that was handled by Stateville's ubiquitous inmate clerks, as my informant explained:

> In investigating, they've got to take a statement off that guy and some information has to go through a convict clerk's hands, and consequently, you've got to find out who set the man up.

While these typical processes are reasonably objective portrayals of what generally happened, they exude an erroneous aura of prescience. In reality, an unknown amount of ongoing bribery was undetected, and no one had precise information about who or how much. My opinion is that it amounted to very little, proportionate to the number of guards and inmates at the prison. But had there been any let down in Warden Ragen's vigilance, bribery would have ballooned.

My memory is that every year I would see a Merit Staff report on smuggling, such as one which detailed:

> Writing a letter which he typed on his typewriter to an ex–convict whose name is John Doe. The letter was addressed to John Doe, 999 North 99 Avenue, Chicago. This letter was information pertaining to drugs, also pertaining to information of people who were using and selling drugs. This inmate Smith admitted writing the letter and also he intended to get the letter out of the institution other than by the regular channel, which is through the Mail Office. He also admitted to writing John Doe previously, which had to be sent out of the institution through channels which were illegal, because the mail office doesn't have any record where Inmate Smith has ever written to a John Doe.

This was typical. Probably this inmate was unable to transact his business by personal visits; perhaps he had none, or he could not trust those who did. Nor do I know any details of his *route* for illegal letters, but the report suggests some guesses. Since no guard was mentioned, the inmate was likely caught before he made the *pass*. Once he was caught, handwriting could be checked because samples of each inmate's handwriting were in his record jacket. Or in using a typewriter, each convict was carefully controlled. Moreover, since the report indicates previous letters had gone out undetected, a guard was undoubtedly involved, and probably the inmate *burned* the guard, for his punishment was limited to a reduction to the lowest of conduct grades. Conspicuous by its absence was any revocation of statutory good time.

However, this discovery did not mean the guard was automatically accused. Warden Ragen would not move without evidence, as my informant explained:

> They can't just fire him. They know the convict's liable to be lying. The only thing to do is wait it out, even six months or a year. He [the guard] won't stop; they'll get a convict who's smart enough to get next to him and set him up.

Only the lone guard who stole by himself could be difficult to detect, if he were prudent. For example, my clerks told me about an industrial foreman of 20 years service who was fired when the Warden discovered he had been pilfering from his inventory (stored outside the walls) for an undetermined period. Less discrete theft by more than one guard was more quickly detected. One case involved a bolder theft where some guards once stole quantities of scrap metal from an outside storage shed.

These examples illustrate the myriad ways in which inmates and guards in steps D and E cooperated to *beat* the Warden, and how guards (with an anonymous *drop* such as a post office box) could *do business* with an inmate's family (steps F and G), or by extension, in steps H, I, and J with other inmates' families. Once money moved around in these steps, it was easy for the families involved to recycle the funds back into the prison's Official Economy (steps K and L) by sending them to the prison's business office for the inmate's account. These last three steps were also the way in which inmates extorted or swindled other inmates, by having their victims instruct their families to forward money.

Part 3:The Underground Economy

Inside the Walls

Now let's consider Part 3 of Figure 11.1, which is relatively simple to diagram. After step A, the Warden's control of the inmate's account on deposit in the business office, Step B shows the amount released to the inmate's commissary account, and then comes step C, the purchase of goods by inmates. Steps D, E and F are really abstractions because the inmates who bought or sold services were often the same person: the *gallery boy* who delivered papers in the cellhouse might charge to deliver *kites* slid inside the papers or magazines he delivered, and he in turn might tip his inmate barber.

This analysis of the three parts of the inmate economy make it clear that Part II, the Underground Economy Tied To The Outside World was a minor factor in Warden Ragen's Stateville. It was limited to the most mundane goods and services. Were this not so, the inmate economy in general would have been impossible for him to control.

We also see that both in Part 1 and Part 2, the crucial financial intermediary was the inmates' commissary, which was the source of cigarettes and sundries, the barter money of the system. This arrangement impacted the entire world in the prison, including the inmate subculture. Thus, Warden Ragen suppressed the inmate subculture because he controlled the inmate economy, and this in turn was based upon his control of the inmate commissary.

This sounds easy, but it wasn't. It took him years to accomplish, and in the end it was one of the pillars of his control, his ability to run a prison while suppressing inmate leaders and violence. It is important to understand how he controlled the commissary and how difficult it was.

The Commissary

In Stateville's barter economy, the commissary was the central financial institution, as it would be in any modern prison. Lest anyone think an ordinary warden today could control its operation, I analyze it in detail in Appendices 11.A and 11.B. This detail explains how the inmates controlled one another, and assisted Warden Ragen's operation. But first the operation must be outlined.

Warden Ragen used the commissary to control the prisoners, buttress his budget, and dispense largesse to outside businesses. The availability of commissary goods certainly motivated the inmates to earn money in Stateville's factories, which in turn motivated them to obey his rules in order to be permitted to spend their money. Befitting its importance, Warden Ragen made the commissary one of the best jobs in the prison. Inmate employees were paid $12.00 ($60 in 1995 dollars) per month, a daily pack of cigarettes, all they could eat, a quart of milk delivered to their cell every night, and two pints of ice cream and a pie in their cell every Sunday.

The commissary also provided Warden Ragen with large profits for purchases and for financing programs. Knowledgeable inmates claimed that most purchases were with favored suppliers, and most funds passed through favored local banks. But the Warden controlled this expenditure efficiently and prudently, the result of tightening up the prison operation over decades. In the past it was a much looser operation with much less accountability of funds. Sometime in this past, inmates nearly managed to embarrass him publically over his management, but these earlier events lived only in the memory of some inmates.

Inside the prison, these funds bankrolled pay jobs for the inmates assigned to the commissary. It funded inmate clerks to a captain of the guards and the Veterans Affairs office. The funds also enabled him to expand programs in athletics, the academic and vocational schools, the library, the band, the prison radio, religious programs (for approved religions), holiday celebrations, and some postage costs.

However, the commissary as a cash cow was secondary to control. Until 1962 inmates were allowed to purchase $5.00 ($26 in 1995 dollars) per week, but Ragen exempted extensive lists of luxuries from this limit, allowing inmates with funds to spend large sums. The commissary sold a multitude of sundries: canned chicken and cranberry sauce in food; wind–up shavers and wristwatches in appliances; tweezers and talcum powder in toiletries; undershirts and footwear in clothing. Then in 1962, Warden Pate changed the regulations so the limit was $6.00 ($30 in 1995 dollars) per week, but virtually nothing was exempt from this limit: inmate spending plummeted. The consequences were bankruptcy and devaluation in the inmate economy as the money supply contracted. Now, nearly all goods were consumed by their purchasers, leaving little for barter. Also, trade such as pay-offs to the inmate barbers by their customers was drastically reduced. The *ante* in gambling dropped as inmates bet fewer packs of cigarettes on sports.

Control of the commissary took years to develop. Up until the late 1940's stealing was widespread. The inmates pilfered goods and distributed them to their friends, as did some guards. Then the same thing happened in the commissary that inmates told me happened in many other assignments, such as the Detention

Hospital, which enabled Warden Ragen to take over. A trustworthy, intelligent inmate who was devoted to the Warden's interests was put in the commissary. I assume this inmate was rewarded by the Warden, but this was lost in legend. This inmate learned its operation and the organization of *the steal*. Then he and Warden Ragen began to organize the structure of control that was in operation by the time of my employ, and allowed one vigilant guard to oversee a tightly controlled operation. Warden Ragen needed an inmate to lead him to control, but it was his vigilant guard force which maintained it. As one inmate explained to me:

> There ain't much stealing going on now. A few years ago I couldn't say that, but now it's sewed up pretty tight. You get an operation doing about five, 6,000 dollars a week and maybe 15 or 20 dollars short, you know there ain't much stolen. He [the officer in charge] gets more than that short, he gets mad, he gets hot and he begins looking, and he'll find somebody to blame. I guess it's a hot place. I don't do much anymore. All we get now is 12 dollars a month and seven packs of cigarettes a week; anything else I want, I buy. Oh, I'll eat a candy bar or drink a can of pop, but I eat it right out in front of him; I don't sneak it. He keeps a close watch on things. He's sitting right there. If he's looking, he'll watch what a guy gets [an inmate purchasing at the commissary], especially a small order. He can see exactly what's on the counter. After the slip is in, he'll look at it. If it don't match, he'll call the cellhouse and have him *shook down* when he gets there. There's a lot of guys they get in there, they see all that stuff, they don't realize they gotta figure just what they can do and what they can't do. I think he's [the officer in charge] bucking for a lieutenant's job, and I think he'll get it.

By now, I think you can understand what kind of vigilant and aggressive officers made good lieutenants, the basis of Warden Ragen's control.

Control: The Final Turn of the Screw

The situation we have described existed until 1962. When Warden Pate decreased allowable spending, it became even easier for the guard at the commissary to scan the slips as they came through; also, with fewer items passing across the counter, the guard could more easily control what was happening. The decrease in spending limits must have decreased the *steal* to nearly zero.

The new limits strangled the inmate economy, as one inmate explained to me:

> You'd be surprised how the joint's changed since 1957. The food's better. In the barbershop, let's see, there's I guess 60 barbers. I bet there's no more than five of them smoking tailor mades [factory manufactured cigarettes]. It wasn't like that then. Maybe it's a different type of con coming in. The guys on pay jobs don't pay off like they used to. There's still a lot of guys in the barber shop are *pack hungry*, but they don't get it. There's still some old–timers' *lay out*, but it's changed.

It is interesting that my informant speculated about "a different type of con," suggesting that the belief in an earlier "golden age" of prisoners is a myth among inmates as well as among those corrections administrators who claim "a different type of con" is the blame for their inability to control prisons nowadays. But in the next sentence, my informant explained the truth in the details:

> I think it's mostly the commissary limit. It used to be a five dollar limit with exempted items, now it's six bucks with nothing exempt. I remember I used to spend 13, 14 bucks a week: I'd buy shrimp cocktail and lots of food. Now I can't do that. I went to commissary today, I bought eight packs [of cigarettes], [instant] coffee—that's off the top every time—a can of Bugler [loose tobacco to roll cigarettes by hand] if guys want to borrow, a half-dozen sweet rolls for tonight. My cell partners go Friday. Then soap and hair oil. I *score* for shampoo on the job. That's six bucks. I got nothing to trade off. I use it myself.

The reverberations of the commissary change were felt throughout the prison. For example, prior to this tightening, the inmate softball teams would bet player–to–player (for example, shortstop–against–shortstop), with perhaps two to three hundred packs of cigarettes changing hands among the players; add to this bets made by spectators, and over 500 packs probably changed hands. With the tightening of the commissary limits this was reduced to less than 200 packs. Moreover, small entepreneurs, such as the inmate who normally charged one pack to shine a pair of shoes, would either have to lower prices to a few cigarettes or go out of business. Over and over this rippled through: the money supply tightened, and Warden Pate created a depression, with devaluation and bankruptcy throughout the inmate barter economy. Changing the commisary rule probably had further consequences for the inmate subculture. In that case, norms such as reciprocity had to be based more on social, and less on economic considerations. For example, prisoners could no longer pay a pack of cigarettes to an inmate barber for extra attention to a haircut. The extra attention would have to come, if at all, because the two convicts liked one another.

Endnotes

1. Some quit, but others who later attained high positions under Warden Ragen began playing it safe by trafficking with only a few inmates they trusted.

APPENDIX 11.A
DETAILS OF CONTROL

Introduction

Here I include some micro–detail of how Warden Ragen controlled the commissary. This will provide you with an example of the myriad interlocking controls by which he controlled other assignments. It may also arm you against believing those who may claim there is an easy way to control complex prison operations. Especially if you remember that the system I describe took Warden Ragen years—perhaps a decade—to develop.

To understand the web of control in the commissary we need two perspectives: first, the inmates who purchased at the commissary, and second, how the assignment was administered. Following these extended descriptions in Appendix 11.A is a brief estimate of how much inmates actually were able to steal from the commissary.

Control Orbit One: The Inmates

All inmates in the prison filed through the commissary once a week, locked into the "bath–shave–commissary" schedule whereby they took a shower, got a shave or haircut, and finally, shopped at the commissary. My informants estimated that little more than half the prisoners made a purchase in any week. Those who did were enmeshed in elaborate controls to ensure that they spent only their own money and did not overdraw their accounts.

The first step began in the cellhouse. There, an inmate clerk entered on a commissary slip, a white sheet 5.5" by 8.5", printed on one side, the date, the inmate's prison number, name, cellhouse and cell number. The inmate who was trading was fingerprinted, recording his thumbprint on the back. He then listed the items he wished to purchase. Now, the initial use of the commissary slip was effectively limited to him. Although one inmate might still coerce another into purchasing an item, it prevented one man from picking up another's commissary slip from the cellhouse commissary clerk.

On schedule, guards called out the commissary line, but every man who was going to *make commissary* knew the exact day and hour long in advance, and on assignment had begun to *mark time*. First the group went to the shower room where they disrobed and showered, and thus limited the amount of contraband they could carry for their next stop, the barber shop, which was a contraband switching point. Finally, they entered the commissary. They were in a rectangular room with wire cages at either end; the smaller one by the entrance door enclosed clerks, the larger one to the rear enclosed the inventory storage area and an eating area for the inmates who worked at the commissary. Athwart this was the long sales counter observed by a guard whose desk was midway along its length. In back of the counter were the clerks who dispensed the merchandise; and in back of each counter clerk were shelves of merchandise he was responsible for.

Inmates who purchased went through a series of controls. Each man first went to the desk at the commissary entrance where an inmate clerk entered his day's trading number on his commissary slip, tying him to that day's sequence. Then he walked across to the guard who checked the control card that listed the balance in his account. The guard entered the inmate's total on the commissary slip, signed it, and had him put a second thumbprint on the back of his slip, next to his first. This placed two further controls on the inmate: first he had an upper limit set on the amount of money he could spend, and second, the fingerprints prevented him from giving away (or having taken) his commissary slip.

Then our inmate walked to the counter and shopped. It would often be crowded, two or three deep, and noisy. A counter clerk gave him the merchandise and entered the merchandise item (if the inmate who was trading had not already done so) and price on the commissary slip, totalled the bill, and stamped the slip with his own identification number. Finally, the inmate signed his slip, acknowledging the goods received. It was virtually impossible for the inmate who was trading to cheat the commissary on his own. After completing his purchases, the customer placed them in a paper sack and got back in line. Purchasing was rarely leisurely, since it was controlled by the need to wait on about 1,500 men a week. (That half of the inmates who traded in any given week.) These men came in on lines which had to be rapidly cleared out and sent back to the cellhouse. When a line finished trading and was re–counted by a guard, the men were walked back to their cellhouse, and filed up the stairs to their cells. Guards did not go with them. Each group consisted of men who worked and celled nearby, so the guards could see they all went to the same bank of cells. However, the guards could not see who actually went in which cell, so the inmates had chances to switch cells and escape surveillance. But their time was limited, for they would either have time just to leave their purchases and drop out for another line for somewhere else, or they would have a short time to *lay in* before they had to fall out for recreation or *chow*.

Could the inmates steal from the Warden or from each other? The counter clerk could elude control only if he could change a commissary slip. One inmate explained one such attempt. He had purchased seven items at the commissary, including a bottle of ketchup. After he walked away with his purchases, the counter clerk erased the ketchup notation and wrote in a pack of cigarettes in its place:

> I lost my commissary for a year, [but] I had it [returned] since last December. I was in the commissary and I had seven articles on my slip, which was ketchup, and the clerk he erased that from where I had it down there on the slip and everything was right, and he put a pack of cigarettes on there. He put "pack" so he could put some in his pocket.

When I asked him to explain, the sequence became clear:

> He give me everything on there. I had seven articles on that commissary slip and he give me everything I had down there, and after I left, he erased that and put cigarettes on that.

What happened was the guard became suspicious, so:

> After I walked away from the counter, Mr. Smith [the guard] he called me over and say, "Let me see what you got in there." So he opened my sack and he looked. He find everything I order, all those seven items, but he asked me I had ketchup, where was the cigarettes...I told him I didn't have no cigarettes...I got over to the captain's office, I told them everything, just how it happened, but they take away my commissary for a year...The clerk he got some days in the hole and he was purged.

At the point he received his order, if the inmate who traded wished to have a record of his purchases he had to make his own, since the counter clerk kept the slip. Under the rushed conditions of purchase, few customers made a record, which enabled the counter clerk to falsify the commissary slip. For example, if a bill actually came to $4.67, a false charge entered after the customer left of 30 cents for candy never purchased could be entered and the total bill raised to $4.97. This kind of *steal* enabled counter clerks to make up for what they stole for themselves or their friends, or to make up for the occasional customer who had managed to cheat them.

This system worked effectively for the overwhelming majority, since those few who did *beat* the system were usually close friends of men assigned to the commissary, or the few successful *thieves* in the prison who always had hangers–on who were looking to do things for them. As one informant explained it:

> About two–thirds of the men in here can't ever beat the system...If they want an extra pack of cigarettes, they got to either swap non–exempt food or buy extra exempt items and swap. These guys usually can't beat the system anyplace in here...About all the rest can occasionally get a little bit, and there's a few can get what they want, when they want it.

To beat the system, the inmate had to steal from the counter clerk by *palming* items on the counter (very rare), or he had to get the counter clerk to cooperate by giving out commissary items not on the commissary slip. This made the counter clerk job harried and nerve–wracked, for every day dozens of inmates who gathered at his counter badgered him to cheat for them, and skewered him with curses and insults when he refused. The counter clerk needed the help of the chief clerk and the inventory (or stock) clerk, if he was to cover up anything stolen.

The customer was effectively tied to a single commissary slip by name and number, signature and thumbprint. He could extort from, or provide services (homosexual, or gambling, for example) to other inmates, but Warden Ragen's controls made this risky business.

It is clear that it was virtually impossible for customers to beat the system unless they were given merchandise by the counter clerk, and the guard was not suspicious. But if the guard inspected the paper sack and compared it with the commissary slip, it was all over. The penalty for failure was severe, especially for the counter clerk. The inmate would typically lose his trading privileges for six months. But the counter clerk went to isolation, lost his job, and might be referred to the Merit Staff.

A counter clerk who cheated could *cover up* by claiming he ate an edible item, but this was limited by his stomach. His only other option was to cheat his customers, which required the cooperation of the chief and inventory clerks.

Control Orbit Two: Operation of the Assignment

Consider next the second orbit, the administration of the commissary. The outline of the administrative routine in Figure 11.2 set its limits.

After the inmate who traded surrendered his commissary slip, the counter

Figure 11.2
The Commissary: Flow of Administative Controls

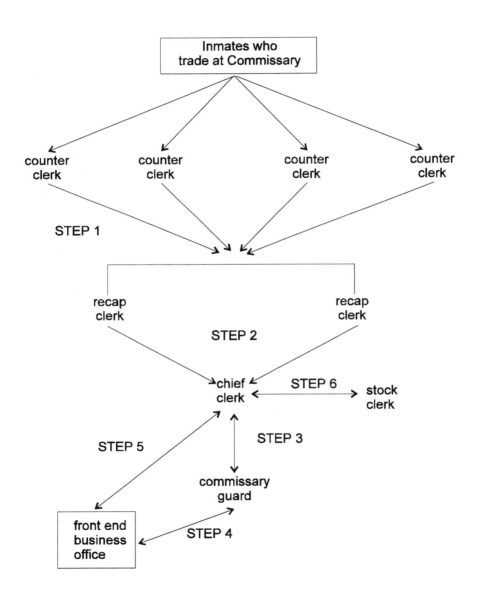

clerk had only a short time to cheat by changing it; all the while he was being hassled by other customers. The slips piled up until one of the two recap clerks picked them up, as shown in Step 1 of Figure 11.2. These men acted as controls on the counter clerks, for they had price sheets for every item sold, against which each commissary slip was checked, item by item, price by price, and then totalled.

Next, in Step 2 of Figure 11.2, the recap clerks brought their slips to the chief clerk who maintained a ledger with an account for every inmate who traded; he entered the total entered on the slip against the customer's account balance, and in Step 3, sent the slip to the inmate who was the assistant to the guard in charge of the commissary. Here, another ledger (in the form of cards) was kept with an account for every inmate who traded. The total shown on his commissary slip was subtracted from the total balance on the guard's books. The guard then stored the slip itself, and (as in Step 4) sent a report for every inmate to the prison's business office listing how much each spent at the commissary that day. After these four steps, there were two additional checks. In Step 5, the books in the business office had to correspond with those in the commissary itself.

The final check involves Step 6 and the stock clerk: what happened if the wrong items, prices, or totals were entered on the commissary slip? If, for example, the customer was really given a 25 cent package of cigarettes instead of the ten cent comb that was entered on the commissary slip? If his actual bill of $5.00 was mis–added to $4.00? (Or vice–versa.) Depending on how it was done, either the prison or the inmate customer would be cheated.

Of the two, the prison was rarely cheated, because of the risk. Figure 11.2 illustrates that the entire pyramid of control had to be climbed to accomplish this. It rarely happened, for the counter clerk, the recap clerk, and the chief clerk all had to cooperate to approve the fraudulent entries on the commissary slip. But even so, if the guard in charge noticed something amiss they all knew they would be before a captain with a Merit Staff referral in the offing.

The stock clerk constituted a final and independent hurdle, for he was the only one with physical access to the locked storage area which contained the stock. He took a physical inventory of each counter clerk's stock every week, and he had to agree to go along in order to readjust any shortfall in the inventory. But if he did this, he had to make up the readjustment out of the inventory for which he was responsible. The only way he could do this was to call it "breakage" or "shrinkage" or have the chief clerk juggle his books so the business office did not learn of it.

I think you can see that the administrative linkages pyramided the counter clerks to the recap clerks to the stock clerk to the chief clerk. No one could steal from the prison without the chief clerk's okay, but if he gave it, he put himself in the vulnerable position of being caught for the actions of any of a dozen men. That didn't happen.

A final way to *cover* the *steal* from the prison was "spoilage." For example, at the end of the week, the chief clerk and the stock clerk divided up such perishables as cake, pies, and pastries, and sent them to the cellhouse commissary clerks who then could eat, give away, or sell what they got. Some stealing from the prison could be covered this way.

What really happened was that the Warden was rarely cheated, but inmates who traded at the commissary were. In fairness, the amount of the *steal* was relatively small, the gains going to the pockets of the inmates who worked in the commissary, under the direction of the chief clerk.

The Steal

These details of how the commissary workers cheated other inmates relate to the earlier system where each inmate was allowed to spend $5.00 per week on non–exempt items (cigarettes and basic foodstuffs) with no limit on exempt items (candy, watches, and other luxuries). This system was severely impacted in 1962 when Warden Pate bankrupted the inmate economy.

The *steal* was run by the chief clerk. His first option was to watch for men who spent large sums, so he could deduct a few cents or even an extra dollar each week the man traded. Naturally, this could be dangerous, and each man was judged individually. There were few *big spenders*, but neither did they watch their pennies closely. A second option for the chief clerk was to raise commissary prices on popular items (except cigarettes, where it would have been immediately noticed) a penny or so until he had accumulated enough to cover the loss and the ledger accounts balanced. The third way to cover the *steal* was to short–weight the packages of prepared meat which the commissary inmates sliced and packaged for sale.

With so complex a set of controls, was it possible for the inmates assigned to the commissary to steal much? I have made an estimate of the maximum that could have been stolen from Warden Ragen's accounts under the guise of shrinkage, spoilage, or food eaten by inmates. I was unable to estimate how much was stolen from other inmates by falsification, juggling prices, and short–weight, but my guess is that it was only a little more than the Warden lost.

As I have detailed in Appendix 11.B, the maximum possible loss to Warden Ragen was about $16,000 ($82,000 in 1995 dollars), or about four percent of his $400,000 ($2 million in 1995 dollars) in annual sales. These approximations are based on commissary pricing sheets and the 1955–56 audit of the commissary profit and loss statement by a Chicago firm of certified public accountants. My personal guess is that the actual loss was perhaps one or two thousand dollars ($5,000 to $10,000 in 1995 dollars).

The same documents enabled me to estimate that the Warden cleared $64,000 ($330,000 in 1995 dollars), or a 16 percent net profit from this $400,000 ($2 million in 1995 dollars) gross sales. He obtained this astonishing net profit margin by marking up his merchandise almost as much as a supermarket, but using his power as a monopolist, he paid his inmate help almost nothing in wages. I have already outlined all the budgetary and political benefits he got from this money, so you would think he would leave well enough alone. But it was not to be. In 1962, Warden Pate put sharp brakes on profitability. I do not know his motives, but as I have explained, one consequence was to bankrupt the underground economy.

APPENDIX 11.B
THE WARDEN'S PROFITS AND THE INMATES' STEAL

A certified public accountant (CPA) firm's audit showed 1955–56 inmate commissary sales (rounded to thousands) of $253,000 at Stateville, $97,000 at Joliet, and $17,000 at the farm, for a total of $367,000 ($2.1 million in 1995 dollars). The equivalent total for 1954–55 was $330,000 and $323,000 for 1953-54.

In addition, friends and family visiting inmates purchased magazine and newspaper subscriptions, typewriters, as well as sundries for them at the officers commissary located in the administration building. These 1955-56 total sales were $86,000 ($480,000 in 1995 dollars) at Stateville and Joliet combined, but I had no way to partition this into sales to guards and sales to inmates. Since there were no transfers shown in the CPA audit from the officer's commissary to the "inmate benefit fund," I assume Warden Ragen kept all profits in the "officer's fund," which showed a balance of $42,000 ($235,000 in 1995 dollars), and which he controlled. To put all this together, I estimate that inmate sales (including those at the officers commissary) were conservatively, $400,000 in 1960 ($2.1 million in 1995 dollars).

What are we to make of these figures? I compared them with the amounts in the 1960 annual report of the Hyde Park Co-op, a consumer owned Rochedale Co-operative in Chicago. This supermarket (the annual report claimed it was the largest in Chicago) had 85 employees and sales of $3,605,489 ($19 million in 1995 dollars). Thus, Warden Ragen ran a grocery store in his prison which was one-tenth the operation of a very large one in the civilian economy.

But the civilian economy could only dream of Warden Ragen's profits. The CPA audit shows Joliet–Stateville inmate commissaries had a 16.74 percent gross profit of sales. (Stateville's gross margin was 16.10 percent.) This gross profit margin was less than the Hyde Park Co-op's 19.96 percent.

But here, the prison and the civilian economies part company. The Hyde Park Co-op's 19.96 percent gross profit was reduced 18.90 points by wages, taxes, and other expenses to 1.05 percent; thus, the net profit for the Co-op on $3,605,489 in sales was 1.05 percent, or $37,858 ($195,000 in 1995 dollars). In comparison, Warden Ragen's 16.74 percent gross profit was reduced a mere 1.04 points by wages and other expenses, so his net profit on $400,000 in sales was 15.70 percent, or about $63,000 ($325,000 in 1995 dollars). In effect, although his gross sales were one-tenth the civilian economy's, his net profit in dollars was nearly double.

These figures enable us to make some educated guesses about the size of the *steal* in the prison commissary. I think I can use the Co-op's gross profit margin of 19.96 percent as a theoretical upper limit. The CPA audit of the prison commissaries showed a gross profit margin of 16.10 for Stateville and 16.74 percent for all branches; the discrepancy between the Co-op and the prison margins was less than four percent. My guess is this equals the maximum possible size of the *steal* from Warden Ragen. (four percent of $400,000 equals $16,000.) My judgement is that it was really no more than one or two thousand dollars.

I am convinced that the numbers in the CPA audit were realistic because it corresponded to the actual invoices of the inmate commissary in the late 1950's. For example, cigarettes which wholesaled for 20.2 cents per pack, retailed for 24 cents, a gross profit on the sales price of 15.8 percent; those which wholesaled for 21.2 cents, retailed for 25 cents. Cigarettes were the highest volume item; candy was next, and had a higher but more variable markup. For example, a low margin was Nestle chocolate which had a 17.4 percent gross profit on sale price, while a more typical one was Hershey's chocolates which returned 31.8 percent. Generally, candy returned a gross margin of more than 30 percent.

12

Conclusion: Where Do We Go from Here?

Introduction

THE era of Warden Joseph E. Ragen is over, never to be resurrected. Much of this is because times have changed. The constitutional rights of convicts have won protection from Supreme Court decisions, and guards have unionized. Neither rights can be cavalierly squashed. But Ragen's brand of control also stems from the right man meeting the right time, which so rarely coincide. Ragen's genius combined with the opportunities he seized are rare combinations. Ragen's genius was his own, but Roger Touhy's prison escape and the pressure on Illinois politicians to get his *frame-up* off the front pages was a rare opportunity. All this was unique. Can we use any of this history to control prisons today?

Imposing a system of close control in a prison will take years. I estimate it took Warden Ragen close to a decade to achieve control of Stateville, after he was re-employed as Warden in 1942. And it will be difficult. Adding to the objective difficulties will be a mindset, particularly among academics, that links beliefs and language. In effect, if you state what has to be done, you know how to do it. An interesting example of this mentality is McConville (1989) in a review of DiIulio's work. In a condescending tone, McConville accurately summarizes DiIulio:

> Effective administration is set out in terms that officials in Victorian England [would] have recognized instantly: DiIulio calls it the "control model." Its components are familiar—a paramilitary staff structure, some *esprit de corps*, an active, perambulatory and personable leader, and a set of unambiguous rules which are strictly enforced. Control is firmly in the hands of the prison management. (p.201)

His first sentence tells us that close control was the ordinary stuff of Victorian prisons; his second sentence begins, "Its components are familiar"— which tells us that we knew about it long before DiIulio. But no one has ever presented evidence that Victorian British governors (that is, wardens) really controlled their prisons as Joseph Ragen controlled Stateville. With regard to his second point, that we have long known how to control prisons—it is too bad the leaders of American penology were never told. After all, the conventional wisdom of American academics for more than a generation after World War II was that close control was impossible. I have elaborated on this in my discussion of Sykes and other sociologists in Chapter 8. The rest of McConville's paragraph is similar to summaries by DiIulio or Useem. All imply that achieving these aims is a straightforward task. It is anything but. I will discuss why it may be a difficult and lengthy process, by no means guaranteed of success.

To learn from Warden Ragen's accomplishment, we will consider several topics. After "Inside Warden Ragen's Stateville," which summarizes how his system actually functioned, "Prisons Of The Future" considers what relevance that massive prison — 3,500 inmates — of 40 years ago has for maximum security prisons now and tomorrow. It has a lot. I will argue that massive institutions are almost certainly in the cards as the American taxpayer continues to insist on imprisonment as a solution to social ills. But taxpayers are now beginning to shrink from the astronomical costs of imprisonment, and future prisons will resemble Stateville in their massive size, and in the taxpayers' emphasis on running them as cheaply as possible.

The following section, "The American Correctional Association," looks for guidance from professionals who work in the field of corrections. Here, we survey the publications of an occupational association dominated by the nation's wardens and upper-level correctional administrators. Like any occupational group, it is an interest group which mingles self-interest with genuine competence and service to society.[1]

Next, we look at "The Judiciary and Prison Control," to discuss the parameters set on prisons by the courts, particularly the federal courts and the U.S. Supreme Court. Then, in light of these strictures, we turn to what lessons we may learn from Warden Ragen's system directly. In "The Prison Operation" I will apply Warden Ragen's methods to the internal operation of the maximum security prison.

Finally, in "The Social Context of Imposing Control," I will discuss what questions have to be considered if politicians are to accept the compromises and power shifts that are necessary for modern wardens to control penitentiaries. Any solution must take place in the maelstrom of practical politics. This may not sit well with those who pursue the goal of "professionalization" which ascends to the heights of rationalism and science. My suggestions exist in a pragmatic world where politicians sometimes grovel for money, pander for votes, and compromise abstract ideals to strike deals. This money and vote grubbing devolves to the conflicts and compromises between interest groups: the haves and have-nots of society, those of racial and ethnic politics, the demands of labor unions for guards, of business interests in the profits from bond issues and contracts, and between liberal and conservative ideologues. All of these interest groups are focussed to pressure the legislature, the governor and the judiciary. To begin our discussion, we will first outline Warden Ragen's system of control.

Inside Warden Ragen's Stateville

Warden Ragen's control basically flowed from his power in the world of Illinois politics. This gave him the leverage to create the harsh but effective system which controlled the internal world of the Stateville Penitentiary.

The external factors of his political standing enabled him to attain his longevity in office, and to develop his status as an effective warden, something recounted in Chapter 2. He used his political standing to fight his enemies, the political liberals, both in the Democratic Party and in the field of corrections. He was also the beneficiary of the penal law of the time. For example, Illinois imposed indeterminate sentences, with inmates incarcerated under sentences such as a one year minimum and a ten year maximum, so the inmate was faced with nine years of his life held hostage to the Parole Board and, if parole were refused, almost four years to the accumulation of good time. Warden Ragen was the gatekeeper to those benefits.

Playing these cards, Ragen perfected his system of control during the decade after his re-employment as Stateville Warden in 1942. Not only was his system effective, but it was publicized and puffed up by conservative newspaper publishers and their reporters.

All of this allowed him the power to pick and train his proteges as deputy wardens, captains, and lieutenants. They became his alter ego in browbeating and welding into a disciplined force the working class young men who were hired as guards. The basis of his control was punishment: whenever a mistake occurred, a guard was punished, usually, through suspension for some number of hours or days without pay. With Warden Ragen's praetorian guard of lieutenants ceaselessly prowling the prison, the slightest oversight could lead to punishment. The constant turnover this entailed did not deter the Warden because the hardscrabble counties of southern Illinois constantly replenished his supply of poor young men. Since guards were expendable, they developed alliances with few inmates and violated relatively few of Warden Ragen's more important rules.

This ever vigilant guard force controlled the inmates the same way: with punishment. Beginning with minor penalties such as loss of an hour's recreation, this punishment escalated to isolation and segregation placements, and if necessary to loss of good time, the time deducted from prison sentences for "good behavior." It meant that inmate leaders were suppressed because Warden Ragen's intelligence about the prison was so efficient and his punishments so draconian that few inmates would follow a leader. When Warden Ragen managed to wrest control of an assignment from inmates, he had a guard force who kept it that way. Ragen used renegade inmates who betrayed their fellows (I am sure he rewarded them) to gain control of crucial assignments. Thus, for example, over the years Warden Ragen managed to find inmates who taught him how the inmate commissary was run by the inmates, and helped him develop a system of control; then his ever vigilant guard force kept inmate leaders from working their way back. One assignment at a time, over the years, Warden Ragen took over.

When necessary his control rested on physical violence, as it does in any maximum security prison. Paradoxically, there was little overt violence in Stateville because Warden Ragen had the prison so firmly in his grasp. In his own way, he created a moral community, accepted as such by the guards and inmates, much as both chafed under his yoke. Dominance in any maximum security prison rests either with the warden, or it devolves downward to fiefdoms of guards and inmates; and this dominance is based upon face-to-face physical violence—either the warden controls it or inmates and guards do. In a prison, this is as natural a force as gravity. Generally, in Stateville inmates were beaten only for hitting a guard, and even then only by lieutenants. Exceptions to this were rare. Moreover, the close control dried up the supply of knives so that fights between inmates were fist-fights, or on occasion, with weapons of opportunity seized of whatever was handy. Similarly, rape and assault were minimized.

The social justice of his regime inhered in one fact: that he, the warden, acting for the wider society, really controlled the prison. Moreover, that close and just control assured the correctional staff they were safe from danger and in charge of the convicts. Finally, it diminished the everyday fear for the average convict of being knifed, raped, beaten, bullied, extorted or demeaned, while eating bad food among roaches and filth. This was so because his convicts were safe from guards who might take a dislike to them and harass them, or get inmate thugs to do it. They were safe from inmate predators. The only thing both guards and inmates were not safe from was Warden Ragen's merciless control. Thus it was that Stateville under Warden Ragen was, in the terms of a maximum security prison, a moral universe. Both guards and inmates groaned under their yoke, but they knew the rules, and they knew these were Warden Ragen's rules.

In the end, Warden Ragen was toppled by political forces. First he was elevated. In 1961 a newly elected liberal Democratic Governor Otto Kerner named him Director of Public Safety. Then after re-election in 1965, Governor Kerner eased him out. Jacobs suggests (1977:54) that Ragen may have suffered a mental breakdown. A liberal political movement took over the prison system and Warden Ragen's era became a memory.

Prisons of the Future

In the past two decades the American people poured much of the nation's treasure into prisons, so that now over one million men (and some women) are in penitentiaries and a half-million are in local jails. They are watched over by about half a million guards, plus numbers of supervisors and civilian employees. I expect it will continue. In my 1976 manuscript I wrote:

> I think we may safely assume that for at least the next generation, the United States will continue to be a nation of great civil disorder, part of which will be expressed as common street crime, the source of our common prison fodder. Moreover, the criminal justice system will continue to use prisons as the ultimate bastions of coercion against men who hail primarily from the lower social classes who have not been controlled by more humanitarian measures such as probation. And this will be particularly so in the state prisons which have been for a century the cesspools for our great urban slums. Perhaps this should not be, but it is and will continue so. Thus we may expect that prisons will continue to be the dumping ground for young men who are violent, rebellious, predatory, as well as many who have been cheated by life or society of any chance to be other than pathetic misfits. Moreover, should our nation continue to experience a stagnant or declining material standard of living, the taxpayers are hardly likely to vote the largesse they did in the 1960's for prison construction and maintenance, so that a small cadre of less well paid custodians on reduced budgets may very well be responsible for containing a large body of restive convicts.

The only difference I anticipate between the last two decades and the next two is that the money is now running out. American taxpayers will still rely on imprisonment, but they will be less willing to pay for it. The signs are summarized by Penelope Lemov in *Governing*, a magazine for people who are professional city managers (March 1995:25):

> A couple of things you can say with confidence about the prison of the future in America. It will have to be cheap, and in order to be cheap it will have to be big.

The only let-down for the taxpayers will be controlling the inmates. Today, the panacea being promoted to accomplish control is expensive, elaborate technology and architecture. We will learn from experience that there is no substitute for a disciplined and vigilant correctional staff. And with such a staff, perhaps a cheaper, simpler technology and architecture may suffice. Another expensive attempt at control, the "super max" prison of small and very expensive perpetual lockups hold only a very small percentage of convicts. But with money running out, taxpayers will increasingly opt for large prisons, the cheaper the better.

While comparative costs are beyond the scope of this book, it is worth noting that as dollars dominate the future, Warden Ragen's regime may be a good benchmark for comparisons. As it is now, some maximum security prisons may operate in the same world of "money-is-no-object" as the military did during the cold war. The current fashion is to propose prisons run by the "unit management" system. For example, modern Stateville is run this way. In general, as DiIulio (1991:17) described it:

Unit management is an approach to correctional management in which a team of uniformed security staff and counselors work together in a given cellblock or wing of an institution under the direction of a unit manager, a sort of mini-warden. Each team is responsible for managing the inmates in its unit, including everything from counting, locking, frisking, and cell searching to monitoring inmates' disciplinary records, keeping track of their program activities and release dates, maintaining sanitation, and so on.

Such elaboration takes considerably more labor than did Warden Ragen's system. For comparison, we consider King's (1991) account of a maximum security prison in Minnesota which was built around 1982 for 359 inmates. King lauds the prison for its emphasis on the latest in unit management, technology and architecture. It is a prison with a ratio of one uniformed staff for every two inmates (a slight understatement: the precise numbers are ten guards to 19 inmates). Furthermore, one-third of the staff have college degrees. The non-custodial or non-uniformed staff are not enumerated, but their number may be lowered by extensive contracting out. For example, inmate food is provided by a catering service, and the prison maintains microwaves and "pantries."

In contrast, Warden Ragen's Joliet-Stateville complex consisted of several prisons which held (in 1960) over 5,000 inmates controlled by 493 custodial staff. I don't think any of the staff had college degrees. I don't know how many non-uniformed staff were employed, but just using the custodial staff for comparison, if Warden Ragen had the same ratio as our Minnesota prison, he would have employed more than 2,500 correctional officers and supervisors. Differences such as 2,500 guards versus 493 are worth thinking about. Ragen parlayed his control into more inmate and less employee labor.

For example, medical care and food preparation at the Stateville Penitentiary today requires large numbers of civilian employees who carry out tasks that were done under Joseph Ragen just as adequately by small numbers of civilians and guards aided by large numbers of inmates. There is no requirement by the United States Supreme Court for a specific ratio of civilian to inmate help to bake bread in a prison, even though past failures may have led lower courts to be involved in such minutiae.

We face a difficult task in relating Warden Ragen's Stateville to modern prisons. Another source of guidance is the collective wisdom of wardens and other high level correctional administrators that is incorporated in the publications of the American Correctional Association (ACA). I do not believe the ACA's publications help understand how to control prisons. But I wish to emphasize that the ACA covers all aspects of corrections, and close control of maximum security prisons is but one part of the ACA's work.

The American Correctional Association

The American Correctional Association (ACA) is an interest group of persons employed in the field of corrections and it is dominated by prison wardens and other upper level administrators. In common with other occupational associations such as the American Medical Association, the American Association of University Professors, or the Teamsters Union, the ACA claims to uplift its practitioners and simultaneously serve society.

For the ACA, this self-interest is exemplified in their 1990 report "Causes ... of ... Riots and Disturbances." Chapter 2 lists nine underlying reasons for disturbances, among them inadequate funding, in a sentence where the first phrase denies what the second asserts: "No single factor is most important in considering the causes of institutional disturbances, but inadequate financing is an underlying cause in many, if not most." Then they continue:

> Hand-to-mouth budget practices and deficit financing, usually stemming from political considerations, are at the root of many of the personnel, physical plant, and program deficiencies that set the stage for major problems of this type.

This observation is noteworthy because this claim that correctional expenditures were inadequate came in the midst of exponential increases in correctional budgets throughout the United States. For example, in 1995, the *New York Times* reported on finances for California. It noted: on April 12 that the corrections budgets exceeded those for higher education; on November 7th, that salaries for prison guards exceeded those of public school teachers. Corrections is certainly not a wallflower at the budget prom. Also noteworthy is the ACA phrase "usually stemming from political considerations," a not very subtle way of blaming politicians for the shortfall.

Also in this 1990 report, all nine underlying conditions underlying riots specified by the ACA are plausible, as are the generalizations of the remaining chapters. But nowhere do they include inadequate management by wardens and staff. In one form or another, such generalizations permeate the ACA literature, from their 1981 *Guidelines For the Development of Policies and Procedures: Adult Correctional Institutions*, to the 1991 *Public Policy For Corrections*.

The ACA has become an economic force, something headlined in a May 22, 1994 front page article in the *Wall Street Journal*, where the writer, Paulette Thomas, concluded, "America's fear of crime is creating a new version of the old military-industrial complex, an infrastructure born amid political rhetoric and a shower of federal, state, and local dollars." The quality of the ACA mindset is alluded to in an article by Steven Holmes in the *New York Times* of November 6, 1994, an evaluation of *Corrections Today*, the ACA's official magazine. The reporter begins with: "Cross Orwell with the wireless-digital age and a Madison Avenue sensibility and you might come close to some of the ads appearing in *Corrections Today*." And he ends with:

> Flipping through *Corrections Today* brings to mind the defense journal *Aviation Week and Space Technology* in the heady days of climbing military budgets, in that its ads leave the unmistakable impression of contractors on the make for government largess.

All advertising reflects shrewd guesses about its audience, and taps into reasons and emotions, conscious and subliminal. The newspaper reporter recognized that military and corrections ads tap the mental worlds of generals and wardens. Perhaps the reporter exaggerated, but he did capture a world of self-glorification, just as he might among physicians or professors.

These are the ACA gestalt, the images that wardens have of themselves. These images are put into practice during the accreditation process, modeled after those of other kinds of institutions such as hospitals or universities.

The bibles for this process are the ACA's *Manuals of Standards*. Each of these books is quite specific, and begins with a title *Standards For....* Then, the subject of each Standards is a separate manual. For examples: *Standards For Adult Correctional Institutions* (1990); or *Standards For Administration of Correctional Institutions* (1993). *The Standards For Correctional Training Academies* (1993), covers the use of force on p.72. This complements the "Physical Handling" section of the 1981 *Guidelines For The Development Of Policies And Procedures*. In the next section on "The Judiciary and Prison Control," I compare these with Warden Ragen's bureaucratic language to indicate that filling out the ACA's forms does not necessarily equate with the reality of control in prison.

These manuals burden the useful idea of providing comprehensive checklists with a formal bureaucratic ritualism. Each manual has hundreds of "standards" which are really maxims, each classified as mandatory or not, compounded by a plethora of numerical weights which add to a final score, topical classifications, cross references, comments, explanations and justifications, supplemented by appendices and glossaries of definitions. The material is endless.

Accreditation doesn't come cheap. Fees to cover the cost of evaluating site visits by ACA inspectors are dwarfed by the labor costs in the prison itself. Since reaccreditation is required every three years, the ACA recommends the prison begin the process after two years to have it completed by the third. This requires staff time just for the paper work of accreditation.

Just what does completing these forms attain? Certainly, completing these forms is no guaranty of control. There may be areas in which filling out these "standards" may be useful in corrections, but the prevention of violence is not among them. We saw this in Chapter 8, where our discussion of today's Stateville Penitentiary illustrates a prison awash in violence which was repeatedly certified as a model prison by the ACA.

This leads to another justification, that being accredited will act as a shield against lawsuits by prisoner rights advocates. That is, if an inmate alleges guard brutality, one of the warden's defenses can be that the charge is baseless, since his prison is "accredited." This does make sense, for the issue of intervention by the judiciary hangs heavy over prison administration, and lawyers on both sides of any lawsuit look for claims they can raise, no matter how ephemeral. This then raises the question: what do we know of the role of the judiciary in the control of the prison?

The Judiciary and Prison Control

For some people, even some of its proponents, the judiciary's relationship to prisons carries the aura of the interloper. This is because many accounts focus on the dramatic recent past, with its landmark Supreme Court decisions. For example, Jacobs (1983b), in a sympathetic and scholarly study, begins by stating: "In the past two decades prisoners have besieged the federal courts with civil rights suits." This emphasis on the 1960-1980 period implies, especially to unsympathetic observers, that it might never have happened, except for those tumultuous days of the 1960's. In reality the evolution of judicial intervention into prison operation is a natural phenomenon of American life and follows Alexis De Tocqueville's precept that from the beginning of the Republic, political and social questions ultimately become judicial ones.

Moreover, the judiciary does not operate in a vacuum insulated from American history. Historically, there have been numerous experiments to improve the status of prisoners and other wards of the state (Simpson 1975). Baker (1974) enumerates many correctional experiments which involved inmates in governance, from the end of the 18th century and into the 19th century, before such efforts ended around 1930.

There have been occasions when the Federal Bureau of Prisons has worked to give its prisoners some additional voice. In 1929 the United States Penitentiary at Leavenworth (Robbins 1994:120) placed a mailbox in the prison where convicts could drop letters to be sent directly to the Superintendent of Prisons. In 1930 the newly organized Federal Bureau of Prisons expanded the idea throughout their system with the inmates able to send letters directly to the United States Attorney General or the Director of the Bureau of Prisons.

More recently, Cripe (1990) reports that in 1965, ten years before the federal judiciary required it, the U.S. Bureau of Prisons adopted (and some states copied) elaborate due process safeguards for inmates who were undergoing disciplinary hearings. It is obvious that the prisoners' rights movement since the 1960s has made many changes through the federal judiciary. But these changes grew out of the history of corrections in America, not in a vacuum.

Such changes return us to the central question: has judicial intrusion restricted the ability of wardens to control prisons? It will soon be obvious that the answer is no. Judicial intervention has made control more cumbersome and bureaucratic, but no less effective. Granted, in some cases an intransigent federal judge may create chaos, or intransigent judges and correctional administrators jointly create chaos. This seemed to be the case in the Texas prisons during the 1970's. But this is to be expected in the way Americans often make social policy, with an axe rather than a scalpel.

This turbulence is built into the structure of the judiciary. To begin with, tension exists between the federal and state courts, something foreshadowed as early as the *Federalist* Essay 82. Each state's courts have at least some base in local politics. (State and local judges are elected, or appointed by politicians for a set number of years.) State courts may also be jealous of the pressure of the federal courts. While the federal courts are more independent of politicians—federal judges, once appointed, have lifetime tenure—their original appointments hinge on their political connections. Examples of the personal and ideological tensions which extend to the U.S. Supreme Court are legion. One example is Anthony Lewis' narrative in his *Gideon's Trumpet*, which detailed the jockeying leading to the decision in the Gideon case: that even the poorest among us must be represented by competent counsel when a criminal charge is brought. Or see Simon's (1995) discussion of the ideologies and personalities of the Current Court. Justices of the Supreme Court may wait decades, perhaps their entire tenures, for a confluence of the right case, the right time in the ideological composition of the court, and the right political temper in the nation before they can push their ideological agendas. By and large, such delays appear to benefit the nation, for whatever ills of ideology they may suffer, the Justices of the Supreme Court are not fools.

This is evident in their rulings on disciplinary proceedings against inmates who have been written up by prison guards for rule violations. The Court required numerous changes in the name of due process which required wardens to create bureaucratic procedures. For example, the Court required that inmates had some right to advice in answering charges, but they restricted the advice givers to correctional staff. Most importantly, inmates had no right to an outside lawyer or to the courtroom rules of legal proceedings. Thus, none of these changes subverted a warden's ability to control the prison.

In addition to ideological and personal tensions among the Justices of the Supreme Court, there is the structure of the federal court system. The Supreme Court is itself the apex of a complex pyramid of specialized courts ranging from military or tax courts to those of international trade. Considering just criminal cases, trials take place before 649 judges assigned to 94 courts of trial, called district courts. These district courts are grouped by geography into 13 Courts of Appeal, (12 by state, and one for the District of Columbia), numbering 179 judges. At the apex, all courts are answerable to the nine judges of the Supreme Court itself. Once a case comes to trial, or a petition is accepted by any federal judge, the results may rocket to an appeals court and the Supreme Court itself—or it may languish in judicial limbo for years. (Or the United States Congress may pass laws which impinge on the subject.) Thus the district courts in one region of the United States may be bound by decisions of their appellate court which conflict with decisions of another appellate court. This will continue unless the Supreme Court chooses to resolve the issue. During interregnums, a hot-headed federal judge may bully a prison system, an intransigent prison director may stonewall a judge, or struggles may break out between them. Perhaps a political deal, called a consent order, may be agreed to by a state's director of corrections and the prisoner rights lawyers to get themselves out of this judicial purgatory.

Like all political deals, it may be based upon expediency, not merit; thus, a corrections director may bow to an unwise consent order because his governor had to accommodate interest groups.

This messy situation—like all political conflict—results in a variety of accommodations and injustices while the issues await decisions by the Supreme Court. Often when we discuss the effects of judicial intervention, we refer to a small number of cases which the Supreme Court brought to closure. Glossed over are the battles still waged in the federal appeals and district courts, and those in state court systems. Overall the system may be a patchwork of conflicting appeals courts' decisions, consent orders, stipulations and other arcane minutae. Lives may be blighted as in Dickens' *Bleak House*, unless the Supreme Court decides. Even then, the United States Congress may pass legislation changing the rules.

The analysis of these key cases already decided by the Supreme Court constitutes an academic industry in itself. Excellent analyses exist, as in Jacobs (1983b), and in Feeley and Hanson (1990). The result of all these decisions by the Court are bureaucratic requirements which can be viewed two ways: one is the abstract requirements as postulated by the American Correctional Association; the other flows from empirical analyses of how it really works in practice as described by writers such as Rhine (1990), or Howard et al. (1994).

Viewed abstractly, it hardly seems possible that prisons can be controlled under the burden of judicial restraints. The American Correctional Association's 1981 Guidelines contained 15 single-spaced pages of do's and don'ts to cope with the burden of the judiciary. But in the end, the Guidelines is a massive bulk of words with little content. For example, the first procedure, Physical Handling begins:

> The first level of force available to a Correctional Officer is the use of his/ her hands. Physical handling is justified to subdue unruly inmates, to separate participants in a fight, in self defense and in defending staff, inmates or other persons. It may also be employed to move inmates who fail to comply with lawful orders.....As with any type of force, the amount of force used in physical handling shall be only as much as is reasonable and necessary in the circumstances.

Now compare this with Warden Ragen's memo to me when he objected to one question in one of my research projects, a linguistic questionnaire, as I related in Chapter 1. My original question read: "What names are there for a guard whose job is to use force to subdue inmates?" Warden Ragen's memorandum read:

> Mr. Kantrowitz: With reference to No. 96 of your proposed questionnaire - "A guard whose job is to use force to subdue inmates?" - I do not believe this is properly phrased. We do not use force at this institution to subdue inmates; however, if an inmates assaults or attacks a guard, proper restraint is used to stop him. I think by all means that question should be reworded if used at all. It is misleading and would be wrongfully interpreted I am afraid.

My solution was to reword the question paraphrasing Warden Ragen's language: "What names are there for a guard who may have to—if the occasion arises (fights, attacks, etc.)—use physical restraint, or force, to restrain or subdue an inmate?" This minor rewording satisfied him, for I was no longer asking a question which could be construed as a slur. On the other hand he was content to have the inmates think or say whatever they chose, while I, the inmates, and probably Warden Ragen knew there was not one whit difference in the answers I would get from either wording. As I make clear in Chapter 9, under carefully controlled conditions, inmates certainly were beaten in Warden Ragen's prison, his formalistic prose to the contrary.

In this regard, social research provides invaluable empirical evidence that while the weight of judicial decisions creates a bureaucratic procedure of due process, it does not obstruct control. Exemplifying this are a multitude of articles, such as Flanagan (1982), Jones and Rhine (1985), Mays and Olszta (1989), or Thomas, et al (1991). We can use two other recent articles to illustrate that judicially mandated due process in prison does not obstruct control.

Edward Rhine's 1990 discussion of disciplinary practices at the Rahway, New Jersey State prison minutely examined such issues as the charges, investigations, the hearings process, representation, witnesses, confrontation and cross examination, dispositions, evidence used, the reasons for actions taken, and appeals. His focus was on fairness and due process, but entirely absent was any reference, even parenthetical, that control by the warden's staff was handicapped by the procedure.

Similarly, Howard, et al, in 1994 carried out a statistical analysis of punishment at a federal medium-security prison. His focus was on the effect of such social variables as age and race on punishment, but as with Rhine, there is no mention of a loss of control in his paper. In the numerous papers in the same vein as Howard or Rhine which minutely examine the disciplinary process for fairness or bias, there is no evidence, statistical or anecdotal, that control by the authorities had been compromised.

To understand this, consider punishment in Warden Ragen's Stateville. There a guard wrote a ticket describing what an inmate had done to break a rule, after which the inmate appeared before a captain who informed the inmate of his alleged transgression, listened to the inmate's point of view, and then assessed a punishment. The punishment was carried out and that was the end of it.

Now, because of the decisions of the United States Supreme Court, prison authorities are required to follow some procedures which stem from the limited rights of inmates to due process. The guard writes a rule violation, much as before. After this, the guard has no role other than as a witness.

The inmate must have a hearing quickly. The warden still has the right to put the accused under some restraint such as administrative isolation if he poses a risk to others or to order in the prison. The inmate is provided the opportunity to admit or deny the charge and provide his side of the argument. While the inmate has some limited rights to have another inmate or correctional staff to advise him, he has no right to a lawyer or to courtroom procedures.

Then the process begins. In the Federal Bureau of Prisons, the process uses staff (Howard, *et al*: 13-14). Within 24 hours an Investigating Officer (usually a lieutenant) forwards his conclusions to a Unit Discipline Committee which holds a hearing. For more serious offenses, the case is referred to a Discipline Hearing Officer. The inmate may appeal the verdicts, beginning with the Warden, Regional Director, or General Counsel.

This is bureaucratic. But an inmate who poses a threat to others can be immobilized while the case undergoes a hearing. And the hearing itself cannot be dragged on to cause the pipeline to be jammed with a multitude of cases. Finally, there is limited ability to appeal after a decision. Other than an additional investment of staff time, punishments do not disrupt the institutional schedule, nor can they drag on to eventually clog the system with backlog and delay. In addition to these procedures, federal prisons have Segregation Review Officials who keep tabs on inmates placed in isolation or segregation.

Similarly, other Supreme Court decisions such as inmates' rights to approach the courts do not necessarily cripple a warden's ability to control. Even the right of inmates to petition for writs of *habeas corpus*, the most central of all rights, is a matter which can be addressed by the United States Congress. The *New York Times* of June 3, 1996 noted that the Justices of the Supreme Court, badly split by ideology, were grappling with recent enactments by the United States Congress (and signed by the President) restricting convicts' use of *habeas corpus*. Then the June 29, 1996 *Times* reported that the court overcame its internal dissensions and found enough common ground to unanimously uphold the new law. If a prison is handicapped by unwise consent orders agreed to by a state corrections department, then the solution to that is a political one of appeals and lobbying.

Whenever we find the judiciary at loggerheads with correctional officials, we find temperaments in collision, or liberal and conservative ideologies in conflict. They lead to political confrontations, compromises and solutions; some problems may never be solved. All this is to say that managing prisons is in the same league with managing any governmental entity.

Finally, prisoner rights and prison control will become even more strictured by the Supreme Court for medical reasons, as AIDS and drug-resistant tuberculosis spreads. This will be confounded with the rights of correctional officers, who will also demand the right to be protected. Eventually this situation will cause inmates and guards alike to sue for protection against violent inmates who may be dangerous for reasons of disease. Some guards hope they can legislate protection. For example, an Associated Press wire service story of May 31, 1996 reported that New York State has just made it a felony, punishable by up to a five year sentence, for a convict to throw feces, urine, blood, or semen at a corrections employee.

Perhaps the changes I suggest are not practical, for they postulate too many political deals between too many vested interests. The theory is easy; the hard part is finding the politicians capable of cutting the deals to do it. My guess is that if changes do come, it will be the result of the slow accretion resulting from prisoner rights lawyers suing for protection from inmate predators. The visceral revulsion of the public over prisoners being raped by other inmates may lead the courts to rule against wardens who do not provide sufficient control to prevent it. This issue of prison rape may be the force which carries along other major questions of control: killings, knifings, and beatings. I hope this book plays a role in persuading the courts that all of these can be minimized, if not eliminated.

The Lessons of Warden Ragen's System

The most difficult part of applying any lessons from Warden Ragen's system of control are the political issues which will have to be settled in the public arena by the governor, legislators, and judges of a state. Setting aside these external issues for the moment, the lessons of Warden Ragen's system devolve to a few precepts.

These are first to create a guard force which is disciplined and ever-vigilant; then to simplify the programs (and the architecture) of the prison; and finally to control physical violence between guards and inmates as well as between inmates. Before these can be implemented, however, there is the task of selecting the prison warden, the leading actor on this stage. Auditioning for the part involves the political establishment, something we will discuss later; but the role itself needs to be defined.

Unfortunately for specifications, the warden who can control the maximum security prison I envision will have to be a master of improvisation. Perhaps if experience produces a number of successes, some specifics will emerge so a more ordinary bureaucrat can become warden, but not yet. Initially, this warden must be a dynamic leader, capable of molding a custodial staff into a disciplined and vigilant work force. Prudence suggests a warden who is 40 rather than 60, a career bureaucrat in corrections rather than a patronage appointee from outside. Not that an elderly patronage appointee would necessarily be a poor choice, but it may take a decade of driving energy to succeed, and elderly or patronage appointees rarely have such longevity.

The paramount task of the warden will be to create a custodial staff capable of being ever alert and responsive. Warden Ragen did this with his praetorian guard of lieutenants who instilled fear into a body of ordinary working class men. Our modern warden must also develop his own equivalent to Warden Ragen's captains and lieutenants, and work some magic to transform ordinary working class men into a coherent, disciplined force. Warden Ragen's age of unalloyed punishment and fear among guards is over, so perhaps some model based upon military elite units such as Rangers or the Marines will evolve.

I don't think anyone can predict the details of how it would be accomplished, and that is the reason the warden must be a leader. A few thoughts may be in order however. First, if corruption or intransigence is deeply imbedded in an existing prison's staff, the state might have to resort to undercover police work to root it out. Second, it is inevitable that a campfollowing of consultants will emerge. Some few may have limited merit. But the political reality argues against it. Many maximum security prisons are located in remote areas where the correctional staff (or at least the guards) must be drawn from ordinary working class men; many will be locals and others will be those who can't get a better job. The warden will have to make whatever compromises necessary to work with what he is given, for politicians locate prisons where they provide jobs for local residents. But compromises only go so far. As soon as guards are disciplined and punished for mistakes and derelictions, labor unions for the guards, local politicians and state legislators will begin pressuring to change the rules of the game. Without strong leadership in high places, a disciplined guard force will never develop.

As a corollary to this control, the warden must control the physical violence of the prison. I expect a modern warden will develop some version of Warden Ragen's operation: only when an inmate hit a guard was he beaten, and then only by lieutenants. Because he will not have Warden Ragen's latitude, the modern warden will have to develop variations on beating errant inmates, perhaps using riot squads on the spot rather than enclosing it within Ragen's segregation building. The other side of the coin is that guards must be disciplined to not harass inmates, or use inmates as their enforcers. One result of this web of controls will be that deadly weapons such as knives will disappear, and as in Warden Ragen's prison, the endemic fights will be with fists and weapons of opportunity. And, as in Ragen's prison, other dangers such as rape and extortion will be contained.

Paradoxically, out of this will grow a tacit acceptance of the warden's control as a morally justified system. The guards will bear the burden of their discipline because they will be safe and in charge. The inmates will try to subvert the system simply as a matter of autonomy, but they will accept the safety they live under and the fact that they are not harassed by guards or other inmates.

Another guideline specifies that in order to make the modern warden's job possible, the prison must be simplified in programs, and where possible, in architecture. Often architecture follows programs, so if, for instance, the warden simplifies prison industries by closing them down, the factory buildings can be gutted and rebuilt for some other purpose with clear sight lines for the guards.

This simplification is necessary because every factory, every school, every other program creates a system of complex controls. It is hard to imagine the avalanche of forms, memos, rules and regulations which Warden Ragen imposed on his prison. An indication of this occurs in Ragen and Finston (1962) which provides facsimiles of some hundreds of Stateville's forms. Naturally, any prison requires many forms, but the excess must be cut down. Moreover, the Ragen and Finston compendium omits the multitude of other material which buried Stateville's custodial staff until no one could remember them all. Anyone who is going to really control a maximum security prison today with all the industries and programs that Warden Ragen had will have to produce a similar paper blizzard. But no modern warden could have the power to humiliate and browbeat his custodial staff to enforce this as Warden Ragen did. The only answer is to simplify programs.

In order to simplify, we must consider what is essential. Here, we have clear mandates to keep inmates in good health, which requires food, clothing, shelter, and medical care. There are also subsidiary mandates such as access to the courts. Another class of rights are to be left alone, which requires inmates be free of physical and psychological abuse by either the custodial staff or by other inmates. Parenthetically, there should be another right, this time of the custodial staff, to be in charge over the convicts and free of assaults and other abuse by the inmates.

Thus the first order in eliminating complexity is the elimination of the inmate commissary, industries, and schools. This, of course, does not preclude their availability at other prisons of the state. Likewise the luxury of inmates as servants for politicians or wardens can be eliminated. The elimination of the commissary would mean crippling the inmate economy, and limiting the possibilities of extortion between inmates. Eliminating factories and schools would cut down on the clerical complexity needed to keep track of assignments, wages and other financial complexities, while restricting the machinery available to manufacture knives and other weapons. This would free up time for meals, recreation and other activities which did not require more complexity.

The resulting human warehousing of the inmates would then devolve to a kind of spartan leisure society. The warden could provide and encourage activities that did not require elaborate physical structures (with hallways and rooms, equipment and machines, nooks and crannies) or an organization of control. Activities could range from television viewing to sports and recreation, from religious services to correspondence courses. The touchstone would be that it did not interfere with control.

Here is where a warden who is gifted as an executive may change the rules. I have repeatedly suggested eliminating programs to simplify the prison's operation. My suggestions, however, are analytic abstractions, a framework for control. A warden who has achieved control over his prison may bend this framework. For example, a warden might consider allowing gambling or conjugal visits. The collection of gambling debts can lead to violence. But if there is no money in the prison and no way for inmates to organize gambling, the warden may decide the trade-off in morale is worth the change. Similarly, sex may be worth a compromise. Conjugal visits will lead to some drug smuggling, but it may give the warden a cadre of inmates who will help him run the prison. Similarly, other simplifications such as the availability of candy or cigarettes may be adjusted by the warden.

The Social Context of Imposing a System of Control

In the previous sections we have discussed what is probably the easiest part of achieving control, the changes within the prison. The hard part is political negotiations with interest groups in the outside world. Success requires that outside groups with special interests in prisons agree to a program of control. This includes participation of the guards, their unions, and political representatives, as well as the political representatives of the inmates themselves, their families, and their communities in the free world. Nor is the general voting public absent from the equation. For example, the warden will be greatly aided if the legislature permits indeterminate sentences, a parole board, and the accrual of good time, the remission of time in prison for good behavior. Indeterminate sentences such as one year minimums and ten year maximums in conjunction with the possibility of parole and generous good time accrual for those who are not paroled provide the warden a powerful weapon of control. They helped Warden Ragen mightily because he was the gatekeeper to those benefits. If a legislature limits such benefits, it will make control that much harder.

In the end all these matters are funneled through the practical politics of decisions which have to be made in the state Capitol by the governor, the legislature, and the judiciary. The governor as the state's chief executive has a major stake because prisons are his responsibility. As Adlai Stevenson, Governor of Illinois, learned from his prison riots of 1952 and Nelson Rockefeller, Governor of New York, learned from the Attica riot of 1971, prisons can be a nail in the coffin of political ambition. It is no wonder that a major responsibility of a state commissioner of corrections is to protect his governor's career by seeing to it that the lid is kept on the prisons: garner whatever good publicity is possible, but above all see to it that there is no bad publicity. This in turn requires appointing prison wardens who are politically connected and "safe:" they will do as told by the commissioner, and are competent to avoid media disasters.

Thus the thought of appointing a warden who has the personal qualities and the authority to genuinely control a maximum security prison is a major break in the existing arrangement of power. It may also be a risk for the governor, for after all there is no guarantee it will succeed.

Such a break with the existing balance of power also affects the legislature: those politicians elected from districts where the prison is located, those who are allied with guards whether by labor unions or otherwise, or those who are allied with inmates, perhaps through racial politics. Also, there are many interest groups such as the businessmen who sell to the prisons, lawyers, as well as conservative and liberal activists, to name but a few who have a stake in the existing system.

Since the ensuing contests are sure to wind up in court, the judiciary, by its decisions, the amount of delay it introduces, and the consent orders it brokers, will be a major player. In a rare public outburst, an example of the political infighting which involves the courts erupted on the editorial page of that prime American establishment outlet, the *New York Times*. At issue was the large number of suits filed by prison inmates in federal court; each suit requires time and labor for the attorney general of a given state to defend its department of corrections, and for the federal judiciary to decide the suits. In one exchange, the Attorney General of New York State (March 3 and December 30, 1995) and the Chief Judge of the U.S. Court of Appeals, Hartford, Connecticut (January 3, 1996) barely remained on a civil level.

The conflicts which must be resolved go far beyond choosing the warden. For example, racial politics may come to the fore. Thus if the prison in question is located in a small isolated town where the guard forces are local whites, while the inmate body is primarily black and from a distant metropolis, then black religious and community groups will demand some *quid pro quo*. This might be greater hiring or promotion opportunities for blacks; any number of accommodations would be necessary, likely to be brokered by black legislators in the state capital.

Likewise, political accommodations might be required to deal with corrupt guards. Here the small number of guards involved in smuggling contraband could collaborate with those who have developed corners of power in league with inmate leaders. It would be easy for them to capitalize on the concern of the majority of the corrections staff over job security. What happens to an honest guard who makes a mistake and is faced with punishment or even discharge? All of this must be faced and fought out in the corridors of the state capital.

The irony of all this is that success in control of such a large maximum security prison would be, in the larger sense, a confession of failure. Just as a successful "super max" is a confession of failure in running the ordinary maximum security prisons of the state, so is a successfully controlled maximum security prison a confession of failure in running the less controlled prisons. Success in escalating the level of coercion creates a paradox that social justice in prison is achieved against the wishes of the governed. Because those bearing the brunt of all this are from the have-nots and racial minorities of our society, we accept the contradiction that we impose coercion in the name of social justice.

The question of social justice and prisons is an important one for the United States. In recent decades, our people have absentmindedly created an American Gulag, an archipelago of prisons which reaches from sea to shining sea. It is an ironic end to this millenium, for more than a century ago, Alexis de Toqueville arrived in our new nation to study its prisons, and returned home to France to explain democracy to the world. If we are somehow to adjust our Gulag to democracy, we must bring some measure of justice — fairness, order, and safety — to our Gulag's epitome, the maximum security prison. I hope this book provides some progress toward that purpose.

Endnotes

1. We will not discuss the International Association of Correctional Officers (IACO). The IACO has an unique objective, to raise the self esteem of correctional officers and to instill in them a self image as "professionals." The membership is the lower ranks of the custodial staff, those who I have usually called "guards" or "officers" in this book. I have used these terms because they were the usual name for correctional officer in the Stateville of my day, where it had no pejorative connotation.

Bibliography

Administrative Office of the United States Courts. [no date]. *Understanding the Federal Courts*. Second Edition. Washington, D.C.

Allsop, K. 1961. *The Bootleggers: The Story of Chicago's Prohibition Era*. Garden City, N.Y.: Doubleday.

American Correctional Association. 1966. *Manual of Correctional Standards*. Washington, D.C.

American Correctional Association. 1981. *Guidelines for the Development of Policies and Procedures: Adult Correctional Institutions*. College Park, Md.

American Correctional Association. 1990. *Standards For Adult Correctional Institutions*. 3rd Edition. Laurel, Md.

American Correctional Association. 1990. *Causes, Preventive Measures, and Methods of Controlling Riots and Disturbances in Correctional Institutions*. 3rd Edition. Laurel, Md.

American Correctional Association. 1991. *Public Policy For Corrections*. Laurel, Md.

American Correctional Assocation. 1993. *Gangs in Correctional Facilities: A National Assessment*. Laurel, Md.

American Correctional Association. 1993. *Standards For Correctional Training Academies*. Laurel, Md.

American Correctional Association. 1993. *Standards For Administration of Correctional Agencies*. Laurel, Md.

Angle, P.M. 1952. *Bloody Williamson*. N.Y.: Knopf.(Reprinted 1992, U. Illinois.)

Baker, J.E. 1974. *The Right To Participate: Inmate Involvement In Prison Administration*. Metuchen, N.J.: Scarecrow Press.

Barnes, J.B. 1954. *United States of America* ex. rel. Roger Touhy vs Joseph Ragen. Case No. 48 C448, August 9, 1954. U.S. District Court, Northeastern District of Illinois, Eastern Division. [U.S. Archives, Chicago].

Bateman, N. 1920. *Historical Encyclopedia of Illinois*. Chicago: Munsell Publishing Co.

Bennett, L. 1976. "The Study of Violence in California Prisons: A Review With Policy Implications." In A.K. Cohen, *et. al.*, *Prison Violence*.

BNA's Directory of State and Local Courts, Judges, and Clerks. 1994-95 Edition. Washington, D.C.: Bureau of National Affairs, Inc.

Bowker, L.H. 1980. *Prison Victimization*. N.Y.: Elsevier.

Buchanan, R.A., C.A. Unger, and K.L. Whitlow. 1987. *Management of Inmate Violence: A Case Study*. Kansas City, Mo.: Correctional Services Group, Inc.

Buchanan, R.A, C.A Unger, and K.L Whitlow. 1988. *Disruptive Maximum Security Inmate Management Guide.* Washington, D.C.: U.S. National Institute of Corrections.

Carlson, N. 1992. Review of P. Earley, "The Hot House", *Corrections Today.* 59:86.

Carroll, L. 1974. *Hacks, Blacks, and Cons: Race Relations In a Maximum Security Prison.* Lexington, Mass.: Lexington Books.

Chonco, N.R. 1989."Sexual Assaults Among Male Inmates: A Descriptive Study." *The Prison Journal.* 69:72-82.

Christopher, H., L.T. Winfree, G.L. Mays, M.K. Stohr and D.L. Clason. 1994. "Processing Inmate Disciplinary Infractions in a Federal Correctional Institution: Legal and Extralegal Correlates of Prison-Based Legal Decisions." *The Prison Journal.* 73:5-31.

Citizen's Police Committee, Chicago. 1931. *Chicago Police Problems.* Chicago: University of Chicago Press.

Clemmer, D. 1940. *The Prison Community.* Boston: Christopher. (Reprinted 1958 N.Y.: Rinehart).

Cloward, R.A., R. Cressey, G.H Grosser, R. McCleery, L.E. Ohlin, G.M. Sykes, and S. Messinger, eds. 1960. *Theoretical Studies in Social Organization of the Prison.* N.Y.: Social Science Research Council.

Cohen, A., G.F. Cole, and R.G. Bailey, eds. 1976. *Prison Violence*, Lexington, Mass.: D.C. Heath.

Colvin, M. 1992. *The Penitentiary in Crisis: From Accommodation to Riot in New Mexico.* Albany: State University of N.Y.

Cressey, D., ed. 1961. *The Prison: Studies in Institutional Organization and Change.* N.Y.: Holt, Rinehart, Winston.

Cressey, D. 1965. "Prison Organization." Chapter 24 in J.G. March, ed, *Handbook of Organizations.* Chicago: Rand-McNally.

Cripe, C.A. 1990. "Courts, Corrections, and the Constitution: A Practitioner's View," in DiIulio, *Courts, Corrections and The Constitution.*

Crouch, B.M. 1985. "The Significance of Minority Status to Disciplinary Severity in Prison." *Sociological Focus.* 18:221-233.

Crouch, B.M. and J.W. Marquart. 1989. *An Appeal To Justice: Litigated Reform of Texas Prisons.* Austin: University of Texas Press.

DiIulio, J. 1987. *Governing Prisons: A Comparative Study of Prison Management.* N.Y.: Free Press.

DiIulio, J. 1989. *Prisons That Work: An Overview of Management In the Federal Bureau of Prisons.* Washington, D.C.: National Institute of Corrections.

DiIulio, J., ed. 1990. *Courts, Corrections, and the Constitution: The Impact of Judicial Intervention on Prisons and Jails.* N.Y.: Oxford.

DiIulio, J. 1991. *No Escape: The Future of American Corrections.* N.Y.: Basic Books.

Earley, P. 1992. *The Hot House.* N.Y.: Bantam Books.

Ellis, D., H.G. Grasmick, and B. Gilman. 1974. "Violence in Prisons: A Sociological Analysis." *American Journal of Sociology.* 80:16-43.

Erickson, G. 1957. *Warden Ragen of Joliet.* N.Y.: Dutton.

Erwin, M. 1876. *The History of Williamson County.* Illinois. No publisher listed.

Feeley, M. & R. Hanson. 1990. "The Impact of Judicial Intervention on Prisons and Jails: A Review of the Literature." In DiIulio, *Courts, Corrections, and the Constitution.*

Feinman, C. 1994. *Women in the Criminal Justice System.* Westport, Conn.: Praeger.

Flanagan, T.J. 1982. "Discretion in the Prison Justice System: A Study of Sentencing in Institutional Disciplinary Proceedings." *Journal of Research in Crime and Delinquency*. 19:216-237.

Fleisher, M.S. 1989. *Warehousing Violence*. Newbury Park Calif.: Sage.

Gaes, G.G. and W. McGuire. 1985. "Prison Violence: The Contribution of Crowding versus other Determinants of Prison Assault Rates." *Journal of Research in Crime and Delinquency*. 22:41-65.

Gaes, G.G. 1994."Prison Crowding Research Reexamined." *The Prison Journal*. 74:329-363.

Garson, G.D. 1972. "The Disruption of Prison Administration." *Law and Society Review*. 6:531-561.

Girardin, G.R., with W.J. Helmer. 1994. *Dillinger: The Untold Story*. Bloomington: Indiana University Press.

Godinez, S. 1995. "Revisiting a Hero: The Complete C.O." *The Keepers Voice*. 6:7.

Gottfried, A. 1962. *Boss Cermak of Chicago*. Seattle: University of Washington Press.

Haas, K.C. and G.P. Alpert, eds. 1986. *The Dilemmas of Punishment: Readings in Contemporary Corrections*. Prospect Heights, Illinois: Waveland Press.

Hoffman, D. E. 1993. *Scarface Al and the Crime Crusaders: Chicago's Private War Against Capone*. Carbondale: Southern Illinois University Press.

Illinois Department of Corrections. 1993. Fact Sheet-September 1993 [of Stateville Correctional Center]. Typescript, photocopied. 11 pages.

Illinois Task Force on Crime and Corrections (Anton R. Valukas, Chairman). 1993. Final Report. Springfield: State of Illinois.

Irwin, J. 1980. *Prisons In Turmoil*. Boston: Little, Brown.

Jacobs, J. 1977. *Stateville: The Penitentiary In Mass Society*. Chicago: University of Chicago Press.

Jacobs, J. and N.M. Crotty. 1978a. *Guard Unions and the Future of the Prisons*. Ithaca, N.Y.: Institute of Public Employment, N.Y. State School of Industrial Relations.

Jacobs, J. 1978b. "What Prison Guards Think: A Profile of the Illinois Force." *Crime and Delinquency*. 24:185-196.

Jacobs, J. 1983a. *New Perspectives on Prison and Imprisonment*. Ithaca, N.Y.: Cornell University Press.

Jacobs, J. 1983b. "The Prisoner Rights Movement and its Impacts, 1960-80." in J. Jacobs, *New Perspectives on Prisons and Imprisonment*.

Jones, C.H. Jr. and E. Rhine. 1985. "Due Process and Prison Disciplinary Practices: From Wolff to Hewitt." *New England Journal on Criminal and Civil Confinement*. 11: 44-122.

Jones, R.S. and T.J. Schmid. 1989. "Inmates' Conception of Prison Sexual Assault." *The Prison Journal*. 69:53-61.

Kalinich, D. 1980. *The Inmate Economy*. Lexington, Mass.: Lexington Books.

Kantrowitz, N. 1969. "The Vocabulary of Race Relations In A Prison." *Publication Of The American Dialect Society*. Number 51:23-34.

Kantrowitz, N. and J.S.Kantrowitz. 1973. "Meet 'Mr. Franklin': An Example of Usage." In A. Dundes, ed., *Mother Wit from the Laughing Barrel: Readings in the Interpretation of Afro-American Folklore*. Englewood Cliffs, New Jersey: Prentice-Hall.

Kaufman, K. 1985. Prison Officers and Their World. PhD dis. Harvard University.

Kenney, D. 1990. *A Political Passage: The Career of Stratton of Illinois*. Carbondale:

Southern Illinois University Press.

Keve, P. W. 1991. *Prisons and the American Conscience: A History of Federal Corrections.* Carbondale: Southern Illinois University Press.

King, R.D. 1991. "Maximum-Security Custody in Britain and the USA: A Study of Gartree and Oak Park Heights." *British Journal of Criminology.*31:126-152.

Landesco, J. 1929. *Organized Crime in Chicago.* Part III of the Illinois Crime Survey. Chicago: University of Chicago Press. Reissued 1968.

Lemov, P. 1995. "Roboprison." *Governing.* 8:24-29.

Leopold, N. 1958. *Life Plus Ninety Nine Years.* N.Y.: Doubleday.

Lewis, A. 1964. *Gideon's Trumpet.* N.Y.: Random House

Light, S. 1991. "Assaults on Prison Officers: Interactional Themes." *Justice Quarterly.* 8:243-261.

Littlewood, T.B. 1969. *Horner of Illinois.* Evanston: Northwestern University Press.

Lockwood, D. 1980. *Prison Sexual Violence.* N.Y.: Elsevier.

Lombardo, L.X. 1989. *Guards Imprisoned: Correctional Officers at Work.* Revised Edition of 1981 work. Cincinnati, Ohio: Anderson.

Lyle, J.R. 1960. *The Dry and Lawless Years.* London: Prentice Hall Intl.

McCall, N. 1994. *Makes Me Wanna Holler.* N.Y.: Random House.

McConville, S. 1989. "Governing Prisons — A Book Review." *British Journal of Criminology.* 29:200-202.

McGee, R.A. 1981. *Prisons and Politics.* Lexington, Mass.: Lexington Books.

Marquart, J. 1986. "Prison Guards and the Use of Physical Coercion as a Mechanism of Social Control." *Criminology.* 24:347-66.

Marquart, J. and B. Couch. 1984. "Co-opting the Kept: Using Inmate Social Control in A Southern Prison." *Justice Quarterly.* 1:491-509.

Marquart, J.W. and J.B. Roebuck. 1986. "Prison Guards and the Snitches: Social Control in a Maximum Security Institution." In Hass, K.C. and G.P. Alpert, eds., *The Dilemmas of Punishment: Readings in Contemporary Corrections.*

Martin, J.B. 1954. *Break Down The Walls.* N.Y.: Ballentine Books.

Martin, R. and S. Zimmerman. 1990. "A Typology of the Causes of Prison Riots and An Analytic Extension to the 1986 West Virginia Riot." *Justice Quarterly.* 7:711-734.

Martin, S. and S. Eckland-Olson. 1987. *The Walls Came Tumbling Down: Texas Prisons.* Austin: Texas Monthly Press.

Mays, G.L. and M. Olszta. 1989. "Prison Litigation: From the 1960's to 1990's." *Criminal Justice Review.* 3:279-298.

Mushlin, M. 1993. *Rights of Prisoners.* 2 vols. N.Y.: McGraw-Hill.

Newman, G. 1979. *Understanding Violence.* N.Y.: J.B. Lippincott.

New York State Commission. 1972. *Attica, the Official Report of the New York State Special Commission on Attica.* N.Y.: Bantam Books.

Owen, B.A. 1988. *The Reproduction of Social Control: A Study of Prison Workers At San Quentin.* N.Y.: Praeger.

Peterson, V.W. 1952. *Barbarians in Our Midst: A History of Chicago Crime and Politics.* Boston: Little, Brown.

Ragen, J.E. May 1963. *Report and Observations on Inspection of Facilities and Operation of the Georgia Penal System.* Typescript, photocopied. "Report Submitted to the Governor's Commission for Efficiency and Improvement in Government, Atlanta, Georgia." [In the New York Public Library.]

Ragen, J.E. and C.Finston. 1962. *Inside The World's Toughest Prison.* Springfield, Ill.:

C.C.Thomas.

Rhine, E.E. 1990. "The Rule of Law, Disciplinary Practices, and Rahway State Prison: A Case Study in Judicial Intervention and Social Control." In J. DiIulio, *Courts, Corrections, And The Constitution.*

Robert, J.W., ed. 1994. *Escaping Prison Myths.* Washington, D.C.: American University Press.

Robbins, I.P. 1994. "The Prisoners Mail Box and the Evolution of Federal Inmate Rights." In Robert, *Escaping Prison Myths.*

Royko, M. 1971. *Boss: Richard J. Daley of Chicago.* N.Y.: Dutton.

Sargent, H. 1953. *The Insight Test.* N.Y.: Grune and Stratton.

Saum, C.A., H.L. Surratt, J.A. Inciardi, and R.E. Bennett. 1995. "Sex in Prison: Exploring the Myths and Realities." *The Prison Journal.* 75:413-430.

Semple, J. 1993. *Bentham's Prison: A Study of the Panopticon Penitentiary.* Oxford: Clarendon Press.

Simon, J.F. 1995. *The Center Holds: The Power Struggle Inside the Rehnquist Court.* N.Y.: Simon and Schuster.

Simpson, A.E. 1975. "Inmate Role in Prison Government." *Law Enforcement News.* 1: 11 *et.seq.*

Sykes, G. 1958. *The Society of Captives.* Princeton, N.J.: Princeton University Press.

Tewksbury, R. 1989. "Fear of Sexual Assault in Prison Inmates." *The Prison Journal.* 69:63-71.

Thomas, J. E. 1972. *The English Prison Officer Since 1850.* London: Routledge & Kegan Paul.

Thomas, J., H. Mika, J. Blakemore, and A. Aylward. 1991. "Exacting Control Through Disciplinary Hearings: 'Making Do' with Prison Rules." *Justice Quarterly.* 8:37-57.

Tingley, D. F. 1980. *The Structuring of a State: The History of Illinois, 1899 to 1928.* Urbana: University of Illinois Press.

Toland, J. 1963. *The Dillinger Days.* N.Y.: Random House.

Touhy, R. with R. Brennan. 1959. *The Stolen Years.* Cleveland: Pennington Press.

Useem, B. 1990. "Correctional Management: Good Prison Administration is Critical." *Corrections Today.* 52: 88-94.

Useem, B. and P.Kimball. 1989. *States of Siege: US Prison Riots, 1971-1986.* N.Y.: Oxford.

U.S. House of Representatives, Judiciary Committee. 1986. *Marion Penitentiary, 1955.* Washington, D.C.: U.S. Govt. Printing Office.

U.S. Senate Committee on Governmental Affairs Permanent Subcommittee on Investigations. 1983. *Organized Crime in Chicago.* Washington, D.C.: U.S. Govt. Printing Office.

U.S. Senate Committee on Governmental Affairs Permanent Subcommittee on Investigations. 1984. *Profile of Organized Crime: Great Lakes Region.* Washington, D.C.: U.S. Govt. Printing Office.

U.S. Senate Committee on Governmental Affairs Permanent Subcommittee on Investigations. 1990. *Organized Crime: 25 Years After Valachi.* Washington, D.C.: U.S. Govt. Printing Office.

Vaughn, M.S. 1996. "Prison Civil Liability For Inmate-Against-Inmate Assault And Breakdown/Disorganization Theory." *Journal of Criminal Justice.* 24:139-152.

Vaughn, M.S. and R.V. DelCarmen. 1995. "Civil Liability Against Prison Officials For

Inmate-On-Inmate Assault: Where Are We and Where Have We Been?" *The Prison Journal*. 75:69-89.

Ward, D. 1995. "A Corrections Dilemma: How To Evaluate Super-Max Regimes." *Corrections Today*. 57:104-108.

Ward, D. and A. Breed. 1984. "The United States Pententiary, Marion, Illinois." *Report To The Judiciary Committee, U.S. House Of Representatives*. Washington D.C.: U.S. Govt. Printing Office.

Warren, P. 1953. *Next Time is For Life*. N.Y.: Dell Publishing Co.

Wooden, W.S and J. Parker. 1982. *Men Behind Bars: Sexual Exploitation in Prison*. N.Y.: De Capo.

Wright, G. and C. Manly. 1955. "A World of Its Own." A series of 11 articles in the Chicago *Daily Tribune*, July 2-12. Reprinted by The John Howard Association, Chicago, with an introduction by Warden Ragen. No date.

Zimmer, L.E. 1986. *Women Guarding Men*. Chicago: University of Chicago Press.

NOTE: Citations to newspaper stories are identified in the text. Newspaper sources are difficult to find for Chicago prior to 1972 when the Chicago *Tribune*'s Index began. Fortunately, that paper's staff created a card file indexing stories about Chicago, primarily (but not exclusively) from the *Tribune*. The file apparently began after World War I and was maintained until after World War II. (Its completeness varies over time.) This file, known as the "Chicago *Tribune* Clipping File" was donated to the Harold Washington Chicago Public Library.

Index

215

Announcing Exciting <u>New</u> Texts from

Harrow and Heston, PUBLISHERS

Representing O.J.: Murder, Criminal Justice and Mass Culture.

Edited by Gregg Barak

IN A FEW WORDS: In postmodern America, this collection of original papers takes a broad-gauged cultural studies approach to understanding the "trial of the century." This book provides a case study of the construction, deconstruction and reconstruction of crime and justice in America. It articulates the conflict among mainstream and marginal interpretations of law and justice, especially as mediated by class, race and sexual identity. A ground-breaking work on the cultural study of newsreporting, entertainment, and the administration of criminal justice.

CONTENTS: PART I. SCIENCE, SUBJECTIVITY, AND CRIMINAL JUSTICE People V. Simpson: Some (IR)Relevant Variables, Research and the Future *Gilbert Geis.* Evidence, Probabilities, and Legal Standards for the Determination of Guilt: Prior to and Beyond O.J. *Brian Forst.* Juror Reciprocal Antagonism and the Intermittent Explosive Disorder: A Plausible Clinical Diagnosis of the O.J. Episode *Laurence Armand French.* The Social Science Significance of the O.J. Simpson Case *Steven Barkan.* PART II. CRIME, CONSUMPTION, AND MASS MEDIA. Slash and Frame *Jeff Ferrell.* The Real Menace to Society *Earl Ofari Hutchinson.* OJ and the Internet: The First Cybertrial *Cecil Greek.* O.J. Simpson and the Trial of the Century? Uncovering a Paradox in Media Coverage *Lynn S. Chancer.* Media, Discourse, and the O.J. Simpson Trial: An Ethnographic Portrait *Gregg Barak.* Media Madness as Crime in the Making: On O.J. Simpson, Consumerism, and Hyperreality *Bruce A. Arrigo.* PART III. EXPRESSIONS AND PERCEPTIONS: On Race, Class, Gender and Justice Overview Ethnic Expressive Style and American Public Opinion: The O.J. Simpson Case *Liza Cerroni-Long.* The Influence of Racial Similarity on the O.J. Simpson Trial *K.D. Mixon, Linda A. Foley, Kelly Orme.* Reality Bites and OJ: Black Protectionism and White Denial *Katheryn K. Russell.* The Matter of O.J. Simpson in Black and White and Green *Risdon N. Slate.* PART IV. CONTRADICTIONS AND DEBATES: On Cameras in Court, Reasonable Doubt, Jury Nullification, and Fair Trials Overview Undercurrents of Judicial Policy: Demystifying the Third Branch of Government and the O.J. Simpson Case *Steve Russell.* A Not-So-Radical Proposal: Eliminate Private Criminal Defense *Thomas J. Bernard.* On Reactionary Reactions to Race and the O.J. Simpson Verdict *James A. Chambers* The O.J. Simpson Trial, Jury Legitimacy, and the Continuing Debate *James N. Gilbert.* Whatever Happened to the Fair Trial in America? Before and After

OJ *Stephen J. Perrello, Jr.* .

RECOMMENDED: Upper division undergraduate courses in law and society, administration of criminal justice. Graduate classes in law and society, sociology of law, crime, justice and the media, administration of criminal justice, sentencing, punishment. Probable release date: November, 1996.

The Rise and Fall of a Violent Crime Wave: Crack Cocaine and the Social Construction of a Crime Problem.

by Henry Brownstein

IN A FEW WORDS: At one level, this is the story of how crime statistics are constructed in New York State, with particular reference to violent crime. And this in itself makes fascinating reading. But at a deeper level, Brownstein raises basic questions about the actual validity of crime statistics, and their abuse. Can crime really be measured by public officials? After reading this book, you will be unable to believe either the official statistics of crime, or their reporting in the media.

Maybe it lacked the drama of an ocean wave, as it rises in the sea and advances thunderously toward the shore. Maybe it lacked the thrill of a progression of thousands of people in a sports arena standing and sitting in sequence, arms raised in applause. Still, the wave of officially documented violent crime that washed over the U.S. and its cities in the waning decades of the twentieth century caught the attention and imagination of public and private citizens alike.

This book tells the story of that wave and the response to it by government policy-makers, law enforcement officials, and the news media. From the perspective of history, the rise and then fall of violent crime that began in the early 1980s was nothing special. Given its moment in history, it became a remarkable event. Following decades of social, political, and economic disruption in the U.S., and finding itself together in time and space with a new variant of cocaine known as crack, this modest wave of violent crime became a symbol of something it was not. In this book, Henry Brownstein, an Associate Professor and Director of the Graduate Program in Criminal Justice at the University of Baltimore, tells the story of how government policy-makers, law enforcement officials, and the news media effectively used modest shifts in the official rate of violent crime to construct a crisis of crime and violence. He demonstrates how crime is a social construction, and why this crisis was constructed.

For more than a decade of the period when this violent crime wave was being constructed, Brownstein worked for New York State government, first doing research and later serving as Chief of the unit responsible for generating official crime statistics for the state. In addition, he spent most of the period conducting federally-funded research on the relationship between drugs and violence. This book is largely based on his experience as an insider during the construction in the U.S. of the last violent crime wave of the twentieth century.

CONTENTS 1. The Wave of Violent Crime. Violence and Violent Crime. The Violent Crime Wave in the United States: 1980 to 1994 . The Crime Wave as an Urban Phenomenon. Violent Crime and Violent Victimizations. Conclusion. 2. The Measurement of Violent Crime . Official Crime Statistics. The Construction of UCR Statistics. The New York Experience. Incident-Based Reporting. Changes in Policy and Practice. The Power of Official Crime Statistics. 3. Crack Cocaine and Violent Crime. The Social Construction of Crime Problems. The Social Origins of the Crack Market in the U.S. Crack Markets and Violent Crime. The Construction of a Crisis of Crack-Related Violence. 4. Making Policy, Making Justice, Making Crime. . Satisfying the Public Demand for Policy and Action on Crack Cocaine. Research and the Internal Generation of Policy on Crack. . Policy-Making and the Definition of the Crack Problem. Policy-Making and the Construction of the Crisis of Crack and Violence.

RECOMMENDED: Excellent text for undergraduate or graduate courses in introductory criminology, social control. Available:Nov./Dec. 1996.

Justice with Prejudice: Race and Criminal Justice in America

Edited by Michael J. Lynch and E. Britt Patterson

IN A FEW WORDS: Extends the articles collected in the widely adopted classic *Race and Criminal Justice.* Emphasis in this volume is on the theoretical and qualitative aspects of the topic. Develops a more profound analysis of the concepts of racism, racial bias and racial discrimination in the crimianl justice setting.

CONTENTS: Editor's Preface viii. 1. Thinking About Race and Criminal Justice *Michael J. Lynch and E. Britt Patterson* 2. Moral Panic as Ideology: Drugs, Violence, Race and Punishment in America *Theodore Chiricos* 3. The "Tangle of Pathology" and the Lower Class African-American Family: Historical and Social Science Perspectives *Frankie Y. Bailey* 4. The Image of Black Women in Criminology: Historical Stereotypes as Theoretical Foundation *Jacklyn Huey and Michael J. Lynch 5.* Race, Popular Culture and the News *Lenny Krzycki* 6. Vice and Social Control: Predispositional Detention and the Juvenile Drug Offender *E. Britt Patterson and Laura Davidson Patterson* 7. Race, Contextual Factors, and the Waiver Decision within Juvenile Court Proceedings: Preliminary Findings From a Test of The Symbolic Threat Thesis *Michael J. Leiber, E. Michele Roudebush and Anne C. Woodrick* 8. Race and Criminal Justice: Employment of Minorities in the Criminal Justice System *Mahesh K. Nalla and Charles Corley* 9. Race and Social Class in the Examination of Punishment *Michael Welch.* Bibliography. Index. 200 pages. ISBN 0-911577-34-3. Paper. $21.50. Now Available!

RECOMMENDED: Undergraduate and graduate classes on race relations, race and criminal justice, minorities and criminal justice, feminist studies.

Just and Painful: A Case for the
Corporal Punishment of Criminals 2ed.

by Graeme Newman.

IN A FEW WORDS: More Outrageous! More Shocking! More Convincing! More Challenging than ever! Substantially revised and extended, Newman takes his argument one further logical step — and treads where no other criminologist has dared to go.

CONTENTS: Prologue to Second Edition. 1. Pain: The Forgotten Punishment . 2. Pain and Punishment .3. On Crimes and Their Punishments: The Psychology of Retribution.4.The Limits of Pain: Barbaric and Civilized Punishments .5. Electric Shock: The Fairest Punishment of All.6. Splitting Crimes from Criminals.7. Prisons as Purgatory .8. Comparing Punishments.9. Choosing the Punishment. 10. Cruel and Unusual?.11. The Moral Superiority of Retribution. 12. Pain is Not Evil.13. Pain is not (Necessarily) Torture. 14. Will Corporal Punishment Deter ? 15. Turning Bad into Good 16. A Punishment Manifesto . 181 pages. Price $23.50, paper. ISBN: 0911577335.

RECOMMENDED: This books will suit any class in which the teacher wants to encourage open, free-for-all discussion. Adopted widely in courses on punishment, corrections, and administration of criminal justice. For those fed up with the current mode of correctional treatment of criminals, this book is welcome relief. You will never think about crime and punishment in the same way ever again. Written in a lively, beautifully clear style. Appropriate for undergraduate and graduate classes of any level.

From Gangs to Gangsters: How American Sociology
Organized Crime, 1918-1994

by Marylee Reynolds

Ever wonder why the famed Chicago School studied juvenile delinquency almost to the exclusion of all else, even though it was at the height of organized crime in Chicago? This book provides an answer, and a penetrating analysis of the "influence" or lack thereof of organized crime on American academic sociology.

CONTENTS: 1. Nature of the problem. 2.The social disorganization paradigm of crime and deviance. 3. Early organized crime in Chicago and the development of American sociology: A chronology. 4. The Landesco study: Its historical and sociological significance. 5. The Landesco study: Its historical and sociological significance. 6. Organized crime as a topic of sociological interest. 7.Organized crime as a topic of sociological interest 8. Academic inattention toward the study of organized crime by American sociologists: some reasons why. Bibliography. Index. ISBN: 911577300. Hard Cover. $48.50

Prison Crisis: Critical Readings

Edited by Edward Sbarbaro and Robert Keller
Foreword by William Chambliss

One can only hope that the publication of this book will usher in a new era of prison studies. -- *From the Foreword by William J. Chambliss*. **CONTENTS: Introduction: Prisons as Social Control of the Powerless**. Overview. 1. Gill Gardner-**Prisons and Capitalism: The New York State Prison Experience**.2. Fay Dowker and Glenn Good-**The Proliferation of Control Unit Prisons in the United States**.3. Michael E. Deutsch, Dennis Cunningham, and Elizabeth M. Fink-**Twenty Years Later—Attica Civil Rights Case Finally Cleared for Trial**. 4. Christina Jose-Kampfner-**Coming to Terms with Existential Death: An Analysis of Women's Adaption to Life in Prison**. 5. Phil Scraton and Kathryn Chadwick-**Speaking III of the Dead: Institutionalized Responses to Deaths in Custody**. 6. Laura T. Fishman-**Visiting at the Prison: Renewed Courtship and the Prisoner's Wife**. 7. David F. Greenberg-**The Cost-Benefit Analysis of Imprisonment**. 8. Edward Sbarbaro-**Teaching 'Criminology' to 'Criminals'**. 9. Robert L. Keller-**From 'Con' to Counselor: Changes in Gender Identity in a Prison Juvenile Awareness Program**.10. Little Rock Reed-**Rehabilitation: Contrasting Cultural Perspectives and the Imposition of Church and State**.11. Mark S. Hamm and Jeffrey L. Schrink-**The Conditions of Effective Implementation: A Guide To Accomplishing Rehabilitative Objectives in Corrections**.12. John Lowman and Brian MacLean-**Prisons and Protest in Canada**.13. Edward Sbarbaro and Robert Keller-**Prisoner Activism as a Mechanism of Struggle for Social Justice. Conclusion**. Bibliography. Index. 1995. 238 pages. Hard $38.50

A Primer in the Politics of Criminal Justice

by Nancy E. Marion

Many "radical" texts on criminal justice and criminology argue that the operations of criminal justice and the definition of criminality are essentially political. These texts are, however, largely ideological and entirely theoretical. In contrast, The Politics of Criminal Justice shows exactly how politics in its everyday sense affects the workings of criminal justice and the generation of criminal definitions. From interest groups to Presidents, this book provides the practical, down-to-earth account of the relationship between political science and criminal justice.**CONTENTS.** 1. Introduction. 2. Congress and Crime. 3. Presidents and Crime. 4. Courts and Criminal Justice. 5. Bureaucracies. 6. Interest Groups . 7. Campaigns, Elections, and the Issue of Crime. 8.The Media and Public Opinion. 9.Conclusion. Bibliography. Index. 1995. ISBN:0911577327. 138 pages. Paperback. $19.50.

Method in Criminology: A Philosophical Primer

by Bruce DiCristina

DiCristina ruthlessly dissects the sacred cows of criminological method, and by force of logic demands a rethinking of the value of the criminological knowledge that has been received.

Introduction. Part One: Common Justifications: The Logic of Privileging Methods in Criminology.. Chapter 1. Causation and the Unreason of the Quest. Causation: A brief description. Hume's challenge to the discovery of causes. On indirect support for causal assertions. Conclusion. **Chapter 2. Probability and the Spirit of Induction**. Two dimensions of induction. Hume's challenge to inductive reasoning and probability. A relative frequency challenge to the logic of probability. On indirect support for inductive reasoning and probability. Conclusion. **Chapter 3. Falsification and the Subjectivity of Facts**. Falsification: origin and nature. On the existence of a world "out there". Physiological limitations on fact-finding. Temporal and spatial limitations on fact-finding. Hermeneutic concepts. The concept-fact connection. Objective observations or subjective constructs?. The language game of falsification. Conclusion. **Chapter 4. The Logic of Privileging: A Final Word**. Causation, probability, and falsification revisited. Alternative standards of justification.Conclusion. **Part two: Criminological Inquiry: Law and Order v. Anarchism.** . **Chapter 5. Scientific Criminology: The Privileged Law and Order**. Evidence of privileging. Foundations for the fall of the scientific methods. Conclusion. **Chapter 6. Reflexive Hermeneutic Criminology: An Alternative Law and Order**. The goal: The greatest happiness. The method: Reflexive hermeneutics. Conclusion. **Chapter 7. Anarchic Criminology: An Alternative to Law and Order**. Anarchism: A plausible "means" to an end. Anarchism: A humanitarian "means" to an end. Additional support for an anarchic criminology. Criminologists for methodological freedom. On pursuing an anarchic criminology. Conclusion. **Summary and Conclusion. References. Index**. 130 Pages. Hard cover. ISBN: 911577-28-9. Price: $28.50. $20.00 for class adoption.

(HH) *Harrow and Heston* PUBLISHERS
1830 Western Avenue, Albany NY 12203
Fax/Phone: (518) 456-4894

S O C I A L
PATHOLOGY
A Journal of Reviews

ISSN:1073-7855 (paper) 1073-8118 (electronic)

A Journal of book and area reviews in deviance, penology, criminology, legal studies, social control, criminal justice, race relations, and social problems. Published 3 times yearly.

Price: Institutional $141.00, individual $48.00

VOL.1. NO.1.
January 1995
Table of Contents

To subscribe, Write or Call:
Harrow and Heston PUBLISHERS
P.O. Box 3934, Stuyvesant Plaza, Albany NY 12203
Telephone/Fax: (518) 456-4894